Practical social work

**Published in conjunction with
the British Association of Social Workers**

Founding editor: Jo Campling

Social Work is a multi-skilled profession, centred on people. Social workers need skills in problem-solving, communication, critical reflection and working with others to be effective in practice.

The British Association of Social Workers (www.basw.co.uk) has always been conscious of its role in setting guidelines for practice and in seeking to raise professional standards. The concept of the Practical Social Work series was developed to fulfil a genuine professional need for a carefully planned, coherent, series of texts that would contribute to practitioners' skills, development and professionalism.

Newly relaunched to meet the ever-changing needs of the social work profession, the series has been reviewed and revised with the help of the BASW Editorial Advisory Board:

Peter Beresford
Jim Campbell
Monica Dowling
Brian Littlechild
Mark Lymbery
Fraser Mitchell
Steve Moore

Under their guidance each book marries practice issues with theory and research in a compact and applied format: perfect for students, practitioners and educators.

A comprehensive list of titles available in the series can be found online at: www.palgravehighered.com/socialwork/basw

D1452433

Practical social work series

Founding Editor: Jo Campling

New and best-selling titles

Robert Adams *Empowerment, Participation and Social Work* (**4th edition**)

Sarah Banks *Ethics and Values in Social Work* (**4th edition**)

James G. Barber *Social Work with Addictions* (**2nd edition**)

Christine Bigby and Patsie Frawley *Social Work Practice and Intellectual Disability*

Suzy Braye and Michael Preston-Shoot *Practising Social Work Law* (**4th edition**)

Jennifer Burton *Practise Learning in Social Work*

Veronica Coulshed and Audrey Mullender with David N. Jones and Neil Thompson *Management in Social work* (**3rd edition**)

Veronica Coulshed and Joan Orme *Social Work Practice* (**5th edition**)

Lena Dominelli *Anti-Racist Social Work* (**4th edition**)

Celia Doyle *Working with Abused Children* (**4th edition**)

Richard Ingram, Jane Fenton, Ann Hodson and Divya Jindal-Snape *Reflective Social Work Practice*

Gordon Jack and Helen Donnell *Social Work with Children*

Tony Jeffs and Mark K. Smith (editors) *Youth Work Practice*

Joyce Lishman *Communication in Social Work* (**2nd edition**)

Paula Nicolson and Rowan Bayne: *Psychology for Social Work Theory and Practice* (**4th edition**)

Michael Oliver, Bob Sapey and Pam Thomas *Social Work with Disabled People* (**4th edition**)

Joan Orme and David Shemmings *Developing Research Based Social Work Practice*

Terence O'Sullivan *Decision Making in Social Work* (**2nd edition**)

Terence O'Sullivan *Supporting Families*

Mo Ray and Judith Phillips *Social Work with Older People* (**5th edition**)

Michael Preston-Shoot *Effective Groupwork* (**2nd edition**)

Robin Sen *Effective Practice with Looked After Children*

Jerry Tew *Working with Mental Distress*

Neil Thompson *Anti-Discriminatory Practice* (**6th edition**)

Alan Twelvetrees *Community Work* (**5th edition**)

EFFECTIVE PRACTICE WITH LOOKED AFTER CHILDREN

ROBIN SEN

First published 2018 by
PALGRAVE

Palgrave in the UK is an imprint of Macmillan Publishers Limited, registered in England, company number 785998, of 4 Crinan Street, London, N1 9XW.

Palgrave® and Macmillan® are registered trademarks in the United States, the United Kingdom, Europe and other countries.

ISBN 978–1–137–26980–5 paperback

This book is printed on paper suitable for recycling and made from fully managed and sustained forest sources. Logging, pulping and manufacturing processes are expected to conform to the environmental regulations of the country of origin.

A catalogue record for this book is available from the British Library.

A catalog record for this book is available from the Library of Congress.

This text is dedicated to the memory of Barbara Sen and Partha Sen
Shanti, shanti, shanti

CONTENTS

LIST OF FIGURES, TABLES AND BOXES

ACKNOWLEDGEMENTS

This book had a very long gestation period and its arrival was massively overdue. I am thankful to Palgrave for allowing me time to finish it and I am grateful to Peter Hooper and Rita Ondarra for gently but firmly steering me towards the finishing line. I feel fortunate to have an academic home in the Department of Sociological Studies at the University of Sheffield and I would particularly like to thank Bev Jowett, Nora McClelland and Sue White from the social work team for commenting on chapter drafts. Jane Bolan, Team Manager at Nottinghamshire County Council, and Lydia Brown, social worker with Sheffield City Council, also provided very helpful feedback on chapter drafts. I am especially grateful to Malcolm Hill of the University of Strathclyde for providing detailed and, as ever, perceptive comments on a full draft of the manuscript. The usual caveat that all errors are my own, of course, applies. Thanks to Paul for ongoing support and wise counsel. Finally, I would like to note that in the – admittedly lengthy – period between when I was first approached about the book and its completion both my parents passed away. During the writing of a book which is, essentially, about the upbringing of children, it gave me cause to reflect on my own upbringing and what my parents gave to me as I grew up. The text is therefore dedicated to their memory.

INTRODUCTION

Coverage and Terminology

There are multiple influences on social work practice – the most prominent being agency rules, inquiries into child abuse, law, theory, policy, practice wisdom, research, theory and values. This book primarily draws on research evidence within the given legal and policy contexts for practice with looked after children. It also draws, to lesser extents, on my own practice experience as a former social worker working with looked after children, my learning from working closely with practitioners and students since moving into higher education, social work values and theory. While the information in the book will be of relevance to a wider audience of adoptive parents, carers, residential child care workers and social workers and social work students practising in a number of settings, it is worth noting that it is a text which is principally about local authority field social work practice with looked after children.

From the outside looking in, the subject of 'looked after children' may seem narrow. However, the label includes a diverse range of children, contexts and issues and it has not been possible to do justice to them all here. The largest gap is around issues of social identity related to looked after children – particularly issues of class, disability, ethnicity, gender, and sexual orientation. Though some of these are discussed through other material (for example, issues of ethnicity in 'transracial' adoptive placements), there was not space to give them more specific coverage. Secondly, the particular situation of looked after asylum seeking young people is recognised but not covered in any depth. Finally, while some attention is given to looked after young people, offending and 'the secure estate' in Chapter 8 on residential care, this coverage is relatively brief.

This book focuses on relevant policy and law in England, but key inter-UK divergences relevant to practice with looked after children are recognised. While there are certain areas of law which apply to all four countries in the UK – for example, those related to foreign affairs, defence and most national benefits – since devolution in the late 1990s England, Northern Ireland, Scotland and Wales have increasingly developed individual policies and law in the area of child welfare. Additionally, historically, there have been different legal systems in place, with England and Wales subject to 'English Law', Northern Ireland to Northern Irish law and Scotland to Scots law. This is leading to increasing divergence in policy and legislation across the four countries. However, much of 'English' law and a good deal of 'English' policy is still also currently applicable in Wales. In Northern Ireland, and particularly Scotland, there are a considerable number of differences, however the broad thrust of policy and law remains more similar than different, and this is also true of underlying social work practices.

Whether to use the terminology of 'children' or 'young people' is always a quandary. Teenagers and those approaching teenage years tend to feel the use of 'children' is patronising, while 'young people' does not feel right when referring to infants and using 'children and young people' throughout feels clunky. Therefore, in this text where I am primarily referring to children under 12 I use the terminology of 'children' or 'looked after children', where I am primarily referring to those over 12 I use the terminology of 'young people' or 'looked after young people', and where I refer to both age groups together I revert to using the terminology of 'children' or 'looked after children' for simplicity.

Since the Children Act 1989 in England and Wales, the terminology of a 'Looked after Child' and 'Looked after Children' has officially replaced the term 'children in care' in the UK, but the latter term is still widely in use and recognised. In other anglophone countries (Australia, Canada, New Zealand, the USA) the term 'out of home care' tends to be used. I use all of these terms interchangeably within the book, though most frequently I will refer to a 'looked after child' or 'looked after children' or a 'looked after young person' or 'looked after young people', preferring not to capitalise any of the phrases. I sometimes also refer to 'looked after and adopted children' where the discussion specifically relates to both sets of these children. As per the convention, I reserve use of the term 'care leaver' to specifically refer to a young person who has aged out of care, or is shortly to do so, rather than to a child who leaves care at a younger age for other reasons.

I hope you enjoy the book!

CHAPTER 1

LOOKED AFTER CHILDREN CONTEXTS AND PATHWAYS

Chapter Overview

This chapter introduces the role of the social worker with looked after children and the overarching legal context for practice. Government statistical data regarding looked after children in the UK are explored including the placement pathways of looked after children in England, with attention given to particular categories of children within the umbrella term 'looked after children' as well as children who are not formally 'looked after' but who may have similar needs and issues. The application of the children's rights agenda to the lives of looked after children is then considered. The chapter finishes by introducing two complex issues – the question of whether there are too many or too few children in care, and the question of whether or not 'outcomes' for looked after children are poorer then we should expect them to be.

Introduction

Looked after children are a highly significant group because they are among the most deprived and disadvantaged children in the UK. Social work practice within this group of children is likely, one way or another, to have lifelong implications. There are several important roles that field social workers can fulfil with looked after children. Firstly, those based within mainstream local authority teams will be responsible for helping arrive at decisions as to when children should be placed in state care, and when they should be returned to family care or placed in long-term substitute care. When a child is in care a field social worker has a number of responsibilities in respect of their care – these include legal duties to visit them periodically, checking whether the child is settled and that their needs are being met in their care and educational settings, seeing that the child's wishes are reflected in decision-making around their care as far as possible, liaising with birth family members, setting up contact arrangements between the child and family and friends networks and ensuring that birth family members' perspectives are also represented in decision-making. These roles require both 'direct work' involving direct interaction with children in care and their families and 'indirect work' which includes keeping written case notes on the child and their circumstances, compiling assessments of the child, completing formal reports regarding the child for meetings such as Looked After Child Reviews and court hearings, and overseeing that the child's care plan is being put into effect.

Secondly, those working in fostering and adoption local authority teams or for independent fostering agencies – known as 'link social workers' or 'family placement social workers' (hereafter referred to as 'family placement social workers') – have particular roles in helping recruit and assess prospective foster carers and adopters, matching children who need a particular placement with particular carers and adopters, and providing ongoing assessment of and support to foster carers and adopters, in liaison with the child's social worker. Again, this role will be a mixture of 'direct work' – direct interaction principally with carers and adopters, but also sometimes with a looked after or adopted child – and 'indirect work' involving case recording and the completion of written assessments and reports.

Thirdly, social workers working for the Children and Family Court Advisory and Support Service (Cafcass) in England and Wales have a role as Children's Guardians in care proceedings for children in the family court. In this role they appoint a solicitor to represent a child's interests in care proceedings, and directly liaise with a child (as appropriate to their age), relevant birth family members and other professionals in order to undertake an independent assessment of a child's circumstances and the local authority's care plan for a child. The Guardian provides the family court with an independent written assessment and recommendations as to what decisions they think the court should make regarding a child's care.

Finally, some social workers will have a specialist remit to provide direct specialist intervention and support to children in care around specific difficulties or challenges the child is experiencing. This may be in a specialist team within a local authority, but quite often such specialist roles are located within the independent and charitable sector. Mainstream field social workers will then refer looked after children with whom they work to the organisation or specialist team in order to allow them to access the specialist service.

Over and above these field social work roles, it is important to recognise the crucial contributions of adoptive parents, foster and kin carers, residential child care workers and special guardians in providing day-to-day care to looked after and adopted children.

Guiding legal principles in respect of looked after children

Looked after children are children legally looked after by the state via local state agencies – local authorities – in foster, kinship, pre-adoptive and residential placements. Local authorities have specific legal duties in respect of looked after children which include a general duty to safeguard and promote their welfare and a more specific duty to produce and implement a comprehensive care plan detailing what the child's needs are and how they will be met.

The key statutes in respect of children and families practice remain the Children Act 1989 in England and Wales, the NI Order (1995) in Northern Ireland and the Children (Scotland) Act 1995 in Scotland, though each has been substantially amended by subsequent legislation. Worded slightly differently, the relevant statutes, secondary legislation and legislative guidance across the four countries share some overarching legal principles. These are that:

- The welfare of the child should be the paramount consideration in any decision.

- Due consideration should be given to the views of the child in any decision.

- There should be partnership with the parents of a child where services are provided and this is consistent with the welfare of the child.

- Courts should follow a 'no order' principle such that they only impose a court order in respect of a child where it is clearly in the child's interests that it should do so.

- Courts should seek to avoid delay in making decisions about the future upbringing of a child.

- Where a child is in care, the local authority should seek to promote links with family members and significant others, so far as this is consistent with the child's welfare.

- Agencies working with children should have due regard for their cultural, religious and linguistic background.[1]

In all four countries, a child will enter care for two overarching reasons. Either:

1. There are concerns about the child's welfare in the care of their parents such that there are reasonable grounds to believe a child will suffer, or has already suffered, significant harm.

Or:

2. If there is no one with parental responsibilities for the child, the child is lost or abandoned or the person providing care is not able to provide suitable care or accommodation (the last scenario includes a wide range of situations such as where a parent is unable to care due to imprisonment, ill health, lack of suitable accommodation or because the child is beyond parental control).

The legal manner in which a child enters care will tend to mirror the reasons for entering care. Where a child enters care for type 1 reasons it is likely to be via a more formal process with judicial oversight in England, Northern Ireland and Wales, or via either a judicial process or the Children's Hearing System in Scotland. In England and Wales, this is mostly via a Care Order under s.31 of the Children Act 1989, or the equivalent provision of the NI Order (1995) in Northern Ireland. In Scotland, the Children's Hearing System is a particular feature of the Scottish child welfare system where, rather than a judge in a civil court, a panel of three lay volunteer members of the community decide on what should happen regarding the care of a child when there are welfare or behavioural concerns (Hill et al., 2006). However, evidential issues concerning children's referral to the Children's Hearing

System in the first place, and applications for the emergency removal of children, are still heard by a judge in civil court, similar to the other jurisdictions in the UK.

Where a child enters care for type 2 reasons, this is more likely to be via a 'voluntary arrangement', described as such as the local authority cannot accommodate a child in care by this process if someone with parental responsibilities is able to provide appropriate care and accommodation for the child and objects to their placement in state care. In England, in 2017, 69 per cent of children were looked after on care orders, an increase from 58 per cent in 2014, while the proportion on s.20 voluntary arrangements has fallen from a recent high of 28 per cent of children in care in 2015, to 23 per cent in 2017 (DfE, 2017c).[2] This fall follows increased scrutiny of the use of s.20/s.76 arrangements in England and Wales in recent years.[3] In a 2015 judgement in Re N,[4] Sir James Munby, President of the Family Division, highlighted four issues of concern regarding s.20 use: that local authorities did not always gain informed consent from parents as legally required; that they did not routinely properly record the consent; that s.20 arrangements were allowed to continue too long after a child was placed in care; and that local authorities were reluctant to immediately return children to parents' care when s.20 consent was withdrawn.

Children who are not 'looked after' but with potentially similar needs

There are three groups of children who are not legally 'looked after children', and towards whom the state does not therefore have the same legal duties, but who are likely to have some similar circumstances and needs. The first group are children who were formally looked after but who have legally left care as they have returned to parental care, become subject to a legal order regarding their care designed to last throughout their childhood – for example, adoption or a Special Guardianship Order (SGO) – or they are care leavers who have aged out of care.

The second group are children who are privately fostered. These are children under 16, or under 18 if they have a disability, who have been in the care of a private individual other than their parents or a close relative for 28 days or more. A close relative is defined in the Children Act 1989 as a grandparent, sibling, step-parent or uncle or aunt whether of full blood or half blood, or by marriage or civil partnership. Private fostering arrangements are made between parents and carers without the involvement of state agencies – hence the name of the arrangement and the reason why these children are not 'looked after'. There has, however, been long-standing concern over the welfare of some children in such arrangements (Holman, 2002), which was given further impetus following the death of Victoria Climbié in the care of her great-aunt and the great-aunt's partner – an arrangement that would be classified as a private fostering in England (Laming, 2003). There is a legal obligation on both private foster carers and parents who place their children in such an arrangement to notify the local authority of it. The local authority is obliged to visit and assess that the arrangement is appropriate within seven days of notification. Difficulties with low levels of notification and a lack of professional awareness of private fostering arrangements have been noted as ongoing issues (Shaw et al., 2010).

Thirdly, are those children who are cared for by close relatives in private kinship arrangements. These children differ from children placed in formal 'kinship care' by local authority arrangement, as their placement with relatives is organised by direct arrangement between the birth parents and the relevant family members. Therefore these children do not become 'looked after'. This group of children also differ from privately fostered children as they are cared for by someone designated as a 'close relative' under the Children Act 1989. Though distinctions between formal and private kinship care can blur, carers in private kin arrangements tend to be less regulated, assessed and supported by state agencies than formal kinship carers (Selwyn and Nandy, 2014). A very sizeable number of children – 164,916 – were estimated to be in private kin care according to 2001 census data, and this figure is likely to have increased since. In comparison, only 9,004 looked after children were estimated to be in formal kinship care arrangements on the same date (Selwyn and Nandy, 2014). Notably, the number of children estimated to be in private kinship care in 2001 is far greater than the total number of looked after children in the UK at the time of writing.

While much of the literature and certain policy guidance on 'looked after children' applies to the first category of children defined above, even though they are technically no longer 'looked after', children in the second and third categories are often not considered within it. This is likely because we know relatively little about the second and third groups, and professional involvement with them is traditionally limited. As a text focusing on looked after children this book will not focus on the needs of these two latter groups; however, professionals should still be aware of the possibility of working with children in such caring arrangements and that, as children separated from their parents, they are likely to share some issues and needs in common with children who are formally 'looked after'.

Practice Pointer 1.1

What are the similarities and differences between the needs of children who are in care, children in a private fostering arrangement and children in a private kinship arrangement?

How many children are in care?

There are three sets of statistics which need to be considered regarding the numbers of children in care:

1. The 'point in time' number showing how many children were in care on a particular date when returns on numbers are sent from local authorities to

national governments in the UK (31 March, except for Scotland where it is 31 July).

2. The 'movement numbers' showing how many children came into and left care in a given year.

3. The 'LAC rate', the number of children in care as a proportion of the child population in a given year.

The 'point in time' number

According to official statistics, on 31 March 2017 there were 72,670 children who were looked after in England alone. This number has been steadily rising each year since 2009, while in the directly preceding years the overall numbers in care had been either static or falling, albeit there has been an overall upward trajectory in care numbers in England since the mid-1990s (see Figure 1.1). The general upward trajectory in care numbers from the mid-1990s can partly be explained by the increasing length of time children are spending in care compared to previously, seemingly reflecting the increasing complexity of their needs and difficulties (Biehal, 2006). The figure of 72,670, however, only tells us the number of children in care on the specific date of 31 March 2017. We also need to consider the numbers coming into and leaving the care system during the year to get a better sense of the overall trajectory of care numbers.

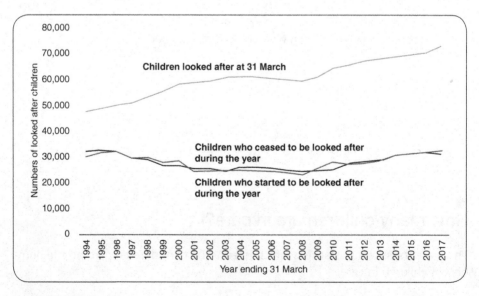

Source: DfE (2017a)

Figure 1.1 Numbers of looked after children in England on 31 March of each year

The 'movement numbers'

These statistics are represented by the two lower lines on the graph in Figure 1.1. These indicate that since 2009 the numbers entering the care system during whole-year periods have been rising, as have the numbers of children leaving care during the year. Children will leave care through, for example, returning to parental care, being adopted or ageing out of care at or close to 18. In 2017, though 72,670 children were in care in England on 31 March, 102,590 children had been in care at some point during the preceding year (DfE, 2017c), the difference between these two figures explained by the numbers of children who had also left care at some point during the preceding year. Figure 1.1 also shows that, while the numbers leaving care have been similar to the numbers entering care, in certain years since 2009 the numbers entering have been greater, supporting a net increase in the number of children in the care system.

The 'LAC rate'

The final statistic to consider is the 'LAC rate' – this shows the number of children in care as a proportion of the child population overall and helps us to better see how the numbers compare across years, between countries and between areas within countries. The LAC rate is given as the number of children in care per 10,000 of the child population in that particular area at that time.

Table 1.1 shows both the numbers of children in care for each of the countries in the UK from 2012 to 2016 and the LAC rates for each of them. It should be noted that a good deal of caution is needed in comparing the figures between the four countries, due to different systems, laws and what constitutes a 'looked after child'. Owing to greater similarity of systems and laws the figures in England and Wales are more easily compared while, by contrast, in Scotland the definition of a looked after child is substantially different and includes those children living at home in parental care on an Interim Supervision Order or Supervision Order through the Children's Hearing System. Between a third and a quarter of 'looked after children' fall into this category (Scottish Government, 2017a). Due to this difference a better, but still partial comparison, can be made by considering only those Scottish children who are looked after 'away from home' (the bottom row of Table 1.1).

Table 1.1 shows that the LAC rate has been rising – slowly – in England since 2010, from 59 per 10,000 children (0.59% of the overall child population) to 60 in 2016 (0.6% of the overall child population). The latest figures for England show this rate rose to 62 or 0.62% of the population on 31 March 2017 (DfE, 2017c). This marks a general increase from a rate of around 55 per 10,000 children in the mid-2000s, but is lower than that during the 1970s when the rate was around 75 (Bullock et al., 2006). Considering the countries in the UK shows that the LAC rate for all children in all the countries in the UK, other than Wales, has been on a

Table 1.1 Looked after child statistics in the UK 2012–2016, statistics given at 31 March each year for all countries

	2012	2013	2014	2015	2016
England	67,070	68,060	68,800	69,540	70,440
Wales	5,730	5,770	5,745	5,615	5,660
Northern Ireland	2,640	2,810	2,860	2,860	2,890
Scotland (All LAC)	16,360	16,170	15,625	15,365	15,330
Scotland (LAC at home)	5,300	4,950	4,255	3,935	3,880
Scotland (LAC away from home)	11,060	11,220	11,370	11,430	11,450
LAC rates per 10,000 children					
England	59	60	60	60	60
Wales	90	91	91	89	90
Northern Ireland	61	65	66	66	67
Scotland (All LAC)	157	156	151	149	149
Scotland (LAC at home)	51	48	41	40	38
Scotland (LAC away from home)	106	108	110	109	111

Source: Scottish Government (2017b)

broadly upward trend from 2012 to 2016. In Wales the LAC rate has been largely static from 2012 to 2016, although taking a slightly longer time frame for Wales shows a substantial rise from an LAC rate of 66 in 2005 (see McGhee et al., 2017) to its current level of 90. It is also noticeable that the LAC rate in Wales, and particularly Scotland, is higher than that in England and Northern Ireland, though additional systemic differences as to whom is considered a looked after child in the four countries do mean this comparison should be made with some degree of caution.

Practice Pointer 1.2

List any reasons you can think of as to why care numbers and the LAC rate may have risen in recent years.

It is hard to conclusively establish why care numbers and the LAC rate have risen over recent years in the UK. However, there are two prominent potential explanations to consider. Firstly, after the financial crisis starting in 2008 there was an economic downturn and, since 2010, very large cuts to public spending, including cuts to welfare benefits and family support services (Churchill, 2013). Since increasing care numbers are likely to have some relationship to the poorest families being less well supported, this is likely to explain some of the rise.

Secondly, the death of Peter Connelly – 'Baby P' – in 2007 and responses to the media reporting of his death in 2008 can be seen as a recent watershed. There was a notable 9 per cent increase in the numbers of children who started to be looked after between 2009 and 2010 in England – the first year after the full ramifications of the case became clear. Parton (2014) identified that a more 'child protection'-orientated stance in government policy and guidance could be found after the case. In support of this point, the Conservative-led governments from 2010 have vigorously promoted the greater use of adoption as a permanence option for children, and it had been suggested that more children experiencing neglect should be removed from parental care, earlier on in their lives, as part of this drive (see Narey, 2011).

However, the devolved governments of Northern Ireland, Scotland and Wales have taken a less overtly child protection-orientated stance than the UK government and yet LAC rates have risen by a larger proportion in these countries than in England from 2005 to 2016 (McGhee et al., 2017; Scottish Government, 2017b). The reasons for this are not currently clear. It should also be acknowledged that there appear to be more recent government moves within the last few years to reduce care numbers in England, with a number of 'Innovation Fund Projects' funded by the Department of Education which have explicit or implicit aims of reducing the numbers of children in care in their local areas (Spring Consortium, 2017).

Why are children in care?

According to government statistics, the principal recorded reasons for why children entered care in England in 2016–2017 are given in Table 1.2.

As can be seen, the main stated reason for over half of those who entered care is abuse or neglect. Some research studies (e.g. Quinton et al., 1998; Wade et al., 2011) have found still higher proportions of looked after children have had

Table 1.2 Principal recorded reasons for why children started to be looked after in England in 2016–2017 (DfE, 2017c)

Principal Reason	%
Abuse or neglect	61
Family dysfunction	15
Family in acute stress	8
Absent parenting	7
Parent's illness or disability	3
Child's disability	3
Socially unacceptable behaviour	1
Low income	0

such experiences. This level of abuse or neglect is greater than the general child population where it is estimated that each year 4–16 per cent of children are subject to physical abuse, 10 per cent to neglect or psychological abuse and 5–10 per cent to penetrative sexual abuse (Gilbert et al., 2011). Younger children are more likely to enter care due to care and protection issues while older children are more likely to enter care due to their own behaviour and family breakdown and exhibit emotional and behavioural difficulties. Regardless of the principal reason for entering care, the vast majority of looked after children will also have had experiences of poor and insecure housing, difficult family settings and poverty (Sinclair, 2005).

Practice Pointer 1.3

Official statistics suggest that the numbers of looked after children entering care due to abuse or neglect have risen since the 1970s. Why do you think this might be?

It is important to note the principal reasons given in Table 1.2 are not the full range of reasons why any child is looked after in England but the administrative 'need code' or category a social worker records as the *principal* reason for a child becoming 'looked after' when they first come into care. As shorthand we might say that 61 per cent of children entered care in England 'due to' abuse or neglect. However, this statistic actually represents the fact that in 61 per cent of cases where a child came into care a, typically very rushed, social worker ticked abuse/neglect as the principal need code for the child's entry into care on their information system.

This is not to say that abuse or neglect were not significant factors for these children, but rather to note that there is individual judgement as to what the principal reason a child entering care is recorded as, and that the UK recording systems do not systematically require a fuller explanation of the reasons for a child's entry into care. In this regard, it is worth considering the cross-comparative analysis of LAC statistics in developed countries as reported by Thoburn (2009b). In contrast to the UK and USA, Swedish data show a very different pattern, with around half of Swedish children recorded as entering care due to behavioural or other child-related problems, and around half because of family or relationship problems. Clearly this difference is not because there is no child abuse or neglect in Sweden, but rather because the category of abuse/neglect is not available as an administrative recording code when children enter the Swedish care system.

Placement pathways

While 'looked after children' are often put together as a single group, they also have diverse needs. Working with an individual child to understand their particular needs and circumstances is an obvious recommendation but it is also possible to identify particular sub-categories of looked after children who have a greater simi-larity of issues and needs. Sinclair and colleagues (2007) undertook a study of the care population in the mid-2000s using a representative sample of looked after children in England. This allowed them to provide various insights into the care population at that time. From their data they identified six distinct categories of looked after children:

- *Young entrants* – children who are aged 10 and under and mainly entered care due to abuse or neglect. They are likely to be experiencing marked difficulties connected to their birth families, but fewer difficulties in terms of school and their behaviour in placement.

- *Adolescent graduates* – young people who entered care as 'young entrants' but then remained in care and are now 11 or older. They are still likely to have home difficulties but are now more likely to be displaying challenging behav-iours in school and placement, and be having some difficulties at school.

- *Adolescents who had experienced abuse* – young people who entered care after the age of 11 primarily due to neglect or abuse. Their behaviour is likely to be more challenging than that of *adolescent graduates*, and they are likely to be doing very poorly educationally. A number of these young people may be open to considering a long-term substitute family placement; however, their behav-ioural problems are likely to make finding a permanent substitute family for them difficult.

- *Adolescent entrants* – young people who entered care after the age of 11, pri-marily because family relationships had broken down, rather than due to abuse or neglect. They are likely to have ongoing, though difficult, relationships with birth family members and many will not want a substitute long-term family placement. Their behaviour tends to be very challenging and they are likely to be doing poorly at school.

- *Unaccompanied asylum seeking* – young people will mainly be aged 11 or older on entry into care. They are in care as they entered the UK without their parents or a guardian and are claiming asylum to remain in the UK long term. As such, they must be treated as a looked after child by the UK state up until reaching adulthood. Their future stay beyond that point depends on whether their claim for asylum is granted. This group of young people is less likely to be displaying challenging behaviour and more likely to be doing well at school than other adolescents in the care system.

- *Children with a disability* – This category of children comprises those whose *primary reason* for being looked after is their disability. These children are less likely to have difficulties connected to the family home, but have high levels of challenging behaviour. They are also the only group of children among the six listed here who are more likely to be placed in residential care rather than foster care.

Practice Pointer 1.4

Think about any looked after children whom you may know. Do they fit into any of these categories? Are there any looked after children you know who would not fit easily into any of these categories and, if so, why?

From the study by Sinclair and colleagues (2007), and the most recent UK government statistics (DfE, 2017c), the following overview of pathways for looked after children in England can be given:

- Close to half of children of the 30,000 leaving care each year will leave within a year of entry into the care system, the largest proportion returning to the care of parents (Sinclair et al., 2007; DfE, 2017c).

- Between a quarter and a third of children leaving care each year will do so via adoption or an SGO (DfE, 2017c).

- Around a tenth of looked after children will age out of care on reaching or approaching adulthood each year (DfE, 2017c).

- At any one point around one-quarter of looked after children will be in place-ments which have lasted two years and 40 per cent of the total number of children in care will be in placements which are intended to be long term (Sinclair et al., 2007).

In recent years, there has been a rise in the proportions of older children in care in England, with over 60 per cent now aged 10–17 (DfE, 2017c). This marks a change from previous years when the proportions were evenly split between those aged over and under 10 (Thoburn, 2009a). In part the change reflects a rising number of unaccompanied asylum seeking young people entering the care system in recent years (DfE, 2017c). It also reflects the fact that children are tending to spend longer periods in the care system than previously (Biehal, 2006), resulting in more children coming into care as *young entrants* and becoming *adolescent graduates*; Bilson (2016) calculated that from 2001 to 2015 there had been a 20 per cent increase in the number of children in England looked after for more than two years.

Children's rights and participation

The United Nations (UN) Convention on the Rights of the Child (UNCRC) was adopted by the UN in 1989 and ratified by the UK in 1991.[5] At the time of writing it has been ratified by all countries other than Somalia, South Sudan and the USA. The UNCRC does not have the status of law within the UK, but its influence on child care legislation is apparent and it has moral force. Children's rights can be viewed as important in terms of recognising children as people who, in and of themselves, can and should expect to be treated by carers and the state in particular ways. The children's rights agenda may also be seen as one mechanism for helping prevent or address abusive care. As a signatory to the UNCRC the UK is also committed to upholding it, and to being inspected by the UN Committee on the Rights of the Child in respect of its implementation of the Convention. The 2016 Committee report on the UK raised concerns that certain groups of children in the UK, including looked after children, 'continue to experience discrimination and social stigmatization, including through the media' (OHCR, 2016, p. 5). A number of the articles, or parts of the articles, of the UNCRC have particular relevance to children in care, most obviously:

- *Article 9* – Children should not be separated from their parents against their will unless it is for their own good. Children whose parents are separated have the right to stay in contact with both parents, unless this might harm them.

- *Article 12* – Children have the right to say what they think should happen, when adults are making decisions that affect them, and to have their opinions considered and taken seriously.

- *Article 20* – Children who cannot be looked after by their own family must be given special protection and assistance by the government, including alternative care which respects their culture, language and religion.

- *Article 21* – Governments must oversee the process of adoption to make sure it is safe, lawful and that it prioritises children's best interests. Children should only be adopted outside of their country if they cannot be placed with a family in their own country.

- And, *Article 25* – Children who are looked after away from home should have their treatment and care regularly reviewed.

Practice Pointer 1.5

Read through the full list of articles of the UNCRC and identify any other articles, or parts of articles, which you think have relevance for practice with looked after children. Can you foresee any difficulties in trying to apply any of these in your local setting?

The development of the children's rights agenda can be linked to the recognition of childhood as a separately defined stage in the life course, and of children as agentic beings who make conscious choices and should be recognised as individuals in and of themselves (James and Prout, 1997). Thomas (2007) presents three core reasons for children's participation: moral (it is the right thing to do);

developmental (it supports children's development); and pragmatic (it helps arrive at better decisions). There are some criticisms of the way in which the children's rights agenda has developed. Some of these are based around the failure of adults and adult-led organisations and structures to live up to claims that they are involving and consulting with children. In turn this can lead to frustration and pessimism among children about their future participation (Borland et al., 2001; Bell, 2011).

More fundamentally there has been criticism of a children's rights-based agenda which emphasises individualistic rather than communitarian principles (Smith, 2009). Featherstone and colleagues (2014) argue that the reification of 'children's rights' within modern UK children's services policy and practice serves not only to obscure consideration of the rights and needs of their birth parents and families, but to overlook the importance of understanding children's needs within the context of their close relationships.

Hart's (1992) ladder of participation provides a gauge of children's involvement in decision-making processes. It has eight steps. The first three steps are all types of non-participation in which adults may claim to be involving children in decisions but are, consciously or unconsciously, not doing so: *Manipulation* – where adults use the involvement of children as a tool to support their own goals. *Decoration* – where children are visually present but have no meaningful influence or role in it. And, *Tokenism* where children's views are formally sought but they have very limited influence on adult plans or actions.

The next five steps on the ladder present increasing levels of genuine child participation: *Assigned but involved* – where adults decide what children's involvement will be in a given setting, but children understand the parameters of their involvement and their involvement is genuine within these parameters. *Consulted but involved* – where children's views on different adult-given options are sought, and their views on these options taken on board. *Adult initiated, shared decisions* – where within an initially adult-established activity, children take decisions jointly with adults. *Child initiated and directed* – where children work autonomously from adults on a particular activity and take all decisions on a particular activity. *Child initiated, shared decisions* – where children set the parameters of the activity after which decisions are taken jointly with adults.

This model is widely referred to but has also been adapted – perhaps most importantly on the grounds that the ladder metaphor suggests that the stages are to be sequentially achieved, with the highest level (*child initiated, shared decisions*) always the ultimate aim. In reality, children may participate in different ways in different activities and any of the five genuine models of participation may be appropriate, depending on the child and the activity in question. Treseder's (1997) adaptation of Hart's model therefore removes the first three types of non-participation, along with the hierarchy of the remaining five, to present a model of the five options for children's genuine participation as ones to choose from depending on factors such as the child's preference, developmental stage and the type of activity involved.

One example of a mechanism for looked after children to influence wider local authority practice is Children in Care Councils (CiCCs) in England. These are made up of groups of children in care who meet with members of their local authority to discuss practice and policy issues related to the care of looked after children. Though it is not mandatory for local authorities to set these up, a review in 2011 found that nearly all local authorities had done so (A National Voice, 2011). However, there was considerable variation in their operation. The most well-established CiCCs reported 'real influence in operational and policy areas such as budget control, Leaving Care Grant and recruitment' (p. 7), while on the other hand a third of CiCCs reported difficulty getting important local authority employees to attend and a lack of clarity about financial resources to support their work – suggesting some level of tokenism.

It is also worth remembering that some looked after children will not want to participate in such forums – a study in Scotland regarding children's views of how they would like to be consulted (Borland et al., 2001) found scepticism about the value of formal participation mechanisms among children who did not participate in them. This study also highlighted that utilising a range of methods to consult children (written and spoken, group and individual) was important to allow for the widest participation, rather than assuming a given group of children would all necessarily prefer a given method such as a group discussion or individual questionnaire.

While the opportunity to influence wider policy and practice is important, looked after children's influence over the decisions about their day-to-day care is the core benchmark of participation. Bell (2011) highlights the central importance of good relationships between practitioners and children in supporting children's participation. She also identifies the central barriers to child participation as adult attitudes, organisational culture and social deprivation – the latter undermining some children's ability to actualise participatory rights. Many children are invited to formal meetings about them, such as Looked After Child Reviews, but often report finding their participation to be tokenistic, or the discussion invasive or uncomfortable (Bell, 2011). This is illustrative of the ongoing challenges which exist in facilitating genuine child participation within structures and formats that are adult-designed and adult-led.

Are there too many or too few children in care?

This is a complex question, to which it is impossible to provide a definitive answer. Most people's answer will depend in part on the context and circumstances of why children are coming into care and the extent to which they believe it might be avoided through more generous welfare and family support. It has been known for some time that children from poorer families are more likely to enter care (Bebbington and Miles, 1989). There are also widespread regional variations in LAC rates in England, ranging, in 2017, from Blackpool with an LAC rate of 184 to Wokingham with an LAC rate of 20 (DfE, 2017b).[6] Such differences can be largely, though not entirely, explained by differences in social deprivation between geographical areas (Bywaters et al., 2016). More recent work by Bywaters and colleagues has identified that children living in deprived areas are ten times as likely to come into care as those living in non-deprived areas (McNicoll, 2017). Such variation may be viewed negatively – as poor families being penalised for their poverty through the removal of their children – or positively – as the increased provision of state resources to those children who are in families in the greatest material need. It is notable, for example, that several of the Western European countries which have been noted to have a greater family support orientation than the UK (Gilbert et al., 2011) also had higher LAC rates than England in the mid-2000s, including Sweden (63), Norway (68), France (102) and Denmark (104) (Thoburn, 2009a). This might suggest that higher proportions of children in the state care system do not necessarily equate with more child protection-orientated policies and welfare systems.

Secondly, views about whether there are too many or too few children in care are likely to be influenced by people's values, particularly what they think the proper relationship between individuals, families and the state should be. Fox Harding (1991) produced an enduring typology of four value positions which are held by people when considering the relationship between the state and family life:

1. *Laissez faire and patriarchy* – that the state should stay out of family life as much as possible and intervene only when it is clearly necessary to prevent harm.

2. *State paternalism and child protection* (also sometimes called the 'child rescue' perspective) – that the state should prioritise the protection and prevention of harm to children within the family home.

3. *Children's rights and child liberation* – that the state should promote the partici-pation and listen to the perspectives of children about their own care as much as possible, seeing them as beings in their own right apart from adults.

4. *Defence of the birth family and family rights* – that the state should respect fami-lies' rights to care for children and support them to do so as much as possible, recognising the socio-economic influences on poor parenting.

This typology is not mutually exclusive – it is possible for a person to adopt ele-ments of more than one of these positions at the same time and, indeed, all four value positions are represented to some degree in the Children Act 1989:

- The 'no order' principle – *Laissez faire and patriarchy perspective*.

- The welfare of the child is the paramount consideration – *Child rescue perspective*.

- The views of the child be taken into consideration by professionals – *Children's rights perspective*.

- And that children should live with their families wherever possible, and where they are in care there should ordinarily be contact with them – *Defence of the birth family perspective*.

However, it is usually possible to identify that one of the four value positions predominates in an individual, agency or policy approach at a given time. Other things being equal, we would associate those adopting the *Laissez faire and patriarchy* and the *Defence of the birth family* perspectives to have, for very different reasons, a more questioning response to rising numbers of children in care than those adopting a *Child rescue* perspective. Those adopting a *Children's rights* perspective would likely take a view dependent on the context of how well children's participation was supported and recognised in a given family or care setting, and children's own views on whether they preferred to remain within their family or be placed in substitute care.

Practice Pointer 1.6

Look at the four above-mentioned value positions outlined by Fox Harding (1991).

Which of the value positions best represent your views and why?

Look at the value position which you think least well represents your views and write down the best arguments you can think of in support of this value position.

Does doing this challenge your views about any area of practice with looked after children at all?

'Outcomes' for looked after children

Indicators of child and adult well-being for children who are and have been in the care system are poor compared to peers in the general population. This includes measures of educational attainment, employment, mental ill health, physical health, involvement in the criminal justice system, homelessness and substance misuse (Meltzer et al., 2003; Wilson et al., 2004; DfE, 2017a, 2017e). Though these discrepancies are striking, comparison with the general child population can be misleading given that children coming into the care system will be among those with the highest levels of need and difficulties. A better guide is arguably provided by considering whether looked after children make progress during the time they are in the care system, or by comparing their progress with children in similar circumstances but who are still living with their parents.

Forrester and colleagues (2009) reviewed 12 UK research studies on children in care spanning the years 1991–2006 and found that they tended to show that foster care, residential care and adoption improved children's welfare over time judged by placement stability, emotional and behavioural, educational, employment and criminality measures. More recent studies which have gathered comparative data on children who entered the care system and then either stayed in care or returned to parental care (Wade et al., 2011; Lutman and Farmer, 2012) have found those returning home tend to fare worse. Research into educational attainment in England and Scotland has also found that those in the care system long term do better than those with social work support living at home (McClung and Gayle, 2010; Sebba et al., 2015). A contrasting finding, however, came from a large-scale survey of mental illness by Ford and colleagues (2007) which found notably higher rates of mental health disorder among looked after children than a comparison group of children living in social deprivation in the community. This contrast may in part be explicable by the higher rates of abuse and neglect experienced by children who are in the care system.

Though not entirely uniform, these findings do then suggest that the 'care system' has a broadly positive impact on children's welfare. This is, however, what we should expect bearing in mind that children are placed in state care on the grounds that it is in their welfare interests and that placing children in state care involves the state spending considerably more money on their care than if they had remained with their parents. In 2010 it was estimated that it cost £763 a month to maintain a child in family care with social work supervision; £1914 per month to maintain them in kinship care; £5951.85 to maintain them in local authority foster care; and £14,662 per month to maintain them in residential care (Hannon et al., 2010). Given that considerably greater resources are invested in children living away from parental care it would be concerning if it did not lead to some improvement in children's well-being. At the same time it is important to note that, while some former looked after children do very well, a good number experience marked difficulties on leaving care when they reach adulthood.

Key messages for practice

- In all four countries in the UK a child will enter care for two overarching reasons: either because there are significant concerns about their welfare in parental care, or because their parent is not in a position, or willing, to provide them with appropriate care.

- Children who were previously in care, privately fostered children and children in private kinship care are not formerly 'looked after' but will share some common needs and circumstances with looked after children.

- There has been an increasing emphasis on children's rights and participation over the last 30 years. This is important, but there are challenges to genuinely involving children within the adult structures and processes of the looked after child system.

- The number of children in care and the LAC rate have been rising in all the countries in the UK over recent years, but there is inter-country variation as well as strong regional variation in England.

- Debates over whether more or fewer children should be in the care system are complex, and views on this topic are conditioned by values concerning the balance between state and family life, the impact of poverty on parenting and interpretations of whether children's entry into the care system improves their welfare and supports their families.

Suggested reading

English law: Brammer, A. (2015) *Social Work Law (4th Edition)*. London: Pearson; and, Ball, C. (2014) *Looked After Children*. Basingstoke: Palgrave.

Northern Irish law: Long, M. (2013) *Child Care Law Northern Ireland: A Summary*. London: BAAF.

Scots law: Guthrie, T. (2011) *Social Work Law in Scotland*. Haywards Heath: Bloomsbury Professional; and Plumtree, A. (2014) *Child Care Law Scotland: A Summary*. London: BAAF.

Online resources

The NSPCC provides some useful information on the systems in the four countries: www.nspcc.org.uk/preventing-abuse/child-protection-system/.

Details of the official looked after child statistics in the four countries of the UK can be found as follows:

England, UK Government. For the year 2016/17, see: www.gov.uk/government/statistics/children-looked-after-in-england-including-adoption-2016-to-2017. For other years, see: https://www.gov.uk/government/collections/statistics-looked-after-children

Northern Ireland, Northern Irish Government (2016/17): www.health-ni.gov.uk/topics/dhssps-statistics-and-research/childrens-services-statistics

Scotland, Scottish Government figures for the year 2015/16 (most current, at the time of writing): www.gov.scot/Publications/2017/03/6791/downloads

Wales, Welsh Government (2016/17 figures): https://statswales.gov.wales/Catalogue/Health-and-Social-Care/Social-Services/Childrens-Services/Children-Looked-After

Notes

1   The Children and Families Act 2014 has now removed this as a legal duty for adoption agencies placing children for adoption in England.

2   For the English care statistics the latest figures at the time of writing are provided. For overall care numbers these are for the year 2016/17 (DfE, 2017c); however, for some outcome data only figures for 2015/16 were available (DfE, 2017a, 2017d). For Scottish figures the latest year available at the time of writing is 2015/16 (Scottish Government, 2017a, 2017b).

3   From 2016, s.76 of the Social Services and Well-being Wales Act 2014 replaced s. 20 of the Children Act 1989 in Wales.

4   *Re N (Children) (Adoption: Jurisdiction)* [2015] EWCA Civ 1112.

5   The United Nations Convention on the Rights of the Child (UNCRC) (1989) may be accessed at: https://downloads.unicef.org.uk/wp-content/uploads/2010/05/UNCRC_united_nations_convention_on_the_rights_of_the_child.pdf?_ga=2.118231691.341736116.1516824749-690257340.1516824749

6   This excludes the Isles of Scilly which have an LAC rate of 0 but a very small population, making comparisons inappropriate.

CHAPTER 2

ASSESSMENT AND LOOKED AFTER CHILDREN

Chapter Overview

This chapter considers assessing the needs, wishes and feelings of looked after children. It starts by reviewing the Department of Health *Framework for the Assessment of Children in Need and their Families* (DOH, 2000a) and the Scottish Government Integrated Assessment Framework (IAF), developed as part of the Getting It Right for Every Child (GIRFEC) policy initiative (Scottish Executive, 2005), and the application of these frameworks to the contexts of looked after children. It reviews the 'ecological' character of these frameworks, discussing ways in which social workers can elicit children's views and take account of a child's wider networks, while also illustrating some of the ways in which the current practice context makes the application of a truly ecological approach difficult. The chapter then provides a critical introduction to three further influential theoretical perspectives with relevance to looked after children – attachment theory, resilience theory and the social studies of childhood. It finishes by considering how insights from these four theories may be combined.

Assessment and professional judgement

When undertaking assessment of looked after children, it is useful to bear in mind some of the broader guidance on assessment in social work. Milner and colleagues (2015) provide a useful overview of the key stages involved in assessment: (1) preparation; (2) collecting information; (3) interpreting information; (4) making judgements based on the information; and (5) deciding what should be done. That assessment should be an ongoing process rather than a one-off event (Coulshed and Orme, 2012) is often emphasised, while the latest version of child protection guidance, *Working Together*, lists key qualities of assessment within children and families work to include participation, child centredness, an orientation towards action and that they be 'transparent and open to challenge' (HM Government, 2015, p. 21).

The importance of practitioners reflecting on their own assumptions in children and families assessment practice is underlined. Research has found that there are some common errors that tend to occur in assessment practice. These include the tendency for practitioners to focus on information which is most readily available, rather than the most crucial, and to be slow to question initial judgements about children and families – typically by looking for information which confirms the initial judgement and ignoring information which might undermine it (Munro, 1999). These tendencies arise, in part, because of heuristics – the cognitive shortcuts people need to take when making sense of complex information. This therefore highlights the need for systemic contextual supports which allow practitioners to engage in more effective assessment practice. Such factors include a working culture which allows space for reflective practice, particularly the questioning of underlying assumptions on which judgements are based; good quality supervision; and organisational systems which encourage the development of practitioner judgement (Helm, 2010; Munro, 2011).

Practice Pointer 2.1

Practitioners identifying the assumptions they are making, and being willing to question them, is a key recommendation across the social work literature on assessment. This is, though, more difficult than it might sound. Think of a practice situation where you made an assumption about a situation which turned out to be incorrect. Why did you make the assumption? What was the impact of the assumption on your practice? What caused you to change your mind?

There are several assessment frameworks which are commonly used in child and family social work practice. *The Framework for the Assessment of Children in Need and their Families* (DOH, 2000a) (hereafter the 'DOH Framework', see Figure 2.1) contains a universal framework of child need, and its use was mandated in child and family social work practice in England and Wales until 2013. The framework was also influential in the development of other national frameworks including the Scottish framework, Integrated Assessment Planning and Recording Framework (IAF) (Scottish Executive, 2005, see Figure 2.1).

The DOH Framework organises assessment around the three domains of a *Child's Developmental Needs, Parenting Capacity* and *Family & Environmental Factors* with the child's needs at the centre. Children's developmental needs are categorised into the seven dimensions of:

- Health
- Education
- Emotional and Behavioural Development
- Identity
- Family and Social Relationships
- Social Presentation
- Self-care Skills.

The seven dimensions are the same as those set out in the *Looking after Children Materials* contained in the Action and Assessment Records (AAR) (DOH, 1995),

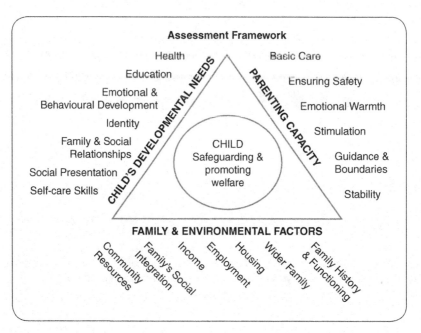

Figure 2.1 The DOH Framework (DOH, 2000a)

versions of which are still used in some areas in the UK. The Scottish IAF (Scottish Executive, 2005) labels the seven dimensions in more concrete terminology and a slightly different order: Being healthy; Learning and achieving; Being able to communicate; Confidence in who I am; Learning to be responsible; Becoming independent, looking after myself and, Enjoying family and friends see Figure 2.2). The IAF links to the *Getting It Right for Every Child* (GIRFEC) policy framework (Scottish Executive, 2005) and eight child-focused indicators designed to apply universally to all children in Scotland. These are that a child should be Safe, Healthy, Achieving, Nurtured, Active, Respected and Responsible, and Included. The equivalent framework in England and Wales is *Every Child Matters* (ECM) (DfES, 2003), which sets out five universal indicators for child well-being. These are that children Stay Safe; Be Healthy; Enjoy and Achieve; Make a Positive Contribution; and Achieve Economic Well-being. There is currently no named equivalent policy in Northern Ireland, but *The Children and Young People's Strategic Partnership* has responsibility for bringing agencies together to work towards five child outcomes – Health, Safety, Learning, Economic well-being and Play (CYPSP, 2017).

The introduction of the *Looking after Children Materials* (Ward, 1995) in the UK over 20 years ago was generally praised as a mechanism for helping monitor and improve outcomes for looked after children and care leavers (Jackson, 1998). However, questions have also been raised about the use of such universal frameworks. Firstly, there is an 'in principle' criticism regarding the compatibility of predefined categories of child need with tailored assessment

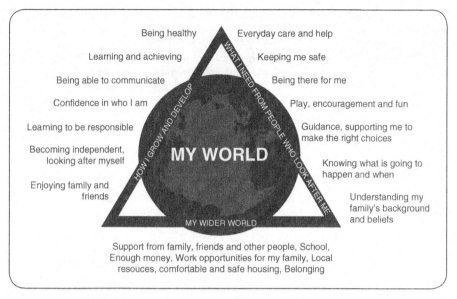

Figure 2.2 The Scottish IAF (Scottish Executive, 2005)

which is genuinely responsive to a child's individual circumstances and life (Woodhead, 1997).

Secondly, there has been a criticism of the application of assessment frameworks within a context of managerialism and performance indicator-led practice. The *Munro Review* identified that the rigid, prescriptive, use of assessment frameworks was one of the factors which had resulted in compliance-driven practice in child and family social work (Munro, 2011). Higgins and colleagues (2015) argue that such criticisms apply equally well to practice with looked after children. The upshot of these criticisms is that standardised assessment frameworks and decision-aiding tools can support effective practice, but only when they are used in a way which augments rather than supplants professional judgement (Sen et al., 2014). Two important messages should be emphasised: the need for busy practitioners to have the time, head space and willingness to fit assessment categories around children's individual, complex and varied needs, rather than vice versa; and, secondly, the need to recognise the emotional and psychological, as well as the technical-rational, aspects of assessment within child and family practice (Helm, 2010).

Assessment contexts relating to looked after children

The particular contexts relating to the assessment of looked after children are set out in Table 2.1. Particular consideration needs to be given to children's membership of at least two care networks – their current placement and their birth family,

Table 2.1 Key assessment foci and contexts relating to looked after children

Focus of Assessment	Key Assessment Contexts
Children's Needs	• Care planning: how well are the child's needs being met within current placement and care arrangements? • The role that birth family members should play in meeting the child's needs while outside of the family's care. • Placement moves where needed: (1) What placement type and what specific placement will be best suited to meeting the child's needs? (2) Whom should the child be placed with (e.g. sibling co-placement; other children in the placement)? • Young person's support needs on transitioning to adulthood.
Parenting/Caring Capacity	• Assessment of carers and adopters. Where placement moves are considered, what future carers will best meet this child's needs? • Consideration of the role of birth family members while the child is outside the family network, including levels and types of contact. • Assessment of birth parents' ability to meet the child's needs if the child returns to their full-time care.
Family and Environmental Factors	• The interaction of the child within adult, peer and other relationships in placement and birth family contexts; should include consideration of previous significant relationships from home and previous placements. • Community influences in placement and birth family settings and how they impact on the child. • Cultural, legal and social influences relevant to the child.

as well as previous carers in the case of some children. The needs of most looked after children, then, will not be met entirely within their placement setting – in particular, issues of identity and family and social relationships will require consideration of the ongoing role that the child's birth family and friends from their home community continue to play. Even where there is no direct contact with birth family members, a child's memory, awareness and ability to come to terms with prior relationships will be important factors in their life. Equally, when considering the domains of Parenting Capacity and Family and Environmental Factors it is important to think through the different contributions that are made through the placement setting as well as the child's birth family.

There are different points, purposes and types of assessment for looked after children. The major decisional points at which more formalised assessment is required are:

● Whether a child should be placed in care and if so what type of placement will meet their needs.

● Whether a child can return to parental care or extended family care if a return to parental care is not possible.

- What type of longer-term placement is best suited to a child if they are not returning to birth family care.

- Planning for a child to exit care, either via a return home, adoption, Special Guardianship Order (SGO) or as a care leaver.

Parts of such assessment require a social worker to write formal reports to develop and justify a particular course of action and to draw up written child care plans which are discussed and approved at Looked After Child Reviews. The local authority must ordinarily hold a review of a looked after child's care within four weeks (20 working days) of their placement,[1] and then three months after this and thereafter six-monthly. Looked After Child Reviews have the overall purpose of formally reviewing a child's care and education. Between such reviews, social workers should be regularly communicating with children and their carers to assess how they are faring on a more informal basis.

Key transition points can be a potential source of stress or anxiety for a child, but they may also present new developmental opportunities which are important to consider (Gilligan, 1997). These points are not limited to, but commonly occur for looked after children where there is consideration of reuniting a child with their birth family, a placement change and when a young person is ageing out of care. At such points thought is required as to how a child's needs will be best met in the new context. In terms of reunification, for example, there should be a focus on how a child's presenting needs and development will be supported within the new care arrangements if they were to return to birth family care, and how both sets of carers and the relevant professionals in placement and home settings will work together to meet these needs.

Tools for eliciting children's wishes, feelings and aspirations

The discussion so far has emphasised children's needs which may suggest a paternalistic and adult-dominated view of determining what is in children's best interests. As noted, however, the children's rights agenda has focused attention on the importance of children's participation and views. Particular tools can be helpful in eliciting looked after children's perspectives. Some examples are:

- The *Looking After Children Materials* (Ward, 1995) are organised around the seven dimensions of children's developmental needs, which provide a mechanism for systematically gathering and recording information about looked after children and can be used in participatory ways. The participatory use of the materials is, however, more suited for work with looked after young people than children.

- Activity books, drawing, games and dolls and puppets are widely used to engage younger children and elicit their views – particularly by encouraging and allowing children to express thoughts, feelings and emotions that would be difficult for them to express in direct speech.

- Vera Fahlberg's well-known text (2012) *A Child's Journey Through Placement* contains a range of suggestions for engaging children on their wishes and feelings when in care.

- *The Three Houses* template – based on the three houses of (1) what a child is worried about; (2) what is going well; and (3) what a child wants to happen – is widely used in child and family social work to gain primary school age children's views, while *The Adolescent Wellbeing Scale* contains 18 questions relating to different areas of a young person's life to elicit their views of their current situation. Both of these last two tools, as well as a range of others for engaging children, are freely available and can be downloaded at the SocialWorkersToolbox.com (see the online resources section at the end of this chapter).

Coming prepared with different play and discussion tools (paper, colouring pens, toys, games) that might allow a child to engage in different ways is helpful for such work while being prepared to try different methods to ascertain a child's views – or indeed get a sense of why they are reluctant to give their views – is also important. Social workers may of course develop their own tailor-made exercises that they find work well with children or that they construct for a particular child, age group or situation. As with all practice tools it is wise to have done a trial run in using them before they are first used in a live practice situation with a child.

Looked after children's views and aspirations may align with professional assessment of their needs, but as with other children, there will be times when they do not. There is an expectation that professional assessment of what children's needs are will be influenced, though not necessarily determined, by what children want for themselves. The tensions there might be between what children want for themselves and what is thought best for them are likely to be more acute for looked after children, because they are not living with their parents and also because of the very significant decisions that will be being made about their future care. It is part of a social worker's role to try and help reconcile these two things. In my experience there will be times when children will accept decisions which do not agree with what they themselves would have chosen, so long as it is clearly explained how their views have been considered and why decisions were taken in the way they were. In other situations, particularly with older young people, this can be more difficult. In such cases clearly acknowledging that a young person's views differ from the decisions taken by professionals, respecting a young person's right to hold and express differing opinions and continuing to try and engage the young person around the issue in question is important.

Practice Pointer 2.2

Ben (10) is an articulate child in a long-term foster placement. He is settled in his placement but has a strong sense of connection to his birth family. However, his birth parents are struggling with addiction issues and do not always attend the monthly contact sessions or give prior notice of being unable to attend. On these occasions Ben returns from contact sessions highly distressed and his behaviour towards his carers in placement is very chal-lenging for the following week. A Looked After Child Review is approaching and Ben has voiced a wish for contact with his birth parents to be increased. You are Ben's social worker and do not think this is in his interests. How might you approach discussing this with Ben?

Children's wider networks – an ecological approach

Frameworks such as the DOH Framework and the IAF are said to be 'ecological' in that they encourage consideration of the different 'systems' which interact in a child's life and, in particular, how changes in one system in a child's life are likely to affect other systems. Bronfenbrenner's (1979) ecological theory outlined five 'sys-tems' operating within an individual child's life. Firstly, the *Microsystem* of direct individual relationships (e.g. parents, carers, wider family members, friends, teach-ers, social workers and other practitioners directly working with them). Secondly, the *Mesosystem* in which relationships in the Microsystem interact in a way that directly impacts upon a child. A common example is of how the interaction between a child's experience of home relationships and school relationships will impact on the child's experience of both. Thirdly, the *Exosystem* of wider institutional factors which are not direct individual relationships but which have a direct impact on a child. Local community resources, local community culture and the child's school, taken as an organisational whole, rather than manifested in particular relationships with individual school staff, are examples of this. Fourthly, the *Macrosystem*, the broader social, cultural and socio-economic contexts which set the broader param-eters of the world in which a child lives. Finally, the *Chronosystem*, representing change over the course of childhood, including important historical events in the child's life which might condition how they respond to present and future issues.

Applying an ecological approach

The ecological model encourages practitioners to think about the key dynamics in different parts of a looked after child's systems, including those in their wider net-works such as birth family and friendship networks. A child's networks are likely to include a child's relationship with different adults and children on placement, the relationships the child has, or can build, in the local area with peers and adults

(Daniel et al., 2010), and the relationship between placement and birth family settings (Cleaver, 2000). Outside of placement, the child's relationship to school and schooling, the relationship between the school and the carers and the interaction of both impacting on the child have been identified as key (Gilligan, 2000; Sinclair et al., 2005b). The relationship between a child and their social worker can be highly significant, not only relationally and in terms of decision-making around placement, but as a link between the birth family and the placement settings (Schofield and Stevenson, 2009) which may otherwise become split into separated worlds for the child (Cleaver, 2000). Health professionals (for example, a school nurse, the named GP, the named health professional and mental health professionals if involved) are also worth considering as potentially significant people in a looked after child's life for periods of time.

Particular tools and ways of working can aid practitioners to gain a sense of children's wider networks. Family network diagrams (for example, ecomaps and genograms) are widely used as tools to gain an appreciation of children's networks and their sense and understanding of their networks. Their application is explored in some detail by Hill (2002). The application of an ecological approach to child and family social work is particularly associated with the work of Gordon Jack, and his co-authored text in this series with Helen Donnellan (Jack and Donnellan, 2013) foregrounds the application of ecological theory to child and family practice. Jack (2015) has also illustrated the importance of practitioners recognising the significance of place and belonging in their work with children.

Family Group Conferences (FGCs) are family-led decision-making processes which can identify and galvanise a child's wider network of family support. Their focus is on giving birth family members opportunity to draw up their own plans to address child welfare concerns. Though their primary use has been to try to prevent the need for children's entry into care, they can be used alongside all stages of social work assessment and planning, including to look at kinship care options or contact plans when a child is already in care. Originating in the late 1980s in New Zealand, drawing on practices within Maori culture, FGCs have operated in the UK since the mid-1990s (Marsh and Crow, 1998) and there has been a recent growth in their use in England (Mason et al., 2017; Spring Consortium, 2017). In the UK, FGCs are sometimes provided 'in-house' by local authorities and sometimes by voluntary sector agencies to whom local authorities refer families. The FGC model in the UK draws substantially on their original usage in New Zealand. The UK model comprises an FGC convenor, independent of the child and family social work service, attempting to engage the child, their birth parents and the wider family and friends network around the child welfare issues of concern raised by the social worker. The FGC provides the family with an opportunity to come together to formulate a plan to address the child welfare issues at a family-led meeting. The FGC meeting itself consists of three key parts:

1. An information-giving session facilitated by the FGC co-ordinator where professionals (the child's social worker and other relevant professionals) provide the family with key information about agency concerns.

2. Private Family Time where all professionals, including the FGC co-ordinator, leave the room and the family are left to devise a Family Plan to address the identified concerns. This may involve requesting additional resources from involved agencies to facilitate the Family Plan.

3. Feedback time where the family present the Family Plan to professionals and the professionals approve whether it addresses the core child welfare concerns. An underlying assumption of FGCs is that professionals will agree to support a Family Plan where it is legal, feasible and likely to safeguard the child's welfare (Marsh and Crow, 1998).

Families participating in FGCs tend to rate the experience highly, feeling their perspectives are better heard than at traditional social work meetings (Marsh and Crow, 1998; Holland et al., 2005b; Mason et al., 2017). FGCs have also generally been found to be successful in widening the family network of support for a child (Ashley and Nixon, 2007).

Practice Pointer 2.3

Returning to Ben (Practice Pointer 2.2): Though he clearly feels a strong connection to his birth family, the only contact sessions set up are with his birth parents. How might a social worker go about gaining a sense of his wider birth family network and of whom in it might play a positive supportive role in his life?

The importance of recognising wider social, cultural, economic and community-level initiatives within child and family social work practice has been emphasised within an ecological approach (Jack and Donnellan, 2013). There are some strong traditions of doing so in some European countries, as well as particular examples of such neighbourhood and community-level working in the UK (Henderson and Thomas, 2013), including the *Sure Start* programme and community-level planning of future service needs (Holland et al., 2011). There have also been good local-level examples of social work practitioners working closely with community-level health initiatives, community-wide parenting support initiatives and community-generated safety initiatives (Jack and Gill, 2009; Nelson, 2015), while links between community development work and child and family social work focused on anti-poverty initiatives, neighbourhood regeneration and youth engagement have sometimes been made (Henderson and Thomas, 2013). However, such links are currently weak and examples remain notable more for their exceptionality than their prevalence. Despite repeated acknowledgement of the ecological nature of the DOH Framework, policy and practice focus within child and family social work in the UK remains heavily focused on the individual child and family, usually to the exclusion of consideration of wider community-level and societal factors (Featherstone et al., 2014). In the language of Bronfenbrenner's (1979) model, while the

DOH Framework encourages practitioners to also consider *Exosystem-* and *Macrosystem-*level factors, child welfare policy, funding and practice remain rooted in particular *Microsystem* responses focused on individual parents and children.

Effective practice with looked after children nonetheless requires that attention is given to how structural-level factors affect individual well-being. This includes consideration of the social position of looked after children in wider society, and the impact of this on how a child conceives of themselves and their looked-after status. The potential stigma attached to being a looked after child in the UK has been noted (OHCR, 2016) and the social isolation faced by many care leavers on leaving the care system remains a concern (Stein, 2012). Altering societal, policy and legal mandates is not within the gift of individual social work practice in the *microsystem*; however, supporting an individual child to develop a positive self-identity within the structural constraints which exist is. It is also worth remembering that progressive societal, policy and legal change for looked after children has also been influenced by organisations led by, working with or working for looked after children and care leavers. Children in Care Councils (CiCCs), mentioned in Chapter 1, exist in most local authorities and there are also a number of national organisations with a specific remit to support and campaign on behalf of looked after children and care leavers – examples of these are provided in the list of online resources at the end of this chapter.

Theoretical influences on the assessment of children's needs and views

Attachment theory

Attachment theory is a universal theory of child development. As a theory which has evolved from exploring the impact of children's separation from their primary carers on them (Bowlby, 1951, 1997 [1969]) it has obvious relevance to the lives of looked after children. Attachment theory has also advanced explanations of the impact of abusive and neglectful care on children's development and therefore has potential relevance in this respect as well, given the majority of looked after children will have experienced some form of abuse or neglect. Attachment theory has provided persuasive explanations of child development and draws on an extensive international research base from the last 75 years (Shemmings and Shemmings, 2011). It has also helped give unprecedented focus to the importance of early social relationships and emotional care in a child's psychological development. Attachment theory-derived concepts have been applied to research on looked after children as both a measure of adjustment (e.g. Quinton and Rutter, 1988; Quinton et al., 1998) and an explanatory framework of children's progress and development in care placements (e.g. Schofield et al., 2000; Beek and Schofield, 2004). Respected guides to practice with looked after children (e.g. Fahlberg, 2012; Schofield and Beek, 2014) have also been heavily influenced by the theory.

Indeed, attachment theory is probably the pre-eminent theory, in respect of not only looked after children, but children and families work more broadly in the UK (Milner et al., 2015). This can, however, be a weakness as well as a strength, as is considered below.

Attachment theory holds that infants seek to develop and maintain closeness to their primary carer. In ordinary secure attachment formation, from 0 to 2 months children show limited preference as to their carer; from 2 to 8 months they develop a more focused attachment; and between 8 and 12 months they tend to form a fully discriminating attachment to their primary carer, exhibiting distress on separation from them and comfort when their presence returns (Schaffer and Rudolph, 1990; Zeanah and Smyke, 2015). From three years upwards toddlers begin to distinguish between their own cognitions and those of their carer and begin to act with increasing autonomy (Howe et al., 1999). The nature, quality and consistency of the attachment relationship between the growing child and their primary carer is held to have significant influence on later ability to form and maintain future social relationships, as well as on cognitive and personality development (Rutter, 2000). Bowlby (1997) explained this through the concept of the internal working model. A young child's early experience of the world is conditioned through the responses provided when they signal their needs for touch, nutrition, physical care, attention and affection. When a carer consistently responds to these needs the child develops a positive internal working model of themselves and others in which their needs are construed as important in the world around them. The child moves to later infancy (up until 18 months) and early childhood (18 months to 4 years) with a 'secure base' from which they feel safe to explore the world around them, confident that their carer will be there for them if and when they need them. A child whose carer does not respond in this way will develop an internal working model in which there are questions about the validity of their needs and the likelihood of them being met in the outside world. Researchers have identified four types of attachment; the first three were identified by Ainsworth and colleagues (1971) and the fourth, disorganised attachment, later, by Main and Solomon (1986):

Secure Attachment

When children experience consistently responsive care they are likely to develop a secure attachment. As infants they will explore from a secure base and seek comfort from their primary carer when distressed. On separation from their primary carer they will tend to display distress but will be easily reassured by their returning presence.

Insecure Avoidant Attachment

When children experience responses to their needs which are consistently rejecting they will develop an avoidant pattern of attachment. An infant with an avoidant attachment will hide or downplay the expression of their feelings as an adaptive response to the rejecting responses of their caregiver. They will not tend to display obvious distress on separation from their primary carer.

Insecure Resistant/Ambivalent Attachment

When children experience responses to their needs which are inconsistently unresponsive they will develop an ambivalent pattern of attachment. An infant with such an attachment pattern will magnify the signalling of their needs – through, for example, amplifying distress – in order to increase the likelihood of generating a nurturing response from their caregiver. A child of this attachment type will typically exhibit extreme distress on separation from their carer but will not be easily reassured when their carer returns.

Insecure Disorganised Attachment

Children receiving responses they experience as consistently dangerous or frightening will develop a disorganised attachment. Disorganised attachment is particularly associated with the receipt of abusive or highly neglectful caregiving. While the three previous attachment types are adaptive responses to caregivers' behaviour, disorganised attachment is characterised by the lack of an adaptive strategy. This is because '[w]hatever strategy the child uses will not bring proximity, care or comfort' (Howe, 2011, p. 47). A child with a disorganised attachment will display contradictory strategies when approaching their caregiver including avoidance, displays of distress, fear or even freezing.

Disorganised attachment has received significant recent attention because of its claimed links both to prior child abuse and to future psychopathology (mental distress or ill health) (Byrne et al., 2005; Shemmings and Shemmings, 2011). Disorganised attachment *throughout childhood* has been found to be *linked with* later mental ill health and behavioural problems, including disruptive and controlling behaviour, dissociative disorders, borderline personality disorders and anti-social personality disorders. However, the connection is not causal and the evidence base is still developing; indeed, a recent review of disorganised attachment strongly cautioned against the view that it can be used as a diagnostic category to indicate the existence of child abuse (Granqvist et al., 2017).

The diagnostic constructs of Reactive Attachment Disorder (RAD) and Disinhibited Social Engagement Disorder (DSED) are separate to the classifications of attachment security described above. They have been increasingly, and sometimes controversially, used in the classification of looked after children's behaviours and are discussed further in Chapter 9.

Questions about attachment theory

Two questions are considered here. The first regards the application of attachment security classifications in practice. In my own practice experience, attachment labels could be applied to children by practitioners based on limited periods of observation in emotionally charged and challenging situations, such as supervised contact sessions between parents and children or contact sessions between siblings in care. This raises a question about the rigour of the classifications that may be routinely applied in practice. It is due to this concern that one proponent of attachment theory in social work has suggested that practitioners avoid using the term 'attachment' to describe carer–child interaction and instead use the term 'relationship' as a better way of describing the behaviours they observe (Shemmings, 2016).

Formal classification of attachment types should take place through clinical observation. However, this requires specific training and detailed knowledge of the history of a child and their relationship(s) with previous carers which is not always available (Byrne et al., 2005; Quinton, 2012) – particularly for a looked after child where information about their early childhood may be incomplete or contested. Even here, however, there is some uncertainty. While attachment classification assessments have been found to be reliable in controlled research studies, their use in clinical practice has been slow and uneven (Byrne et al., 2005; O'Connor and Byrne, 2007). There is also some inconsistency between different methods of assessing attachment. An examination by Crittenden and colleagues (2007) of three commonly used methods of assessing attachment type (the Ainsworth-extended method, the Cassidy-Marvin method and the Preschool Assessment of Attachment) found limited agreement between them. As a result the authors concluded that 'if applied in clinical settings, these three methods would result in very different groups of children being seen as safe and at risk' (p. 78). This discussion suggests that rather than focusing on the application of a particular attachment label to a child, a social worker's assessment should rather focus on describing relational interaction, as well as supporting children and their carers to develop the basis for secure attachment formation (Barth et al., 2005).

Secondly, there is a broader question as to whether attachment theorists have tended to overstate the causality of early childhood experiences on later human development, in particular future psychopathology (Barth et al., 2005; Granqvist et al., 2017). This is neatly summarised by Deklyen and Greenberg's comment (2008, p. 638 cited in Shemmings and Shemmings, 2011, p. 62) that 'enthusiasm to utilize attachment theory has at times led to over-interpretation of the findings and a fruitless search for a "Holy Grail" of psychopathology'. To illustrate this debate further two other theoretical perspectives will be drawn upon: resilience theory and the social studies of childhood.

Practice Pointer 2.4

What do you think are the key strengths and weaknesses of attachment theory as applied to practice with looked after children?

Resilience theory

A debate has developed within the social work field regarding the policy applications of neuro-scientific evidence on the impact of abuse and neglect in early childhood on children's later development. The central contention being around the claimed irreversibility of early childhood developmental delay and the implications of this for work with children deemed to be at risk (Wastell and White, 2012; Brown and Ward, 2013; Ward and Brown, 2013). The debate has parallels with earlier debates about the research base for attachment theory and its claims about the impact of early childhood adversity on later childhood development (Wootton, 1959).

Both debates concern the theory of resilience, or the extent of children's ability to display 'normal development under difficult conditions' (Fonagy et al., 1994, p. 1). The concept of resilience developed as a way of explaining why and how some children made remarkable progress despite marked adversity in earlier life, compared to peers in similarly adverse circumstances (Rutter, 1981). Rutter questioned Bowlby's (1951) assertion that there was a 'critical period' of around two years from birth in which a child needed to develop a primary attachment if they were to develop 'normally'. While acknowledging that brain development early in a child's life can be highly influential on their later development, resilience-influenced perspectives have also emphasised that personality and development are subject to change even into adulthood, rather than fixed during early childhood (Rutter and Rutter, 1993). Therefore it is argued that while early childhood deprivation may be associated with later psychopathology, patterns of development are not deterministic (Wastell and White, 2012; Granqvist et al., 2017).

Subsequent research has lent some support to Rutter's views and it is now widely accepted that insecure attachment opens up 'pathways' which may lead to later mental ill health rather than directly 'causing' it (Sroufe et al., 1999). Contemporary attachment research has therefore started to look at the interaction between early childhood attachment, family relationships and other social factors which might influence whether certain developmental pathways are more likely (Lee and Hankin, 2009).

Within social work, the theory of resilience has been most meaningfully applied to consider the factors which can support children who have faced adversity to progress (Gilligan, 1997, 2000; Daniel et al., 2010; Ungar, 2015). It has emphasised the psychological, relational and environmental factors which can help promote healthy development in children's lives and thereby support them to overcome adversities. Daniel and colleagues (2010) outline a number of individual child-level characteristics which are linked to resilience including:

- A secure attachment

- Articulateness

- Self-confidence

- Self-efficacy

- A positive self-image

- And a cheerful and optimistic disposition.

Practice Pointer 2.5

What activities can you think of which a social worker or carer might undertake with a looked after child to support their resilience?

However, a child's ability to develop such characteristics will depend on an interaction between individual-, family-, community-level and broader cultural and societal factors in the first place (Wright and Masten, 2015). In other words, a child's ability to develop characteristics which insulate them from the worst impacts of adversity, will itself be influenced by an interaction between a child's innate characteristics and the broader environment around them (Daniel et al., 2010). This recognition has led to an emphasis on the contextual factors that can support children to develop the characteristics which will allow them to be resilient. In particular there is a focus on the attachment-related concept of a child having a 'secure base' with their primary carers; the promotion of positive relationships between a child and significant adult figures and peers, including significant positive figures from their past; recognition of the therapeutic potential of everyday positive educational experiences and the pursuit of interests and hobbies; and recognition of the developmental potential of providing a child with socially important and responsible roles (Daniel et al., 2010).

The social studies of childhood

The social studies of childhood developed in the 1980s and 1990s in response to the recognition of limitations within earlier studies of children and family life (Moran-Ellis, 2010). Though not synonymous with the children's rights agenda, the social studies of childhood approach shares a focus on recognising children as active participants within their own lives. The approach provides a challenge to models from developmental psychology, including attachment theory, which delineate predefined goals and stages of universal child development (Walker, 2005). Those influenced by the social sciences of childhood approach argue that such models of universal development tend to adopt a deficit approach, adversely labelling any child who is not found to fall within the parameters of 'normal' development. As such, it is held that such universal models fail to acknowledge the diversity of children's capabilities and developmental pathways (Winter, 2006; Goodyer, 2011).

Underpinning the social sciences of childhood approach is a view of childhood as a social construction: different times and different cultures construe childhood differently; indeed, historically some societies have not clearly distinguished 'childhood' from 'adulthood' at all (Ariès, 1982). This gives focus to exploring the particular ways childhood is constructed in our society. Secondly, in distinction to many developmental psychological models which heavily emphasise the biological aspects of growing up, the approach gives attention to theory and evidence that familial, social and cultural contexts are also key to the way children learn and develop (Rogoff, 1990, 2003). Finally, the approach argues that children have often been positioned as passive recipients of processes of socialisation (Corsaro, 2004; James, 2013) with the consequence that their agency in their own development has been overlooked (Goodyer, 2011). The social sciences of childhood therefore emphasises children as active agents who not only receive cultural ideas and social values, but influence and shape them (James and Prout, 1997; Corsaro, 2004). It therefore encourages approaches to childhood that are grounded in children's lived experiences, recognising the social contexts which influence child development and children's agency within their own development.

One recent application is found in the work of Katz (2015) who explored the relationships between mothers and children after mothers had experienced prolonged domestic violence and separated from their partners. She found that these relationships were marked by the choices and behaviours both children and mothers made, and the interaction between them, contrasting with previous accounts which had solely focused on adult choices and behaviours in this context. Work within this tradition has also helped influence more nuanced notions of child participation – for example, in respect of family court proceedings and parental separation, practice and research utilising the social studies of childhood approach have helped develop the understanding that most children usually want to participate and have their voice influence proceedings, but this does not mean they think their views should necessarily be decisive in the conclusions that are reached on hugely significant matters such as contact and residency with their parents (Smart et al., 2001; Coyle, 2008).

Strengths and questions regarding the social studies of childhood

The emphasis on the diversity of children's developmental pathways and children's agency within the social studies of childhood approach can be viewed as a countervailing influence to developmental psychology-influenced models (Goodyer, 2011). The focus on children as active agents in their lives is consistent with a children's rights agenda and a child participation philosophy. It has been argued that, by contrast, models of childhood based within developmental psychology only tend to emphasise children's rights to protection rather than their rights to participation and choice (Winter, 2006). Goodyer (2011) argues that consideration of the contextual influences on childhood advocated by the social studies of childhood also importantly encourages consideration of the wider social, political and socio-economic dimensions of looked after children's lives.

Like attachment theory, there are also criticisms. While the social studies of childhood has provided a fruitful way of approaching the study and understanding of childhood, its primary influence has been in the domain of research rather than practice (e.g. James and Prout, 1997; Qvortup et al., 1994; James, 2013). Given its emphasis on recognising and exploring the diversity of children's lived experience it is doubtful whether the approach could provide detailed practice guidance over and above the commitment to exploring children's lives from their own perspectives, recognising them as social actors in their own right and supporting their participation as fully as possible. This commitment is not to be scoffed at. It does, though, bring to mind Forrester and colleagues' (2012) reflection that '[i]t sometimes appears as if the theory of social work is drawn largely from sociology and the practice from psychology' (p. 124).

A second critical consideration is that though the recognition of child agency appears an empowering position to take, it can also lead to attribution of blame for the choices which children do then take. Moran-Ellis (2010) argues that the 'demonization' of teenagers has become an increasing political theme in the UK, revealing the tension between a perspective which emphasises young people's participation and dominant political and policy orientations in the UK. This is not to say that the recognition of child agency is itself misplaced. It is to acknowledge that such recognition is not always empowering for marginalised young people within the context of prevailing political and policy discourse.

Finally, if a criticism of models rooted in developmental psychology is that they tend to overstate the case for universal paths of child development then a parallel question can be asked of the social studies of childhood, namely if children develop in such diverse ways and make, at least some, choices about their own development then how does the social studies of childhood account for similarities in children's development or even the coherence of the concept of 'childhood' at all? As James (2013, p. 47) puts it, this is the challenge of:

[H]ow to account for the heterogeneity of children's individual lives, together with experiences of being children and of belonging to a particular generational category that is embedded in the social world in particular ways.

Practice Pointer 2.6

How do you think the social studies of childhood approach might be applied to practice with looked after children?

Bringing the threads together

This chapter concludes by suggesting that practitioners working with looked after children can learn from all four theoretical perspectives discussed here – ecological theory, attachment theory, resilience theory and the social studies of childhood. Attachment theory focuses attention on the importance of children's early experiences of being cared for and the quality of nurturing relationships in supporting their future development. Most notably, application of the theory emphasises the need for children to be supported to develop strong, trusting relationships with their current carers in order to support their wider development (Sinclair et al., 2005a). It is suggested, however, that practitioners should be wary of using the theory to apply attachment classifications to looked after children with whom they are working; while an attachment theory-influenced focus on children's interaction with the significant people in their lives is important, using insights from the theory to describe a child's behaviours, rather than seeking to definitively classify attachment types, should be the focus for practitioners. It is also worth remembering the critique from the social studies of childhood that attachment theory, like other areas of developmental psychology, can lead to an overly deterministic, deficit-focused, view of early childhood adversity which may imply there is little room for the possibility of later positive development (Goodyer, 2011).

Resilience theory highlights the particular relationship qualities and wider supports which will best aid children to develop characteristics to overcome adversity (Daniel et al., 2010). Building resilience entails consideration of the different relationships in the child's *microsystem* and their interaction in the child's *mesosystem*, remembering that for most looked after children their relationships with both primary carers and birth family members will be highly significant. At the same time ecological theory reminds us that community-level, social and structural factors will also impact on a child's life (Bronfenbrenner, 1979). While individual practice cannot address such macro-level factors alone, an approach which recognises the constraints that exist and looks to support children to develop community links and social support that will help foster their resilience is emphasised. Finally, the social studies of childhood emphasises the importance of practitioners engaging with children's perspectives and agency about their situation in grounded ways. Its insights suggest the importance of a strengths-based approach to children's development that avoids framing divergence from perceived developmental norms pathologically, and which seeks to engage and support looked after children to identify what their own aspirations for their lives are, and how they might realise them.

Key messages for practice

- A holistic assessment of children's needs requires an appreciation of the key areas of children's development, but also requires the application of professional judgement and an openness to recognising the different developmental paths children's lives can take alongside children's own views and aspirations.

- The quality of the relationship a looked after child has with their current primary carers is likely to be crucial to their progress, as is the integration of the child's experience of birth family connections, directly or indirectly, within placement life.

- Children's active choices in their lives should be recognised and supported as far as possible.

- Wider relationships with school, peers, professionals and the wider community are also important to consider – they will impact on a child's quality of live and the quality of their social support as they grow. They can also be an important source of support when a child or young person leaves care.

Suggested reading

Daniel, B., Wassell, S. and Gilligan, R. (2010) *Child Development for Child Care and Protection Workers* (2nd Edition). London: Jessica Kingsley – Provides comprehensive coverage of a wide range of issues with a strong practice application.

Howe, D. (2011) *Attachment across the Lifecourse: A Brief Introduction.* Basingstoke: Palgrave – A good, short, exploration of the application of attachment theory.

Winter, K. (2006) 'Widening our knowledge concerning young looked after children: the case for research using sociological models of childhood', *Child & Family Social Work, 11* (1): 55–64 – Article strongly setting out the case for applying a sociological understanding when considering the lives of looked after children.

Online resources

An excellent repository of freely accessible resources for direct social work practice, with specific sections on tools for engaging children is available at: www.socialworkerstoolbox. com/the-adolescentt-wellbeing-scale/

Examples of two organisations working with looked after children:

Become (formerly The Who Cares? Trust) offers advice around practical, policy and legal issues connected to looked after children and also runs a mentoring scheme for young people in care. It makes regular submissions to the UK government on policy and legislative matters concerning looked after children: www.becomecharity.org.uk

Coram Voice facilitates a network of national advocates for children in care and undertakes campaign work and practitioner training around issues relating to looked after children have: www.coramvoice.org.uk

Note

1   It is within six weeks in Scotland.

CHAPTER 3

DIRECT WORK, THERAPEUTIC WORK AND INDIRECT WORK

Chapter Overview

This chapter considers what 'direct work' and 'therapeutic work' consist of and also outlines the 'indirect work' tasks which are a core part of a social worker's role with looked after children. The chapter emphasises the centrality of relationships to effective practice, before examining the main types of ways of working with looked after children. Some of these ways of working will be delivered by a therapist specifically trained in a given method while others will be used by social workers with or without specific therapeutic training who are directly working with a child in care and their birth family. The end of the chapter provides an overview of risk factors and intervention priorities for young people affected by Child Sexual Exploitation (CSE) – an issue which has been found to affect young people in care disproportionately.

Direct and therapeutic work

'Direct work' is any form of interactional work undertaken by social workers with children and birth family members and can be understood as the process of building and sustaining relationships with a child and their family, with the aims of promoting a child's behavioural, emotional, psychological and relational well-being (Luckock and Lefevre, 2008). Social workers' role in undertaking direct work with children is underpinned by statutory requirements in England which specify the minimum number of times a social worker must visit a child in placement: on the first day of the placement, within a week of its start and thereafter at least every six weeks while the placement is not considered a long-term one (DfE, 2015b).

Therapeutic work has the same aims as direct work. This may lead to the question of how 'direct work' undertaken by social workers with children and their birth families differs from 'therapeutic work'. The answer is not always clear-cut. Social workers regularly undertake life story work, for example, but the Adoption Support Fund in 2015 distinguished between 'basic life story work' and 'extensive therapeutic life story work'. When I asked a class of child and family social workers with experience of using the Adoption Support Fund what the differences between the two types of life story work were, the reply came back that 'basic life story work' was conducted by social workers while 'therapeutic life story work' was undertaken by clinical psychologists!

Though the reply was tongue-in-cheek, it provides some insight. Therapeutic work is traditionally carried out with a child by someone with specific training in a therapeutic method who tends to deliver the therapy in a specific, controlled environment – for example, a number of weekly therapy sessions of a set duration between the therapist and child at the therapist's office. A child is usually referred for therapeutic work to help them address particularly difficult, deep-seated or troubling issues. A distinction may be made between therapeutic interventions that are shorter-term with task and treatment focused goals targeting undesirable thinking and behaviour (e.g. anger management sessions), and therapeutic interventions focused on feelings and relationships (e.g. therapy in response to past trauma) which will typically be less narrowly focused and longer-term. By contrast, social workers will undertake direct work with all children and their birth parents as part of their role and this work will be more multifaceted and less clearly boundaried than therapeutic work – for example, direct work may range from discussing a child's wishes and feelings with them about an important aspect of their future care, to discussing important past issues with them, to discussing practicalities regarding contact arrangements with a birth parent to discussing everyday issues such as how they enjoyed their last week at school.

Outside of 'direct work' and 'therapeutic work', a child's developing relationships with their carers, birth family members and others will be central to a child's progress and may have a 'therapeutic effect' in that they promote a child's behavioural, emotional, psychological and relational well-being. It is for this reason that a move to a secure, stable and nurturing placement may be described as 'therapeutic' (Dozier et al., 2001; Prior and Glaser, 2006) and many interventions focused on working with children in care now emphasise the importance of working with both children and their carers, as well as sometimes also the child's birth family. Relationships with other professionals – such as teachers at school or key workers in residential care – may also be particularly important for a child. While it makes sense to specifically delineate direct work undertaken by social workers, and therapeutic work delivered by trained therapists, it is also important therefore to recognise that the ordinary day-to-day activities that a child engages in with those around them can foster and sustain their well-being and development.

Social worker–child relationships

In recent years there has been a renewed focus on the importance of the relationship between a social worker and a child as a facilitator of change (Munro, 2011). The assertion that relationships are important to humans is axiomatic, but what does this mean for practice? After all, every social worker has a 'relationship' of some kind with every child they work with, even if the relationship is hostile and conflictual! We therefore need to ask what qualities of the working relationship matter in supporting children to make positive change, and what difference a good relationship makes. Fortunately, there is a good degree of consistency in findings about the qualities that underpin a good helping relationship. The move towards describing the 'common factors' and 'common practice elements' (Barth and Lee, 2014) shared by different effective interventions with children has emphasised the importance of a practitioner developing trust, displaying empathy and conveying warmth towards a child. These qualities reinforce the qualities Carl Rogers (1951) argued a counsellor must show an adult client in order to promote their growth through the therapeutic relationship in person-centred counselling.

Practice Pointer 3.1

Read the article below on the helping relationship between social worker Jenni Randall and David Akinsanya:

www.theguardian.com/society/2013/nov/06/social-work-looked-after-children-love-care

- What qualities of effective helping relationships can you identify in Jenni's work with David?

- Do you think it would it be possible for a social worker to build the same kind of close relationship with a child they were working with today? Why/why not?

The second, perhaps trickier question, is how much the relationship matters, as opposed to other factors, such as the particular method of intervention that a practitioner uses, or the circumstances of the child. McKeown (2000) drew on studies from psychotherapy and counselling to present a breakdown of the effectiveness of therapeutic interventions as follows:

- 40 per cent is due to the characteristics and social support of the individual receiving the therapy.

- 15 per cent is due to the therapeutic method used by the therapist.

- 15 per cent is due to the individual client's optimism about change in their life.

- And, 30 per cent is due to the quality of the practitioner's relationship with the client.

Barth and Lee (2014), by contrast, draw on other evidence from psychotherapeutic research to argue that a practitioner's ability to maintain a therapeutic alliance with their client accounts for the majority of therapeutic change, with the unique contribution of a particular intervention method contributing only between 1 and 15 per cent of the change.

While the exact contributions of the different elements of success in a helping intervention may be debated, and there may be questions as to how well findings from adult psychotherapy translate into social work with children, there is a clear and consistent underlying message: a positive relationship or working alliance between a social worker and a child based on genuine warmth, trust and empathy is a necessary condition for supporting a child's positive development. Schofield and colleagues (2000) speak of the need for long-term foster carers to believe a child is special and to be optimistic about their potential. This is also a very good maxim for a social worker working with a child in care.

Direct work with birth family members

Social workers' practice with birth family members tends to be focused on the birth parent(s) in the initial period after a child comes into care, especially when there is the assessment of the possibility of child's return to parental care. The relationships between birth parents and a social worker may be difficult, especially when the social worker is the same one who worked with the parents when their child was placed in care in the first place. Though this can be a very challenging situation for all involved, it is part of a social worker's role to try and overcome these difficulties in order to work constructively with the birth parents regarding their child's well-being. The social worker also has a key role in acting as a bridge between the child's birth family and placement experiences (Schofield and Stevenson, 2009), a particularly important function given children can develop divided loyalties once in care leading them to 'split' their lives between placement experiences and experiences and histories with their birth families (Cleaver, 2000).

In engaging birth parents around their child's future care and well-being, social workers need to give consideration to parents' feelings on their child's placement in care (e.g. anger, guilt, fear, shame), their histories of parenting, being parented and of service engagement and involvement (Cleaver, 2000; Ruch et al., 2010; Sen, 2016). Where relationships between a social worker and birth parents are so difficult that productive working appears impossible it may be necessary to change social worker (Schofield and Stevenson, 2009). However, this should not obscure the need for any social worker to have respectful, but challenging, conversations with parents around child care issues, including what needs to change for it to be possible for their child to return to their care.

Though the focus of direct work will often be on birth parents, practitioners need to also give consideration to a child's wider network. The use of family network diagrams and Family Group Conferences (FGCs), as explored in Chapter 2, can help identify these wider networks, as well as potentially identify alternative carers and/or wider networks of support for a child.

Indirect work

A child's social worker will have a number of ongoing responsibilities to undertake in respect of their care over and above direct work. These tasks include keeping regular case recordings in respect of the child and their circumstances, writing formal reports for court regarding the child's future care, compiling written assessments and care plans for statutory Looked After Child Reviews, completing written assessments of the child's parents' caring capacity where reunification is an ongoing consideration, and completing assessment of other potential family and friends carers where a child cannot, or is unlikely to be able to, return to parental care. Where a child needs another placement, the child's social worker should be involved in discussing, exploring and helping decide which of the available placement options is best suited to the child.

In the situation where a long-term fostering or adoption placement is being pursued, it will be the responsibility of family placement social workers, rather than the child's social worker, to undertake assessments of potential unrelated foster carers and adopters. However, the child's social worker will normally complete the Child's Permanence Report and be involved in discussion with the family placement service as to the potential carers for that child and the best match for them.

Social workers are also tasked with overseeing that a child's day-to-day care is meeting their needs and that their wishes regarding their care are being taken on board. All of the aspects of a child's care set out in the DOH framework (see Chapter 2) need to be considered. Examples of these kind of responsibilities are:

● Ensuring that a looked after child is registered with the appropriate medical professionals and is up to date with vaccinations, medical reviews and appointments.

● Ensuring that the child's school is aware of their changed care arrangements, and where a child changes school that school staff and, as appropriate, the educational psychologist, is aware of their educational support needs.

● Checking how the child is settling in at their placement and monitoring their overall progress, addressing any arising questions and concerns.

● Setting up and overseeing contact arrangements between the child and their birth family and significant others.

Given that social workers will typically have 20–30 children on their caseload at any one time, and the child may be in placement at a considerable distance from them, they will not undertake many of these tasks directly. Carers will undertake many of the day-to-day caring tasks and foster carers also have a family placement social worker to help support, as well as help monitor, their care of the child in the foster placement. Education staff and an educational psychologist, where one is involved, will take the lead around the child's schooling, while many social work teams now have specific 'contact workers' who will supervise and assess most contact sessions between a child and their family. Nonetheless, it is the social worker's responsibility to have oversight of the child's overall care plan, ensuring that it reflects a child's needs and wishes, and that actions agreed by different parties within the care plan are being undertaken.

The evidence base for direct and therapeutic work

There has been a move towards 'evidence based social work practice' internation-ally (Shlonsky and Benbenishty, 2014). This has taken two forms – a wider move towards using research evidence to inform social work practice and policy and a narrower 'what works' drive to only use interventions that have been empirically tested and proven (Hill, 2009). The explicit drivers for using evidence for practice are economic and moral. If an intervention can achieve better results than another with the input of the same resources then it will be more cost-effective to use it. There is also a moral case: that in seeking to help children, professionals and policy makers should seek the best available evidence to support their helping efforts, and avoid using practices which have been shown to have no effect or proven harmful.

While these arguments are uncontroversial in broad terms, the creation and application of an evidence base for practice, particularly the kinds of knowledge it tends to privilege, are more contested. Within programme/intervention research, Randomised Control Trials (RCTs) are generally seen as the most reliable form of evaluation evidence, followed by other types of experimental research designs, while qualitative research is viewed as providing the lowest level of reliability (Gray et al., 2009). However, the place of RCTs as the 'gold standard' in complex social interven-tions, such as social work with children, is more contested. Criticisms include:

- Questions about how well the RCT methodology translates from contained medical interventions to complex social interventions (Featherstone et al., 2014).

- Concerns that the application of evidence from RCTs in social interventions downplays, or even ignores, the importance of context in producing particular outcomes (Gray et al., 2009; Pawson, 2013).

- That the focus on RCTs can overshadow the recognition of other important empirical evidence and other forms of knowledge which are important guides for practice (Rycroft-Malone et al., 2004).

None of the above are arguments against using research evidence in social work practice *per se*. They do suggest the need for a more inclusive approach as to what forms of knowledge are used when practitioners and agencies take decisions about which interventions are best employed in a given case.

Practice Pointer 3.2

You are working with a child in care with emotional and behavioural difficulties. How would you go about deciding what were the best ways of working with them to address these difficulties? What restrictions might there be on your ability to choose from different ways of working with a child?

In terms of the evidence base for therapeutic work, McKeown (2000) presented evidence that therapeutic input makes a positive difference for 70–80 per cent of people receiving It, compared to those receiving no treatment at all. However, it has also been found that particular therapeutic inputs will work for some children in some circumstances, but will not be effective for all children (Fonagy et al., 2002). The number of interventions and therapies which recent UK governments have supported using with looked after and adopted children is large. The National Implementation Service (NIS, 2017), a DfE-funded centre to support the use of evidence-based interventions with children in care and other children with high-level needs, currently supports: AdOpt (a parenting programme for adopters) Functional Family Therapy; Multisystemic Therapy; KEEP (Keeping foster and kin-ship carers trained and supported); RESuLT (a training programme for residential child care workers); and Treatment Foster Care Oregon (TFCO) (also known as, and referred to in this book as, Multisystemic Foster Care (MTFC)). In addition, when the government-funded Adoption Support Fund was first announced in 2015, the following were among the therapies which it was specified would be funded: creative therapies (art, music, drama, play); Dyadic Developmental Psy-chotherapy; extensive therapeutic life story work; Eye Movement Desensitisation and Reprocessing Therapy; Filial Therapy; Multi Systemic Therapy; Non-Violent Resistance (NVR); psychotherapy; Sensory Integration Therapy/Sensory Attach-ment Therapy; Theraplay; and therapeutic parenting training.[1]

The established evidence base for the effectiveness of all these different interven-tions is varied. A recent Welsh review of the evidence in support of interventions with looked after children summed up the current situation by concluding that, though there were many promising interventions, the available evidence base was weak overall (Roberts et al., 2016). In summary, there is evidence that therapeutic input is better than no treatment, and several specific intervention methods, or types of intervention with children, have some evidence in their favour in particular contexts. However, the evidence does not suggest that there is any one intervention or way of working which will always produce better results, irrespective of context.

Therefore, practitioners need to consider both the evidence for a particular way of working and their 'practice wisdom' as to what is likely to work and what is ethical in that specific situation for that particular child. The last two considerations will entail taking account of what preferences children, their carers and their families might have for or against a particular proposed method of working. It should also be emphasised that practitioners will not have a completely free hand in choosing a particular type of intervention, or way of working with a child; organisational preferences for particular ways of working, available funding, staff resources and the policy and legal contexts, will all serve to constrain the range of options which are available.

Consent for treatment

Where psychological inputs are not effective, psychotropic therapies (medica-tion) may be considered alongside or instead of psychological therapy. There tends to be a healthy scepticism towards prescribing psychiatric medication for children in the UK, and psychological alternatives are usually considered first. However, evidence suggests medication can be effective and may be necessary as part of the treatment plan for children with ADHD, severe depression and psychotic symptoms (Taylor, 2015). Meltzer and colleagues (2003) found nearly half of looked after children in England had a mental disorder but just 4 per cent were taking prescribed psychiatric medication – although a fifth of those diagnosed as having hyperkinetic disorders were taking psycho-stimulant drugs.

Issues of consent arise for children in terms of both psychological and psychotropic treatments. Where a local authority, adoptive parents or carers have parental rights (PR) they can give parental consent, though good practice would dictate that any treatment plan would ordinarily be discussed with birth parents who retain PR wherever practicable. Where a child is in care via a voluntary admission, then a birth parent will need to give consent, unless in a situation where treatment was needed and parental consent was not obtainable in a reasonable time frame. In this circumstance, s.3(5) of the Children Act 1989 gives authority to those without PR to 'do what is reasonable in all the circumstances of the case for the purpose of safeguarding or promoting the child's welfare' (Hale and Fortin, 2015).

According to *Gillick* competency a child of any age must give their own consent to a treatment when a doctor deems that that child has 'sufficient understanding of what is involved to give a valid consent in law' (cited in Hale and Fortin, 2015, p. 243). A child who is deemed *Gillick* competent may therefore access treatment without parental consent, but may also refuse it despite parental consent. In cases where a child refuses life-saving treatment, case law has dictated that their refusal may be overridden by someone with PR or via an application from someone else to make the child a ward of court (Hale and Fortin, 2015). In the case of mental disorder, compulsory detention of children under the Mental Health Act 1983 may be possible but only in very particular situations related to risks to the child's health and safety or the health and safety of others. Detention through the Mental Health Act for assessment or treatment must always be considered as the least restrictive alternative available and for children this is often viewed as a last resort. A more likely route for those children on Care Orders who require mental health treatment, but who do not consent to it, is for the local authority to apply to court for leave to apply inherent jurisdiction (see Schwehr, 2016).

Types of therapeutic intervention and direct work with looked after children

This section outlines some of the principal types of intervention/ways of working which are currently used with looked after children. Though the types of intervention are distinct, it is common for a specific programme of work with a looked after child to draw eclectically on more than one way of working.

Psychodynamic psychotherapy for children

Originally influenced by Sigmund Freud's work, psychodynamic psychotherapy is principally a talking intervention which focuses on a child's underlying thoughts and feelings, and the significance of past experiences and relationships on current functioning and relationships. More classical versions of the therapy also emphasise the role of the unconscious in psychic distress, the symbolic meaning of behaviours and notions of transference and counter-transference (Delgado, 2008) – transference and counter-transference referring to the way in which both the child and the therapist's past histories of relationships replicate themselves in patterns of interaction between the child and the therapist in the therapy session itself.

Box 3.1 Psychodynamic psychotherapy key features

- Typically long-term (lasting a year or more) and involving regular planned therapy sessions with the same therapist. Sessions may involve talk only, play or play and talk depending on the age and preferences of the child.

- The therapist's role in psychotherapeutic work is, therefore, very different to the multi-stranded nature of a child and family social work role.

- Some sessions may be held jointly or in parallel sessions with carers.

- The overarching goal of the therapy is to support the child's healthy emotional and psychological development and strengthen the child–carer relationship. The therapy seeks to do this by unpicking underlying patterns of behaviour the child is exhibiting and mental representations of the carer the child has. It seeks to help the child and carer gain insight into what might lie behind the behavioural patterns, with particular consideration given to the influence of past events and relationships.

- Similar unpicking may occur with the carer, exploring their patterns of behaviour towards the child and what might lie behind them.

Potential strengths and weaknesses

The aim of psychodynamic approaches is to resolve underlying emotional conflicts and facilitate deep-seated emotional and personality change rather than just addressing presenting symptoms. They therefore potentially offer the chance of lasting and fundamental change. One weakness is the position of power the psychodynamic approach gives the therapist in interpreting a child's feelings and thoughts, particularly unconscious ones (Rojek et al., 1988). Another arises from long-standing questions about the approach's effectiveness (Milner et al., 2015).

This may be in part due to methodological challenges in evaluating the approach, as it is harder to measure the deep-seated changes the therapy seeks to effect. However, Midgley and Kennedy's (2011) review of the evidence found psychodynamic psychotherapy can be as effective as other interventions for children which have been classed as 'evidence-based'. Psychodynamic therapies are reported to have effectiveness with younger children, children with internalising disorders, such as depression, and children who have experienced trauma. Older children and those with emotional and behavioural disorders have been found to be less responsive to the therapy which may reflect difficulties in engaging the latter two groups in an intensive talking therapy over a prolonged period of time (Midgley and Kennedy, 2011).

Attachment theory-informed interventions

These interventions derive from attachment theory and tend to focus on supporting the relationship between a child and their primary carer through developing the carer's attunement with, and sensitivity towards, the child. In so doing they aim to support the child's self-regulation, self-esteem and secure attachment (Kerr and Cossar, 2014).

Box 3.2 Overview of an attachment-informed intervention

One example of an attachment theory-influenced intervention is the *Video Feedback Intervention to promote Positive Parenting and Sensitive Discipline* (VIPP-SD) developed by Juffer and colleagues (2008, as described in Shemmings and Shemmings, 2011, pp. 181–197). This is targeted at caregivers looking after children between one and four years of age. It aims to support caregivers' sensitivity towards the child they are caring for and promote carers' ability to apply effective disciplinary strategies to reduce behavioural difficulties in children. The programme consists of:

- Seven home visits of around an hour during each of which video footage is taken of the parent and child, with video feedback from the previous session shared in the next. There is a preliminary assessment visit during which the first video recording is taken. Subsequently there are six further visits in three phases.

- Phase one focuses on the child, supporting the caregiver to attune with the child and pick up on the child's behavioural signals.

- Phase two focuses on the carer and their responses to the child, providing the caregiver with strategies to use positive reinforcement, boundaries and sensitive time out to reinforce wanted behaviour and manage unwanted behaviour.

- Phase three reviews previous key ideas and considers any challenges there have been to applying them.

Potential strengths and weaknesses

These interventions will normally be considerably shorter-term than psychodynamic therapy and focus on caregivers with younger children. Two meta-analyses – a particular type of evidence review considering the effectiveness of an intervention – found strong evidence that attachment-based programmes addressing carer sensitivity to the child were the most effective (Bakermans-Kranenburg et al., 2003, 2005). Kerr and Cossar's (2014) review of the evidence found that while there is some evidence of attachment-based interventions positively affecting child behaviour, emotional self-regulation and relational functioning, the evidence is not yet strong enough to draw firm conclusions. Those who have reservations about the widespread use of attachment theory are likely to bring some of the same reservations to the use of attachment-based interventions (see Chapter 2). Barth and colleagues (2005) argue that, rather than a narrow focus on attachment theory-informed interventions, practitioners need to locate them alongside other evidence-based approaches which emphasise different cognitive and social influences on child development, in order to arrive at a more balanced approach to helping children.

A note on Attachment/Holding Therapy

Attachment/Holding Therapy (hereafter 'Holding Therapy') is distinct from the evidence-informed attachment-based interventions discussed above and its use has been highly contentious. Holding Therapy has been particularly used with children in care displaying marked emotional and behavioural difficulties, and in particular those children identified as having attachment disorders. It is, however, considered by many to be associated with treatment that is abusive to children and one version of its use was implicated in the death of an adopted child, Candace Newmaker, in the USA in 2000 (Mercer, 2011). The use of Holding Therapy was also rejected by the American Professional Society on Abuse of Children and the (then) British Association for Adoption and Fostering in the mid-2000s (BAAF, 2006).[2] All versions of Holding Therapy share the view that a child's attachment difficulties need to be resolved by 'regressing' the child to the developmental stage in which the attachment problem began. The regression occurs by re-enacting early childhood experiences, with some form of holding of the child by the therapist(s) an essential part of the treatment (Mercer, 2011).

Some variants of Holding Therapy include the use of sustained eye contact and a view that pain, discomfort and anger should be induced in a child to address unresolved emotions arising from previous childhood experience (Mercer, 2011). Some of the strongest critics of Holding Therapy are those who are enthusiastic proponents of evidence-based attachment theory interventions but who draw a sharp distinction between them and Holding Therapy, which they hold to have no evidential basis (e.g. Dozier, 2003; Prior and Glaser, 2006).

Prior and Glaser (2006, p. 265) state that Holding Therapy stands in contradiction to some of the core tenets of attachment theory, 'not least attachment theory's fundamental and evidence-based statement that [attachment] security is promoted by sensitivity'.

Given these concerns, the continued use of Holding Therapy appears highly questionable in an era focused on both children's rights and evidence-based practice.

Behavioural approaches and Cognitive Behavioural Therapy (CBT)

These interventions, derived from classical behavioural approaches originally formulated by B.F. Skinner, emphasise learning developed through respondent and operant conditioning (Coulshed and Orme, 2012). Respondent conditioning is typically used in the treatment of anxiety and phobias and explains how an individual learns to instinctively associate a stimulus with a response. For example, a child who has been badly bullied at a previous school may refuse to attend their new school due to extreme anxiety about being bullied there; even though they have no experience of being bullied at the new school, they anticipate and expect, instinctively, that they will be. This may be treated by systematic desensitisation – the child is progressively exposed to the new school environment while being supported by a practitioner and/or school professional who teaches the child relaxation techniques to manage the fears or anxious feelings as they arise (Coulshed and Orme, 2012).

Operant learning theories describe learning through the association of consequences with a particular behaviour. Often attention is drawn to caregivers' own behaviour which may unwittingly reinforce unwanted child behaviours. The classic example is of a child who acts out and is given either attention or a treat to stop the behaviour (Kendall et al., 2015). The child then learns that if they misbehave, they are rewarded, so the misbehaviour is reinforced. In parenting programmes influenced by behavioural theory, caregivers are taught the importance of sanctioning unwanted child behaviour and rewarding wanted behaviour, and that the link between the child's behaviour and the positive or negative consequence are made clear to the child. Most parenting programmes now also tend to emphasise the effectiveness of praise and rewarding positive behaviours over sanctioning negative ones (Coulshed and Orme, 2012).

Social learning theory (Bandura, 1977) provides an extension of behavioural theories. It emphasises that children learn through observing the behaviour of those around them. A number of interventions for children and parenting programmes incorporate this element of social learning theory, identifying the importance of carers' and professionals' 'pro-social modelling' behaviours for the child so that the child has opportunity to learn and can then replicate this behaviour themselves. A very simple example might be of a carer who wants a child to say 'please' and 'thank you' regularly when they make requests. The carer might then address the child, and others in front of the child, in the respectful manner they wish to see the child adopt. This allows the child to learn from the carer's way of interaction, and encourages them to respond in a similar way themselves.

CBT adds the dimension of cognitions to behaviour, emphasising the way in which thoughts impact on and interact with feelings and behaviour. Consequently, the emphasis in the therapy is on identifying and rectifying cognitive distortions: irrational thought processes which negatively affect a person's emotional and behavioural responses to a given situation (Beck, 1991). CBT is, for example, prominently used within anger-management work with young people with behavioural problems and conduct disorders.

Box 3.3 Key elements of a therapeutic CBT programme for children

Kendall and colleagues (2015) outline the following features:

- Psychoeducation: Teaching a child about the ways in which their thought responses to given situations affect their emotions and behaviours, developing the child's ability to recognise different emotional states and to express a range of emotions appropriately.

- Problem-solving: Teaching a child how to define a given problem, generate solutions, choose the workable ones, choose the preferred solution, implement it and then evaluate how successful the solution was.

- Cognitive restructuring: Challenging cognitive distortions a child may be prone to including negative thoughts while promoting positive self-talk.

CBT also involves therapeutically integral 'homework tasks' where the therapist asks the child to apply learning from the session to real-life situations they encounter and then discusses the successes and the challenges they faced in doing so in the following session. Role play and modelling (Bandura, 1977 – see above) are also frequently used.

Potential strengths and weaknesses

One criticism of strictly behaviourist approaches is that children may be treated mechanistically rather than as thinking, responsible, agentic beings (Goodman and Scott, 2012). That said, employing behaviourist strategies to address specific behaviours does not preclude the use of other strategies that might support a child to develop their own reflective thinking and judgement. There is good evidence that behaviourist approaches are effective in the treatment of specific issues and narrow behaviour – for example, phobias, eating and sleeping difficulties, enuresis, encopresis and specific disruptive behaviours – but little evidence of their effectiveness with more complex or wide-ranging emotional and behavioural issues (Fonagy et al., 2002; Goodman and Scott, 2012). Evidence does seem to suggest that behavioural approaches augmented by cognitive approaches are generally more effective (Milner et al., 2015).

Fonagy and colleagues' summary of the evidence on CBT (2002) reports there is evidence of its efficacy in treating children with generalised anxiety disorders and simple phobias, depression and mild conduct problems and that CBT combined with social learning theory can be effective in addressing child substance misuse. There is also some evidence that CBT programmes can reduce suicidal ideation and improve coping skills in children who are suicidal but, perhaps oddly given this, little evidence of its efficacy in preventing youth suicide. There is little evidence that CBT by itself is effective in treating more severe conduct problems, ADHD and developmental disorders such as autism, although there is some evidence that in combination with behaviourist interventions it can be of some help.

CBT approaches do require a child to be able to understand the approach and be able, and prepared, to attempt to apply it outside the sessions. As behavioural therapies restrict their efforts to targeting presenting and exhibiting behaviours (and the thoughts and emotions connected to them in CBT) they are easier to evaluate than some other therapeutic methods, and may be more attractive to agencies as they tend to be briefer interventions. This is also a point of criticism – that behaviourist-influenced approaches overly focus on presenting symptoms at the expense of addressing their underlying causes such that any short-term gains may not be sustained longer-term (Kendall et al., 2015). Advocates of CBT would dispute this and the increasing acknowledgement of the importance of the therapeutic alliance within CBT delivery (Milner et al., 2015) may suggest an accommodation between techniques of CBT and more relational ways or working.

Play therapy and play techniques

Play therapy is a specific therapeutic intervention, however play and play techniques are also commonly used by social workers as a means of engaging children in work around their feelings, views and wishes. While the idea of using children's play within therapy can be traced back to those working out of the psychodynamic tradition – particularly the work of Anna Freud, Melanie Klein, Clare Winnicott and Donald Winnicott – there is now a wide variety of play therapy approaches. These vary in the amount of direction/non-direction from the practitioner during the session, the way play sessions are structured and whether the primary focus of the therapy is observation and interpretation of the child's thoughts and behaviour, exploration of the child's feelings or communication with the child (for a more detailed outline of major different approaches, see Wilson and Ryan, 2005).

Box 3.4 Play therapy – shared understandings across different approaches

Wilson and Ryan (2005) outline some common understandings which are shared by the different approaches to play therapy. These are that play as therapy:

- Needs to be delivered in a therapeutic context.

- Has symbolic meaning and allows children to express thoughts, wishes and feelings in a therapeutic context.

- Can enable children to re-process past traumatic or difficult events so they can better manage feelings and thoughts arising from them.

- Can be a vehicle for children to express pent-up feelings and thoughts.

- Can support a child to develop coping skills, management of their feelings, self-esteem and positive self-image.

To briefly illustrate three approaches to the use of play:

- Play therapists influenced by psychodynamic theories will primarily use play to observe and interpret children's behaviour and gain potential insight into their unconscious thoughts and feelings (Levy, 2011).

- Play therapists influenced by attachment theory will primarily see play as a tool to use with caregivers and children together in order to promote the attachment relationship between them. For example, Filial Therapy (Ryan, 2007) and Theraplay (Robinson et al., 2009) are two play therapies which are currently being used with looked after and adopted children. They both seek to utilise the multi-sensory experience of play to engage children, while supporting caregivers to provide appropriate structure and boundaries for the child during play activities. Involving carers in the play aims to promote a child's emotional and behavioural self-regulation, relational closeness and trust in their carer.

- Some social workers without specific play therapy training may use play as a tool to engage children in communication when direct verbal communication is difficult or the use of play might otherwise allow children to open up about their thoughts about particular topics (Lefevre, 2008).

Potential strengths and weaknesses

Not all children will be willing to engage in play, but it does offer different ways of communicating with children and building rapport, particularly with younger children with whom direct talking therapies may be difficult (Bratton et al., 2005). Lefevre (2008) wisely cautions that care is needed in interpreting the way in which a child plays and what this says about their feelings and views about the external world as there is no sure framework for translating how play reflects a child's reality outside of that play.

In the UK there is evidence to suggest that particular types of play therapy have promise as interventions with children, though currently the evidence tends to come from small-scale research undertaken by those who are strong advocates for the play therapies they are studying (e.g. Ryan, 2007; Robinson et al., 2009). It should be noted that this is not, however, unusual in the early stages of a developing intervention. Two meta-analyses by US academics did find there was wider evidence to support play therapy's effectiveness. Bratton and colleagues (2005) reviewed evidence from 93 outcome studies of play therapy published from 1953 to 2000 and found they showed play therapies were highly effective, in particular they improved family functioning and relationships where parents were fully involved in the play therapy sessions. The authors acknowledged, however, that some earlier studies included in the review may not reach the standards of rigour needed for more recently designed evaluations. Subsequently, a second meta-analysis, restricted to more recent studies of play therapy between 1995 and 2010, still nonetheless found play therapy to have a moderate positive impact on children (Lin and Bratton, 2015).

Life story work

Life story work involves a carer or practitioner – often a social worker – working with a looked after or adopted child to help them make sense of their pathway into care and provide them with lasting memories of their life and relationships before their current placement. The work typically also involves the production of a life story book which is kept by the child, or for the child by their carers. Life story books traditionally contain photographs of the child's birth family and previous people and places of significance for them. However, adopters in Watson and colleagues' (2015b) study noted that life story books for their children included, in addition to photographs, adoption orders, a birth certificate, greetings cards, hospital bracelets, a lock of baby hair, letters from extended family members and foster carers, a map of the country in which a child was born and medical information related to a child's birth family.

The *Draft statutory guidance on adoption* in England (DfE, 2014c) stipulated that all children with a plan for adoption must have a life story book which should be prepared along a 'memory box' and a later life letter, giving the child information about their personal and family history of birth. *National Minimum Standards* on adoption state that the finalised life story book and later life letter should be given to the adopter(s) 'within ten working days of the adoption ceremony' (DfE, 2014a, p.14).

Hammond and Cooper (2013) usefully suggest the possibilities of digital life story work. That said, children's narratives have emphasised the value they place on physical objects that are connected to their personal histories and identities being contained within their life story books. This may suggest that social workers combining the tangibility of physical objects and the flexibility of digital objects within life story work is worth consideration.

Box 3.5 Considerations for doing life story work

Ryan and Walker's guide (2007) provides a range of insights into undertaking life story work. These include that:

- The life story book is the child's and no one should look at it without the child's permission. As a result, discussions between the child and the practitioner which form part of life story work should be viewed and understood to be confidential (with the exception of where new safeguarding issues are raised by what the child says).

- Life story work should be viewed as a child's right and not a reward or sanction.

- Life story work is a process not an event and should not finish until both the child and the practitioner agree it is complete. Ryan and Walker caution that if life story work is finished after three or four sessions and has 'turned into little more than a photograph album' (p. 8) then practitioners should question whether the work has been adequately undertaken.

- Life story work is likely to generate further questions for the child which go beyond the actual time frame in which the life story work is undertaken. As a result, practitioners and carers need to be prepared to support a child to address the emotional impact life story work has and when questions arise for them.

The production of a life story book leads to tensions about what delicate information or 'untold stories' (Baynes, 2008) should be included about a looked after child's birth family history and the reasons they came into care. A balance needs to be struck between honesty about difficult parts of a child's past history relating to their birth family, including child abuse, criminality, domestic violence and substance misuse, and the need for that information to be delivered in a way a child can process and manage. Baynes (2008) argues that accounts of a child's birth family history should also be sensitive to the challenges birth parents faced when bringing up the child, such as poverty, poor housing and racism, and acknowledge where professionals or services made errors in the child's previous care.

Practice Pointer 3.3

Think of a child of primary school age (5–11) who has a challenging birth family history. How might you describe that child's history to them, striking a balance between honesty and sensitivity to the child's feelings?

Potential strengths and weaknesses

Rushton (2003) notes the lack of research evidence regarding the efficacy of life story work in supporting children's well-being. He raises the important question of whether reawakening previous experiences of abuse through life story work could in some cases be damaging rather than helpful. On the other hand, qualitative studies have strongly suggested that looked after and adopted young people tend to find life story work highly valuable (Willis and Holland, 2009; Watson et al., 2015a). These findings sit alongside long-standing evidence that firmly identifies the need for children growing up in substitute families to understand their backgrounds and personal histories (Triseliotis, 1973; Triseliotis et al., 2005). Ryan and Walker (2007) do, however, caution that, despite its importance, life story work should not be seen as a substitute for tailored therapeutic work with a child where this is needed.

Strengths-based approaches

These focus on people's strengths and problem-solving abilities rather than the problem itself or people's deficits within their current situation (Saleebey, 2006). Given that much work with looked after children is framed around the deficits identified in their lives, such approaches can provide a counter-weight. Though there are a range of intervention methods which may be described as strengths-based, solution-focused brief therapy (SFBT) (de Shazer, 1994) is probably the most well-known, and solution-focused methods have been developed for use with children (e.g. Milner and Bateman, 2011). There is an overlap between the broad thrust of solution-focused work with children and practice approaches which seek to support children's resilience by identifying the positives, strengths and resources that children have in their lives and building on them (Daniel et al., 2010).

Box 3.6 The core factors underpinning children's resilience

Ungar's 2007 study of children from 11 diverse countries (as reported in Ungar, 2015) found there were seven key identifiable common protective factors in the lives of children who were doing well in spite of adversities. These were:

1. Positive adult and peer relationships.

2. A strong positive identity.

3. A sense of empowerment through the ability to express their views about the world around them and to have these views taken on board.

4. A view that they were treated fairly in their own communities.

5. Access to material resources.

---

6. A sense of cohesion – membership of, and belonging within, a particular social setting, whether that be school or a community or religious group.

7. Identification with a set of group beliefs and norms.

Potential strengths and weaknesses

As strengths-based approaches cover a range of methods I focus these comments on the use of SFBT. Criticisms of SFBT have included concerns as to whether strengths-based approaches can be fully effective where problems are manifold, difficult and entrenched (Milner et al., 2015) – some discussion of what is wrong may be necessary, and perhaps helpful, as well as discussion of the solutions and resources that a child has to build on. A second criticism is not so much about the method in and of itself, but its superficial application, which may fail to acknowledge the depth of difficulties a child and their carer are encountering and lead to suggestions of simplistic solutions (ibid.). However, a systematic review of the effectiveness of SFBT with children (Bond et al., 2013) found that there was 'tentative support' for its effectiveness in respect of internalising and externalising mental health issues (on this distinction, see Chapter 9). While the review noted the need for more robust outcome studies, it did find particular support for the use of SFBT as an early intervention method before severe difficulties had developed.

Child Sexual Exploitation (CSE)

CSE is considered here as an increasingly prominent public concern which has impacted on a number of young people in care (Sen, 2017). There is evidence that looked after young people, and particularly young women in residential care, are disproportionately likely to be victims of CSE (Beckett, 2011). This does not, of course, mean that all young people in care are at high risk of CSE, and far less that they are all victims of it. However, awareness of the heightened risks of CSE is needed. These heightened risks appear to stem from the following factors:

- A young person going missing, particularly overnight, is strongly linked to CSE and young people go missing from care placements, particularly residential ones, more often than from home settings (Wade et al., 1998; Beckett, 2011).

- Some young people will be in care because they were subject to CSE, or at high risk of it, in the community (HOC, 2013).

- There is some evidence that young people in the care system who are already subject to CSE may bring other young people in the care system they befriend into contact with a network of perpetrators (Beckett, 2011; HOC, 2013).

- Some perpetrators expressly target settings like residential child care facilities where there is opportunity to groom vulnerable young people (Beckett, 2011).

- Young people who are placed in 'out-of-area placements' (that is, outside their own local authority area) without adequate help can be more vulnerable to CSE (HOC, 2013). While such placements may be necessary to remove a young person from a circle of exploitation in the local area (Jay, 2014), there is need for close liaison between the placing and receiving authorities to ensure the young person is appropriately supported. There is some evidence that this currently does not routinely happen (HOC, 2013; Jay, 2014).

Practice Pointer 3.4

This a fictionalised case study. Please read it and consider the questions below.

Ahmina and Lauren are both 15 and attend the same school. They are best friends. Ahmina has been in a children's home in the local area for the past two years; Lauren lives with her parents close by. Ahmina came into care following the breakdown of her relationship with her mother, her sole carer, following a number of violent arguments. During the last year both Ahmina and Lauren started to truant from school, at first occasionally, and then more frequently. Over the last two months Ahmina has regularly absconded from her children's home, at first by herself, more recently with Lauren. The last two occasions they returned home together in the early hours intoxicated. The police, social services and the school are all involved, though both young women state that they are not being subject to CSE. Ahmina and Lauren's parents are in conflict, each blaming the other young person for their child's situation.

1. What would your priorities for engagement and support be?

2. Who would you seek to engage and support and how?

Where young people are subject to CSE, persistence and flexible services are needed that fit around their lives, which are likely to be chaotic (Coy, 2009). Paskell (2012) suggests that direct work with young people experiencing CSE should have three main aims:

1. Preventing immediate harm.

2. Helping the young person exit CSE and addressing the impact of the exploitation on them.

3. Supporting the young person through any potential prosecution of the perpetrator(s).

These aims will require a mixture of practical and therapeutic support for the young person. Paskell (2012) outlines Barnardo's 'Four A's approach' for organisations working with children/young people around CSE. This consists of:

- *Access*: Easy referral procedures (including self-referrals) to organisations that are welcoming for the young person.

- *Attention*: A key worker who builds a positive and consistent relationship with the young person.

- *Assertive outreach*: Persistent contact that reaches out to young people where and when they choose to engage.

- *Advocacy*: Sensitively supporting young people to access other services which are needed.

Such support is unlikely to be a short-term fix. Paskell (2012) notes that support is typically offered for at least 18 months, but support for shorter, 6–9-month periods, can sometimes be effective.

Key messages for practice

- Relationships are central to effective practice social work with looked after children. The importance of a practitioner developing a trustful relationship with a child, displaying empathy towards their situation and conveying warmth towards them is key to building a working relationship with a child which supports them to make progress.

- There are a range of intervention methods and ways of working with looked after children which have different strengths and weaknesses. There are additionally a large, and growing number, of tailored interventions for looked after children. Though practitioners are unlikely to have free choice between the different interventions, consideration should be given to the practitioner's assessment of the nature and extent of the presenting problems and how good a fit the proposed intervention is for addressing them; the child, their carers and – as appropriate – their parents' views of the proposed intervention; and the ethics of the proposed intervention method.

- Child Sexual Exploitation (CSE) has emerged as a pressing concern in respect of the welfare of some looked after young people. Practitioners need to strike a balance of being aware of the possibility of CSE among the care population, while not assuming that all young people in care are at risk of, or are being subject to, CSE because of their care status. Where young people are subject to CSE there should be three main aims: to prevent immediate harm; to help the young person exit and address the impact of the exploitation; and to support the young person through any potential prosecution of the perpetrator(s).

Suggested reading

Luckock, B. and Lefevre, M. (eds) (2008) *Direct Work: Social Work with Children and Young People in Care.* London: BAAF – A very helpful edited collection containing a wide range of different approaches and methods to undertaking direct work including with looked after children in care.

Ryan, T. and Walker, R. (2007) *Life Story Work: A Practical Guide to Helping Children Understand Their Past.* London: BAAF – The most comprehensive guide to undertaking life story work.

Tait, A. and Wosu, H. (2012) *Direct Work with Vulnerable Children: Playful Activities and Strategies for Communication.* London: Jessica Kingsley – Very helpful guide providing strategies for engaging children in discussion around important and difficult issues.

Online resources

The government-funded National Implementation Service provides information on a number of government-approved 'evidence-based' interventions which are currently being used with looked after children in England: www.evidencebasedinterventions.org.uk/about/national-implementation-service

Shemmings, D., Shemmings, Y., Wilkins, D., Febrer, Y., Cook, A., Feeley, F. and Denham, C. (no date) 'Tools social workers can use to talk to children' – A useful introduction, including a video demonstration, of some tools for direct work with children on Community Care's website: www.communitycare.co.uk/tools-social-workers-can-use-to-talk-to-children/

Young Minds – the website of a prominent UK charity which provides information and resources to support young people's mental well-being: https://youngminds.org.uk

Notes

1 A brief description of most of these therapies can be found in Lewis, J. and Ghate, D. (2015) *Adoption Support Fund – learning from the prototype.* London: DfE, pp. 114–166.
2 BAAF has since become CoramBAAF.

CHAPTER 4

PATHWAYS AFTER ENTERING CARE

Chapter Overview

This chapter begins by looking at the placement options for children on first entering care and goes on to consider longer-term placement pathways and decision-making for children. The chapter considers different definitions and types of permanence, before summarising the current evidence on the outcomes of different placement options. It is emphasised that while a knowledge of these placement outcomes can be a helpful aid for practitioners, comparison of different placements types is difficult because they tend to be used for children in substantially different situations and they therefore rarely compare 'like with like'.

Placement options on first entering care

One of the presumptions underlying child care legislation in the UK is that when children come into care they should ordinarily return to the care of their parents wherever possible and consistent with their welfare. Therefore, other than in exceptional cases, such as where there has been extreme abuse, or when a child first comes into care it is evident that a parent is unable or unwilling to provide future care, the possibility of reunification with a birth parent is assessed. While such an assessment is ongoing, a child will normally be in one of three types of placement:

- Short-term foster care, where a child is cared for in a family setting by carers who are unrelated to them.

- Short-term kinship care, where a child is cared for by family or friends, or by carers previously known or connected to them.

- Residential care, where a young person will be cared for in a group care setting, rather than a family-based one.

In reality, not all options are available for each child entering care. Due to placement shortages social workers are often scrambling to find *a* placement for a child rather than having a range of placements to choose from (Sen, 2010; The Fostering Network, 2017). Foster care is by far the most likely placement destination for most children entering care. The latest figures in England show that of all children in care on 31 March 2017, 62 per cent were in foster care, with 12 per cent in kinship care and 12 per cent in various residential settings (the remainder of looked after children were either 'looked after' in a placement with their parents, in other specialised community or residential placements or in prospective adoptive placements; DfE, 2017c; see also Figure 4.1 below for 2012–2016 figures). Residential care is now usually only considered as a placement for young people of 12 and over – though there is no legislative requirement to place younger children in family-based care, it is now standard practice to do so.

By contrast, there is both legislative direction (e.g. s.23 Children Act 1989; s.2 Children and Families Act 2014) and policy guidance (e.g. Scottish Government, 2007) in the UK suggesting kinship care should be given preference over other placements where its use is consistent with the welfare and preferences of a child. The use of kinship care may, however, be hindered because social workers are not fully aware of a child's networks on their entry into care, and this may explain why the proportion of children in kinship placements in England has remained largely static, at just over 10 per cent in recent years, although notably greater proportions of looked after children are in kinship care in Scotland and Northern Ireland (McGhee et al., 2017). As noted in Chapter 2, the use of Family Group Conferences (FGCs) may help social workers identify children's wider networks and thereby potential kinship carers.

Concurrent planning or 'foster for adoption' placements

A relatively new placement option for younger children entering the care system is 'foster for adoption'. Fostering for adoption is also known as 'concurrent planning' and was originally developed in the USA in the 1980s, and started to be used in England from the late 1990s (Borthwick and Donnelly, 2013), although children could be previously placed in a foster care 'with a view to adoption' placement

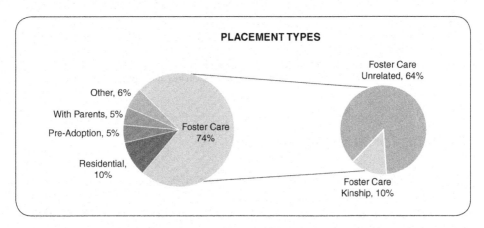

Figure 4.1 Placement usage overview, from data in DfE (2017a) for 2012–2016

which was broadly similar. Fostering for adoption consists of placing a looked after child directly with prospective adopters who are also approved as short-term foster carers for that particular child. Reunification with the child's birth parents is explored after the placement is made but, in the event that reunification is ruled out, the child is the adopted by their current foster carers. This has the potential significant advantages of speeding up the adoption process and avoiding any placement moves for the child prior to, or as part of, the adoption process.

Section 2 of the Children and Families Act 2014 now requires that local authorities in England consider using a foster for adoption placement when deciding on an initial placement for a child for whom they are considering adoption, or for a child whom they think should be placed for adoption.[1] Kenrick's (2009, 2010) study of a concurrent planning project, run by Coram, found children were adopted more quickly and that, based on adopters' self-reports, adopter–child relationships were good. In the study 27 children were placed with 26 prospective adopters and 26 of the children were adopted, with only one reunified with their birth parent. Additionally, only one of the adopted children had direct contact arrangements with their birth parents post-adoption.

The 4 per cent rate of reunification reported in the study is very low; data from across Coram's four concurrent planning projects suggest that a higher, but still low, proportion of children – around 8 per cent – return to their birth families in these arrangements (Laws et al., 2012 cited in Borthwick and Donnelly, 2013). By contrast, 35 per cent of children whose parents went through the Family Drug and Alcohol Court (FDAC) were reunified with their parents (Harwin et al., 2014). The difference may be partly explained by the fact that the children selected for concurrent placements are those whom the local authority already thinks are unlikely to be reunified with their parents. However, Dale (2013) questions whether the development of concurrent planning reflects an unacceptable presumption in favour of adoption before the possibility of reunification with birth parents has been properly explored.

Practice Pointer 4.1

What are the potential advantages and disadvantages in using foster for adoption placements from the point of view of (1) the child; (2) the child's birth parent(s); and (3) the prospective adopters?

Planning for longer-term care

Gaining children's views on their future care

Before seeking to gain children's views social workers need to assess children's understanding and their preferences for communicating their views, according to their stage of development, gender and cultural and linguistic background. It is important for children to know at the outset that their views on their future care are important and will be considered with respect, but that it is ultimately adults' responsibility – in the final analysis a judge's – to make final decisions on children's future care arrangements in their best interests, while taking account of their views. Some children may otherwise feel burdened by the thought that their expressed views could solely determine final decisions on their future care, while others may feel badly let down if they expect their views are going to be decisive and a decision is subsequently made which differs from their expressed wishes.

The play techniques and assessment tools mentioned in Chapter 2 may also be used for engaging children about their views of their future care. Gupta (2008, p. 200), drawing on experience as a Children's Guardian, illustrates examples of more specific exercises for engaging (younger) children about their views on their future care, including the use of a 'what I want to happen ladder' and a game using a toy rabbit, where a six-year-old was asked to help the rabbit think about where it was going to live and how it might feel about this. As with the use of play more generally, practitioners need to be careful about assuming a child's responses to a play scenario translate readily into their views about their own life outside the game. Checking out a child's views after they are expressed is important for clarification, as is seeing whether children's expressed views accord with other indicators of their wishes and feelings – such as how they respond before, during and after contact sessions with parents, or what they may have otherwise communicated to carers and professionals around their hopes, fears and wishes. Some children will express very clear views of their wishes and feelings, others will be more reluctant, or provide less definitive, or even seemingly contradictory, answers. It is important that social workers capture and record children's views as accurately as possible, including reflecting where there is ambiguity, confusion or complexity.

Practice Pointer 4.2

You are social worker to Tariq (11) and Salma (7) who are siblings in a short-term foster placement. Tariq has developmental delay while Salma has been diagnosed as having Selective Mutism. What would you want to know and consider before going out to engage with them on their views and feelings about their future care?

Longer-term placement options and 'permanence'[2]

Differing definitions of permanence

The concept of permanence, which has existed since the 1970s, is the attempt to find longer-term stable care for children who have entered the care system. So far so clear. However, more confusingly, the concept has been variously defined and understood. As Hill (2014) notes the original definitions of permanence for looked after children were primarily concerned with adoption. In other words, in this view permanence is about finding a permanent substitute family placement outside the care system for a looked after child, which will last until adulthood, and beyond. Permanence has, however, also been defined to encompass a broader spectrum of placement options, including adoption at one end of the spectrum, reunification with birth parents at the other end and the 'in-care' option of long-term foster care between the two (Triseliotis, 1991; Marsh and Triseliotis, 2014 [1993]). This broader conception of permanence nonetheless retains the underlying concept of a child having a *lifelong* connection to and support from a *family* whether that be an adoptive, birth or foster family. By implication, fostering would only qualify as a permanence option where young people who have been fostered are able to fall back on their foster family as an ongoing support after ageing out of care as adults, something supported by the 2014 *Staying Put* policy (see Chapter 10).

To complicate matters further, Sinclair and colleagues' (2007) influential study of permanence provides a looser definition of permanence as 'a lasting experience of a family that gives [children in care] opportunity to attach to adults' (p. 18). While this definition suggests that permanence *may* involve a child in care develop-ing long-term connections, it does not insist on permanence as necessarily entail-ing a *lifelong* connection for a child. According to this definition, therefore, long-term foster placements that do not even last throughout a looked after child's childhood might still be considered a 'permanence' option if they offer some longer-term stability to a child in a family-based setting. Boddy's review for the Care Inquiry (2013) went a stage further and suggested that residential care should in some circumstances be viewed as a permanence option. There is some logic here in that a minority of young people will spend several years in residential care and may build very strong – even family-like – relationships there (Kendrick, 2013). However, it is still currently rare for those relationships to last long beyond leaving residential care, and Boddy's suggestion does move us some distance from previ-ous conceptions of permanence as *a lifelong family connection* for a child in care.

In short, the looser the conception of what permanence must entail (for exam-ple, that it need *not* include family-based care or be lifelong) the more placement options this opens up in terms of those which may be regarded as permanence options, and vice versa. There are arguments for using both a looser and a tighter definition of permanence. A looser definition may better reflect the reality that for many looked after children, though a placement may not be lifelong, it still offers significant stability and security over several of their childhood years. A tighter defi-nition of permanence – as a lifelong family-based connection – is closer to what most children growing up in their birth families will have experience of.

Different types of permanence

The question of whether a placement provides a longer-term *home* for a child is a matter not just of whether the placement lasts, but also of that child's sense of belonging within it and how they are viewed by others within the placement. Sinclair and colleagues (2005a) suggest a typology of four core aspects of permanence in foster care which I have slightly adapted here to apply to all placement options for a child in care. These are:

- *Objective permanence*, where a child remains in the same care placement.
- *Subjective permanence*, where the child feels that the placement is a long-term base.
- *Enacted permanence*, where all in the placement treat it as though it is the child's long-term home (for example, the child goes to all family events or has similar experiences as part of a residential care unit).
- *Uncontested permanence*, where a child's sense of their placement and birth family relationships do not conflict with each other.

Practice Pointer 4.3

To what extent will these different aspects of permanence tend to go together? For example, is it realistic for 'subjective permanence' to exist without 'enacted permanence'? Try to illustrate your thoughts by coming up with examples of differing permanent placement scenarios and applying the typology outlined above.

In policy, the focus has often been on achieving 'objective permanence' and seeking a legislative basis to underpin the stability of a child's placement. Normally, those caring for a child long-term will acquire some or all parental responsibility (PR) either directly via a Child Arrangement Order (CAO), Special Guardianship Order (SGO) or Adoption Order, or the local authority will acquire PR via a Care Order. Recent government policy responses have tended to prioritise legally secure arrangements for children's care, mostly outside the care system, and particularly via adoption. There is a rationale for this as evidence does suggest that the lack of objective permanence within the care system is an issue for children's care. Sinclair and colleagues' (2007) study of the care system found that only around a quarter of children who enter the looked after system aged under 11, and who were still in care at 17, had been in the same placement for five years or more. However, it should also be noted that secondary legislation and guidance in 2015 (see DfE, 2015a) created a statutory definition of long-term fostering, as a result of which, the definition of permanence no longer requires permanent caregivers to have legal parental responsibility. Alongside the *Staying Put* policy this change supports the viability of long-term foster care as a permanence option.

Sinclair and colleagues' (2005a) typology of the different kinds of permanence highlights that there are other important dimensions to children's long-term stable care beyond legal and placement stability. In support of this, *The Care Inquiry* (2013, para 3.9) came to the conclusion that too much focus has been given to promoting legally secure arrangements at the expense of a broader understanding of permanence which encapsulates 'security, stability, love and a strong sense of identity and belonging' for a child.

Exploring the placement routes to permanence in more detail

The discussion here relates to England and Wales. A brief overview of key variations in Northern Ireland and Scotland is considered after this section. Employing a looser definition of permanence, Boddy (2013) summarised the main placements routes to permanence as:

- A return to birth parents ('reunification').

- Shared care arrangements.

- Permanence substitute care within the care system via a long-term residential, foster care or kinship care placement.

- And permanent substitute care outside the care system via a Residence Order (since replaced as a CAO), SGO or Adoption Order.

These are summarised in the Table 4.1 below:

Table 4.1 Long-term placement options in overview

1. Reunification A return to the care of one or both birth parents	*Decreasing levels of birth parental rights and involvement*
2. Shared care A return to parental care with care shared either with the local authority via a 'respite care' arrangement or with another adult carer in the child's network	
3. Long-term foster placement, kinship placement or residential placement, legal status remains 'looked after' A child remains in a local authority-provided placement, which is planned to last at least until adulthood, and remains legally 'looked after'	
4. Long-term placement with family or friend carer, ex-foster carer or adopter. Legal status is no longer 'looked after' A child goes to, or remains in, the care of a previous foster carer, family or friend carer or adoptive parent, via a legal order which takes them out of the 'looked after' system	

1. Reunification

This is where a child is returned to either or both birth parents. If the child is subject to a Care Order then this will normally be terminated prior to the child's return, meaning the local authority no longer share PR, though the local authority can request the child be returned under a Supervision Order which gives them particular duties to 'advise, assist and befriend' the child, and may contain specific conditions regarding the child's care (s.35 of the Children Act 1989). Where a child is returned to a birth father who does not have PR then the father may seek a CAO (previously known as a Residence Order) to provide him with these rights.

2. *Shared care*

This refers to situations where the care of the child is divided between birth parents and others. This could be between separated birth parents, between birth parents and other adult carers – for example, family or friend carers whom the child stays with for part of the week – or via a series of short-term breaks provided via the local authority, also known as 'respite care'. This kind of care is frequently provided to children with a disability (DCSF, 2010b), but also has a tradition of being provided as a form of family support for other children (Aldgate and Bradley, 1999).

3. *Long-term foster placement, kinship placement or residential care*

This occurs when the plan is for a child to remain in their care placement until they reach adulthood and possibly beyond. The child will remain legally 'looked after', normally via a Care Order which gives the local authority joint PR with the birth parents, and also gives it power to determine which aspects of PR a birth parent can exercise. There will normally be ongoing direct contact between a child and their birth parents, though its frequency is likely to be substantially less than when there was the possibility of a return to parental care. Traditionally, fostering and kinship care have been thought of as possible permanence options within the care system, but residential child care has not. Boddy (2013) argues that it should be.

4. *Long-term placement with family or friend carers, ex-foster carer or adopter – legal status is no longer 'looked after'*

This occurs when the permanence plan is for the child to either stay with their current carer long-term or move to another long-term carer but the legal order supporting this will take the child out of the looked after system. The legal order in question could be a CAO, SGO or an Adoption Order. For example, a child could be 'looked after' in a long-term placement with a foster carer. The foster carer may then agree to apply to be a Special Guardian for the child, which means they acquire PR. The granting of the SGO terminates the child's Care Order, meaning they are no longer 'looked after', and formal local authority responsibility for the child's care ends.

Permanence timescales

A local authority must ordinarily hold a Looked After Child Review within four weeks (20 working days) of their placement,[3] then three months after this and thereafter six-monthly. In England and Wales, secondary legislation (DfE, 2015b) specifies that there must be a permanence plan for a child by the second Looked After Child Review – around four months after entry into care – while further emphasis on making decisions about children's future care within set timescales was provided by the Children and Families Act 2014 (s.14), which requires that all care proceedings in England and Wales should ordinarily be completed within six months. The court can extend proceedings by up to eight weeks beyond this where it deems that the extension is necessary; however, the legislation specifies that extensions should not be routinely granted and require a specific justification.

The principle of 'no delay' already underlay key child care legislation in the UK before the Children and Families Act 2014 but there were concerns about the time care proceedings were taking despite this. When the Children Act 1989 came into force it was envisaged that care proceedings would take an average of 12 weeks (Shah, 2016), whereas the Family Justice Review (Norgrove, 2011) found that care and supervision cases were taking an average of 56 weeks. Such lengthy proceedings have led to concerns that court and social work timescales are 'out of sync' with the developmental needs of younger children (Brown and Ward, 2013). A range of reasons for delay had previously been identified linked to both local authority practice (delayed social work reports and appointment of local authority legal representatives, repeat assessment of birth parents, additional relative assessment late on in the process) and court-side delays (appointment of additional expert witnesses, legal objections, insufficient court capacity) (Masson et al., 2008; McKeigue and Beckett, 2010; Ofsted, 2012).

Research does indicate that there is a relationship between long-term placement stability and age at placement – the younger a child is when placed, the more likely their placement is to last (Biehal et al., 2010; Selwyn et al., 2014). There is undoubtedly therefore value in trying to reduce *unnecessary* delay. However, the question then becomes what is 'necessary' and what is 'unnecessary' delay? For example, the reduced timescale for proceedings also reduces the time parents have to demonstrate they can resume care of their child. Following judgments in two high-profile family court cases (*Re B* and *Re B-S*),[4] which appeared to reduce the number of children being placed for adoption in England, the National Adoption Leadership Board (2014) clarified that the 26-week rule does not apply to care proceedings where a Placement Order is sought when a local authority is seeking to place a child in a pre-adoptive placement. And it has also been agreed that cases which go through the FDAC are excepted from the 26-week timescale (Harwin et al., 2014).

Practice Pointer 4.4

What do you think are the pros and cons of the move to enshrine a 26-week limit for Care Proceedings in law in England and Wales?

Variations in Northern Ireland and Scotland

Residence Orders still exist in Northern Ireland and Scotland, rather than CAOs, which have replaced Residence Orders in England and Wales. Residence Orders are granted via a court and have similar powers related to them as CAOs – for example, to specify a child's residence and contact with others. SGOs do not exist in Northern Ireland or Scotland, but adoption does and works in similar ways. Two significant differences between Scotland and the rest of the UK are that, firstly, when a child comes into care via a statutory order (for example, a

Supervision Order via the Children's Hearing System) the local authority does not acquire parental rights and responsibilities (PRRs) in Scots law as a local authority acquires PR via a Care Order in the other countries. Secondly, the Adoption and Children (Scotland) Act 2007 introduced 'Permanence Orders' where the plan is for a child to be placed long-term outside birth parental care. This allows a local authority to apply to court to apportion PRRs between the local authority, the birth parents and the child's current carers – who could be foster carers, kinship carers or prospective adopters. Under the same procedure, a local authority may also apply to court for a Permanence Order with Authority to Adopt where the plan for the child is adoption. Where granted this dispenses with the birth parents' right to consent or withhold consent to the child's future adoption. A Scottish case involving the granting of a Permanence Order with Authority to Adopt was, in 2017, appealed to the Supreme Court (*In the matter of EV (A Child) (No 2)* (Scotland) [2017] UKSC 15). In the Supreme Court judgment the authority to adopt, which had been granted by a lower court, was quashed. Concerns were raised by the Supreme Court judges regarding the evidential basis for some of the local authority's claims regarding the parent in question. It appears this judgment may have a similar impact on local authority adoption practice in Scotland to that which *Re B* and *Re B-S* have had in England and Wales.

Children for whom permanence is not a meaningful option

The push towards completing care proceedings in six months in England and Wales is part of a broader push to underpin permanence for children in care. As important as permanence planning will be for many children in care, it is also important to acknowledge it will not apply to all children in the care system. For example, older young people, for whom a return home it is not currently safe but who wish to return home and will not commit to a substitute family as a result – a good number of the *adolescent entrants* described in Chapter 1 – are unlikely to want a permanent placement in many of the ways set out above. They may be in a foster or residential placement which offers some stability of care and relationships, but if a young person's desire to return home is strong, the possibility of reunifying them with their birth parents may be kept open, depending on whether the home situation improves sufficiently for this to happen. As another illustration, asylum seeking minors who enter care in their later teenage years, and who may be placed in foster, residential care or hostel accommodation, may again be unlikely to experience permanence in many of the ways discussed above.

In such cases, seeking to find a young person as much support and stability in their placement should still be the goal. In some cases, relationships may build over time and offer more lasting sources of support to the young person. However, their placements are unlikely to exhibit several of the aspects of permanence described earlier in this chapter due to the nature of their circumstances.

Considering outcomes in longer-term placements

This chapter concludes by considering the research evidence around different placement options. Historically, comparisons have been made between adoption and long-term fostering; between fostering and kinship care; and between reunification and state care generally. There has also been some comparison of fostering and residential care, though the data are limited and dated. Additionally, the relatively recent study by Selwyn and colleagues (2014) compared different legal orders underpinning objective permanence in England, namely Adoption Orders, Residence Orders and SGOs.[5]

The main ways in which placement comparisons have been made is by looking at:

- Placement disruption rates (typically whether placements last as long as they are planned to last).

- And child development outcomes (typically educational attainment, emotional and behavioural well-being and psychological adjustment, and sometimes outcomes related to identity and sense of belonging).

Before discussing particular placement outcomes, it should be noted that any placement is more likely to disrupt the older a child is, the older they were on entry into that placement and where a child has emotional and behaviour difficulties (Schofield and Beek, 2009; Biehal et al., 2010; Selwyn et al., 2014). In turn, placement disruption is itself associated with poorer outcomes for children (Holland et al., 2005a). This leads to a very important consideration underlying any discussion of placement options: that, while knowledge of comparative placement outcomes can be helpful as an aid for practitioners, different placement types offer care to different groups of children and young people. Therefore in discussing placement outcomes we are rarely comparing 'like with like'.

Adoption and long-term fostering

As a placement adoption is more stable than long-term fostering but the younger age of children when placed for adoption underpins this better performance. A national survey of looked after children (Sinclair et al., 2007) found the mean age of those adopted to be 4.83 years, and more than half of those adopted were less than a year old when first coming into the care system. Children going into long-term foster care are on average substantially older than this.

A national survey (Selwyn et al., 2014) of adoption disruptions post-Adoption Order highlighted the low rate of adoption breakdowns, finding a disruption rate of 3.2 per cent over 12 years. The authors conclude that the actual adoption disruption rate in the UK post-Adoption Order lies somewhere between 2 and 9 per cent of all adoptions. This compared favourably with disruptions of 5.7 per cent for

SGOs and 14.7 per cent for Residence Orders over five years (the adoption disruption over five years was a mere 0.7 per cent). This is a positively low figure for all orders, but particularly so for adoptive placement stability. It should be noted that these figures are only post-order. Previous evidence has suggested there is an issue of disruption after a child is placed in a prospective adoptive placement, but before the Adoption Order is granted. For example, Lowe and colleagues (1999) found that of adoption disruptions known to agencies, 92 per cent had occurred before the Adoption Order was granted, while a government White Paper estimated that 18 per cent of adoptions broke down pre-order (Cabinet Office, 2000, p. 15 cited in Triseliotis, 2002b). This does suggest that if pre-Adoption Order adoptions were included, the disruption rate would be substantially higher.

A previous study undertaken by Selwyn and colleagues (2006) allowed for some comparison between long-term fostering and adoption and found adoptive placements were notably less likely to disrupt than foster placements after seven years (only 17 per cent vs. 46 per cent). Schofield and Beek's study of long-term foster care (2009) similarly found that of 52 children placed in long-term foster care aged 3–12, 43 per cent were no longer in their original placement ten years later. However, 19 per cent of young people were noted to be thriving in other settled care placements such that the authors concluded that 76 per cent of the children were 'stable and doing reasonably well' (p. 258). A contrasting finding on long-term foster placement stability comes from a Northern Irish study of McSherry and colleagues (2013) which tracked the placement pathways of 374 children over seven years. While a very high rate of adoptive placements were stable (99%) – consistent with the findings of Selwyn and colleagues (2014) above – a very high proportion of foster placements (87 per cent) were also stable after seven years.

Underpinning foster care's poorer comparative performance is not only the older age of children who go into long-term fostering, but the fact they tend to have greater levels of need. In Schofield and Beek's (2009) study children in long-term foster care had adverse histories at the time of their first placement and 90 per cent were in care due to neglect or abuse. Similarly in the study by Selwyn and colleagues (2006) children placed in long-term foster care were older than adopted children and also had some greater difficulties and needs. Indeed, when comparisons are made between children of similar ages and circumstances in adoption and foster care, the evidence suggests placement stability rates for the two placements are broadly similar (Thoburn et al., 2000; Triseliotis, 2002b; Biehal et al., 2010). By the same token, evidence from adoptions made in later childhood suggest that while they can work well, disruption rates will be notably higher than for adoptions of younger children: Rushton and Dance's (2006) six-year follow-up of a representative sample of 108 children adopted between the ages of 5 and 11 found 49 per cent of placements were continuing positively but 23 per cent had disrupted, and 28 per cent were continuing with difficulties.

In terms of developmental outcomes, adoption again fares comparatively well. Selwyn and colleagues (2006) found developmental outcomes were similar in long-term fostered children and adoptees, but adoptive placements tended to be better at promoting attachment, a finding which was mirrored in the study by Sinclair and colleagues (2005a) which gathered data on 596 children over three years who had been initially fostered. McSherry and colleagues' (2013) study in Northern Ireland again produced contrasting findings. Here, the attachment security of children in foster, kinship care and on Residence Orders was equal to, if not better than, those children who had been adopted. Studies in England do also suggest that, while *stable* long-term foster placements can produce similar developmental outcomes to adoption, where placements are not stable outcomes are notably worse (Sinclair et al., 2007; Biehal et al., 2010).

That adoption generally supports children's developmental catch-up is given further support by international evidence (Van IJzendoorn and Juffer, 2006). Compared to peers in the general child population who had not been in care or adopted, adoptees developmentally caught up to some degree, but not entirely, in respect of cognitive development, educational attainment, physical growth and attachment. Interestingly adoptees had the same, if not better, levels of self-esteem than peers who had not been in care. The best developmental catch-up was of those adopted before they were a year old. A previous review by the same authors (Juffer and Van IJzendoorn, 2005) found that adoptees had greater behavioural problems and mental health needs than non-adoptees but that the differences were small. While these findings do provide additional support to the contention that adoption is generally effective in supporting children's development, some caution does need to be taken in translating such international findings into the UK context as many of the studies on which the paper was based were either international adoptions or adoptions from different legal jurisdictions to the UK, where the process is substantially different.

Practice Pointer 4.5

Think of two potential reasons as to why adoption may be chosen for a looked after child, and two potential reasons why long-term foster care may be chosen for a child.

Kinship and foster placements

Evidence suggests that placement stability rates are similar between kinship and unrelated foster care in the UK. Farmer and Moyers (2008) found placement disruption rates were virtually identical (18 per cent kin vs. 17 per cent unrelated), but the average length of kinship placements was greater. While disruption rates for children over 10 were higher in kinship care, kin carers were also found to be more likely to demonstrate higher levels of commitment to the children in their care. Hunt and colleagues (2008) found reasonably low disruption rates overall in their study of kinship care (28 per cent) but these rates were substantially higher for 5 to 12 year olds (43 per cent) and teenagers (50 per cent). The disruption rates for children 5 and above in kin care found by Hunt and colleagues (2008) were comparable, though slightly worse than, those reported for long-term fostering by Triseliotis (2002b) in a review of UK evidence. By contrast, the study of McSherry and colleagues (2013) found slightly better placement stability rates for kinship care as compared to foster care (95 per cent vs. 87 per cent).

One of the great potential advantages of kinship care is the opportunity to better preserve a child's birth family links and connections. There is evidence that kinship care promotes greater levels of contact with birth family members and where kinship placements do disrupt, children are more likely to move into the care of other family carers, with their original kin carer more likely to remain in touch (Hunt, 2009). This suggests that where disruption occurs in a kinship placement it may be less of a rupture for a child than in unrelated foster care. The greater levels of contact with birth family members can be a double-edged sword though. The most recent large-scale UK studies suggest contact is more likely to be unsupervised in kinship care and yet conflictual relationships between carers and other family members are considerably more likely (Farmer and Moyers, 2008; Hunt et al., 2008), with children distressed by exposure to such conflict (Sinclair et al., 2004).

There is currently a lack of longitudinal data on children's development longer-term in kin placements (Hunt, 2009). In terms of shorter-term data, Farmer and Moyers (2008) found no significant differences between kin and unrelated foster care in respect of children's emotional and behavioural development, despite the fact that a higher proportion of poor quality kin placements had continued. Sinclair and colleagues (2007) similarly found kinship placements were of poorer quality than foster and adoptive placements, but had better outcomes than foster placements. In summary the in-placement data on children's emotional, behavioural development and mental health suggest that kin placements perform similarly or, in some respects, slightly better than unrelated foster care (Brown and Sen, 2014). This is despite the fact that kinship placements are, on average, more poorly supported by social workers, with carers who are less well skilled than in unrelated foster care, and which are characterised by greater levels of poverty and poorer housing conditions (Brown and Sen, 2014).

Practice Pointer 4.6

Think of two potential reasons as to why a kinship placement may be chosen for a looked after child.

Residential child care

The outcomes for young people in residential care tend be the worst of any of the options in the care system. However, young people will typically enter residential child care at an older age, and with a greater level of need and difficulties than other placements. There are also relatively few large-scale studies on placement outcomes in residential care as well as a lack of studies which compare residential care with other placement options for young people with similar backgrounds and needs. Without such comparative evidence, it is difficult to properly evaluate the extent to which the poorer outcomes associated with residential care are related to the residential environment, and to the extent to which they are linked to the circumstances and characteristics of the young people entering residential care.

There is mixed evidence on the effectiveness of residential child care based on the data we do have. Evidence from the 1960s and 1970s pointed to the fact that young people who spent longer periods in residential child care fared badly, but research after those decades has found that most young people make some progress in residential care (Hill, 2000). In a review of post-war UK research until the early 2000s, Forrester and colleagues (2009) found that residential child care did improve the well-being of children within it, but there was less evidence of it doing so than for foster care and adoption.

The comparative data around residential care in the UK are not particularly favourable for the sector. In the three-year follow-up study by Sinclair and colleagues (2005a) social workers were asked to rate the children's then current placements. Only 4 per cent of children were in residential care, and residential placements were rated more poorly than adoption, foster care and care arrangements with the child's birth family – only independent living was rated more poorly. The study did also find, though, that children who had returned to the birth family and those in independent living – rather than residential care – had the greatest difficulties.

Sinclair and Gibbs (1998) found that young people in residential care scored highly in terms of health and moderately in terms of social presentation. However, they were also rated poorly in respect of self-esteem, education and work. The study found that nearly half (44 per cent) of the young people they spoke to were bullied in their stay and 14 per cent reported they had been 'taken advantage of sexually' by peers. Despite this, most of those in the residential homes studied expressed a preference for this type of care rather than foster care. However, few children in current foster placements express a preference to move to residential care (Sinclair, 2005). In one of the few UK studies to directly compare residential care and foster care Colton (1988) found that young people in both placement settings showed behavioural improvements, reduced offending, less violence and better educational performance. However, the performance of those in foster care was better on all but one measure (that of displaying negative behaviour towards carers). Supporting this finding, Colton also found the foster care environment to be significantly more child-orientated.

Walker and colleagues (2002) compared the use of secure care with a pilot scheme where intensive foster placements were instead used. While the outcomes for the young people in the scheme were similar to secure care, the authors point out that they were achieved without the same cost or the restriction of liberty that secure care entails. Sinclair (2006) asks whether the continued use of residential care can be justified given the small proportion of looked after young people in this type of placement, its relative expense as a placement option and the relatively poor outcomes associated with it. He raises the questions of whether foster care might instead accomplish the tasks currently undertaken by residential care but does also acknowledge that some young people prefer residential care, and that it might also be very difficult to support some young people in family settings due to their high-level needs and difficulties.

The latter point of view is supported by previous experience where individual local authorities have closed all their own residential provision but ended up using out-of-area residential placements for some of the young people they placed in care (DOH, 1998a). It should also be borne in mind that a number of other Western European countries make far greater use of residential care for young people than in the UK (Thoburn, 2009a) and the young people in it tend to achieve more positive outcomes than young people in residential care in the UK (Munro and Stein, 2008). This does suggest that it is not the residential child care environment *per se* but its use and delivery which should be the key issue of focus.

Practice Pointer 4.7

Identify two reasons why a residential placement may be chosen for a looked after young person.

Reunification and state care

For a long time in the post-war period, policy and practice emphasis was on reunification to birth families, partly because of concerns about poor outcomes within the care system. This emphasis has been questioned by more recent research on reunification which suggests that children who return home are more likely to experience placement breakdown and poorer developmental outcomes than children who remain in care – such that, in the twenty-first century, Thoburn and Courtney (2011) describe reunification as the least successful permanence option.

Biehal (2006) reviewed research in the UK and USA on reunification and found that approximately 20 per cent of children re-entered care within two years. However, in one UK study Farmer and Parker (1991) found disruption rates of up to 50 per cent, and more recent research in England has found similarly elevated rates. In a further study of reunification led by Farmer 180 children were followed up two years after reunification (Farmer and Wijedasa, 2013; Farmer, 2014). Forty-seven per cent of returns had broken down, and researchers rated a third of those placements which had endured to be characterised by poor-quality parenting. When the children were further followed up five years after return it was found that almost two-thirds of the original returns had broken down (Lutman and Farmer, 2012). It should be noted that this study did exclude from its sample reunifications which occurred within the first six weeks of a child's entry to care – these were likely to have been the least problematic returns so the numbers reported in the study do not fully reflect all attempts at reunification.

Wade and colleagues (2011) looked at the placement pathways of 149 children, 68 of whom children had returned home. Over four years 59 per cent of those 68 had come back into care at least once. Further maltreatment, poor-quality parenting and the failure to manage children's behaviour were behind most returns. Sinclair and colleagues (2005a) found slightly lower, but still high, breakdown rates after reunification: 37 per cent of children had returned to care within two years. The study by McSherry and colleagues (2013) in Northern Ireland is again an outlier. Over seven years 95 per cent of placements with birth parents in their study were stable. It is not clear why there might be such a difference between England and Northern Ireland in this regard.

In terms of outcomes, a number of studies on reunification have gathered data on the 're-abuse rate', the proportion of children returning to parental care who are subject to further abuse and neglect, and these again reveals elevated rates. Farmer and Parker (1991) found one-quarter of one group of children they studied were re-abused, while the more recent UK studies have reported higher rates than this. Sinclair and colleagues (2005a) found some evidence of re-abuse for 42 per cent of children returning home. Lutman and Farmer (2012) reported 59 per cent of the children had been abused or neglected two years after reunification. During the subsequent three years, half of the children (48 per cent) with open cases had been abused or neglected.

Studies have also largely found comparatively poor wider outcomes for children returning home. Sinclair and colleagues (2005a) found those reunified and then returning back to care had higher levels of emotional and behavioural difficulties, mental health problems and poorer educational achievement than children in long-term fostering or adoption. Brandon and Thoburn's (2008) eight-year follow-up of 105 children who had experienced significant harm (s.31 Children Act 1989) found those children who returned home after a short stay in care had poorer well-being than those who remained in care. To assess children's progress in their study, Wade and colleagues (2011) used a well-being tool encompassing measures of risk behaviours, emotional, behavioural and social development, educational attainment and school adjustment. They found children who returned home fared worse than children who remained in care, even those children who returned home and then remained in stable home placements.

These findings on reunification make for depressing reading at first glance. However, underlying them is a complex picture. There are strong ethical, legal and pragmatic considerations supporting a child's return to their family wherever this is consistent with their welfare. In some cases children strongly wish to return home and preventing this – particularly as young people move towards adulthood – is very difficult even where the home situation is not ideal. Moreover, birth family links can be an important source of support for care leavers (Marsh, 1998). The quality of care in a birth family home where there have been marked parenting concerns is, on average, likely to be poorer than that provided by rigorously selected carers in foster and adoptive placements. Birth families are also likely to be materially poorer (Sebba et al., 2015). Taking both of these factors together we might then expect some poorer outcomes for children returning home.

Practitioners may have some sympathy with these points, but also wonder how they can take account of such wide-ranging factors in their practice when considering whether reunification is viable. It is therefore worth emphasising that research also suggests the importance of social work practice in assessing and supporting returns. Farmer (2014) found that between the six local authorities who participated in her study return breakdowns varied from 32 to 75 per cent of returns, and good-quality returns varied from 10 to 64 per cent. This strongly suggests that individual authority-level practice makes a strong difference as to whether returning home works for children or not. Harwin and colleagues (2014) found that re-abuse rates were 25 per cent for parents going through the FDAC compared to 44 per cent for those who had not – illustrating the impact that intensive, purposeful, support can have on supporting successful returns. Some of the international evidence also provides a counterpoint to the current UK evidence. Lloyd and Barth's (2011) US study looked at developmental outcomes for 353 children in care, comparing outcomes for those who stayed in care, those who were adopted and those who were reunified. According to measures of social skill, emotional and behavioural development and cognitive development, children in adoptive and home placements outperformed those in care on most of the eight measures used. Indeed, home placements scored the highest in four of the eight developmental measures. While it is important to recognise the different US context for these findings, these data do illustrate that poor outcomes for children returning to parental care are far from inevitable.

Practice Pointer 4.8
_____

Identify two reasons why reunification may be chosen for a looked after child.

Implications for practice of this research evidence

If we were to construct a simple league table based on the research evidence of placement stability and child developmental outcomes, then adoption would come first, with fostering and kinship care tied in second place, then residential care and finally reunification. However, the validity of the table would be called into doubt by the fact that it does not compare 'like with like'. The different placement options tend to provide care to children of different ages with different levels of need and difficulties. Adoption tends to be used for the youngest children with the least difficulties, and residential care generally for the oldest young people with the greatest difficulties. Equally, there are differences in socio-economic contexts: children who return to birth family care will be more likely to be living with carers who are living in poverty, in poorer quality housing and in communities that are less well-resourced. As a result, researchers have cautioned against making simplistic placement comparisons (Biehal et al., 2010; Lloyd and Barth, 2011; Thoburn and Courtney, 2011). Rather, the realist-influenced question (Pawson, 2013) of which placement options work best for which children in which circumstances, and why, is a more meaningful one to ask.

It will be very rare for a practitioner to have all four placement options available for a looked after child when making future placement decisions. Adoption is only rarely an option for children beyond the age of five or six. Residential child care is only rarely an option for children under 12. Whether kinship or reunification options are available will depend on the circumstances of birth parents and the child's wider network of feasible family and friend carers. However, practitioners will have some choices to make. These might be between pursuing adoption or long-term fostering or long-term kinship care for a child. Or, between trying out a further fostering placement for a young person whose placement has broken down or pursuing a residential placement instead. Or, between pursuing reunification for a child or seeking an adoptive placement or permanence route within the care system. These decisions are never simple and will require detailed individual assessment of a child and their family's circumstances and wishes, alongside consideration of which of the available placement options are best suited for the child. Knowledge of current research findings about particular placement options can aid decision-making but needs to be placed alongside detailed individualised assessment of children's circumstances and needs.

Key messages for practice

- On entry to the care system children will be placed in an initially short-term foster, kinship or residential placement pending assessment of whether they can return to their parents' care. Foster care is currently by far the most common placement option for children in care.

- Permanence is the attempt to find long-term stability of care and relationships for looked after children. There are four main permanence options for children entering the care system: (1) a return to parental care; (2) shared care arrangements; (3) long-term care in the care system; and (4) long-term substitute care outside the care system. Though legal and placement permanence has been the traditional focus of policy there are other aspects to lived and experienced permanence for a child which need to be considered. It is also important to recognise that, despite policy drives towards emphasising the importance of permanence for all children in care, it is unlikely to meaningfully apply to all looked after children due to their circumstances.

- Concern about the length of time care proceedings were taking has led to legislative changes in England and Wales, requiring that care proceedings should ordinarily be completed within 26 weeks.

- If we were to construct a simple league table of placement options based on placement stability and child developmental outcomes then adoption would come first, with fostering and kinship care tied in second place, then residential care and finally reunification. However, such a table does not compare 'like with like' due to the differing circumstances and needs of children entering different placement options.

Suggested reading

The following two major studies of the care system in England provide a number of insights into the way it operates in the early twenty-first century:

Biehal, N., Ellison, S., Baker, C. and Sinclair, I. (2010) *Belonging and Permanence: Outcomes in Long-Term Foster Care and Adoption.* London: BAAF.
Sinclair, I., Baker, C., Lee, J. and Gibbs, I. (2007) *The Pursuit of Permanence: A Study of the English Child Care System.* London: Jessica Kingsley.

Online resources

Research in Practice (2014) 'Placement stability and permanence'. Available at: http://foster-ingandadoption.rip.org.uk/topics/placement/ – This provides a very useful summary of current evidence.
The Transparency Project – Campaigning website of charity run by family law experts in England aiming to shed light on the workings of the family court system in England and Wales: www.transparencyproject.org.uk

Notes

1   England only and not Wales.
2   The 1989 Act and the Children (Northern Ireland) Order 1995 use the terminology of 'Parental Responsibility' (PR) to refer to parental rights and duties, whereas the Children (Scotland) Act 1995 refers to 'Parental Rights and Responsibilities' (PRRs). The terminology of Parental Responsibility (PR) will be used in this chapter unless referring only to the Scottish context.
3   It is within six weeks in Scotland.
4   *Re B (A Child)* [2013] UKSC 33 and *Re B-S (Children)* [2013] EWCA Civ 813.
5   Though Child Arrangement Orders replaced Residence Orders in England and Wales in 2014, the research data gathered by Selwyn and colleagues (2014) were before their introduction.

CHAPTER 5

REUNIFICATION, CONTACT AND FAMILY AND FRIENDS RELATIONSHIPS

Chapter Overview

This chapter considers reunification in more detail – looking at what the research evidence suggests are the difficulties underpinning some of the poorer outcomes following reunification and suggestions on what might be done to improve them. The chapter goes on to explore children's contact with their birth family and friendship networks when they are in care, looking at issues in non-permanent and permanent placement and the impact of digital media on children's contact with their birth families.

Reunification

In the UK, reunification (also sometimes referred to as 'rehabilitation') typically refers to situations where children who are in state care return to the care of at least one of their birth parents. The parent whom the child returns to live with may not be the same parent the child was previously living with. A child may also return to live with one parent where parents have separated since children came into care, or return to live with a parent and a new partner where a birth parent has entered a new relationship. Some definitions of reunification, particularly in the USA, also include situations where children go to live with extended family (what we call in this book 'kinship care') or young people over the age of 16 go back to live with their family (what is termed 'leaving care' in this book) (Thoburn, 2009b). However, the focus here will be on situations where children go back to live with at least one birth parent.

Reunification is an area where social work practice might improve and there have been calls for it to be given more attention (Thoburn, 2009b) and recognised as an area of specialist practice (Fernandez, 2012). Some high-profile tragic cases where children have been killed in parental care have followed reunification to birth parents from care, most notably the deaths of Maria Colwell in 1973, Peter Connelly in 2007 and Ayeeshia Jane Smith in 2014. Though these cases are rare, alongside the evidence of poorer outcomes for children returning home, they do suggest that better practice in assessing and supporting returns to parental care is needed.

Practice Pointer 5.1

'When a child returns to care a further time, having unsuccessfully returned to their parents' care, this suggests social workers made the wrong decision for the child to return home in the first place.' What are the arguments for and against this statement?

The timing of returns

There is a 'leaving care curve' in the UK care system – see Figure 5.1 (Biehal, 2006). Initial research into this phenomenon indicated that if intensive work was not carried out in the first six weeks after a child entered care their chances of a return home drastically reduced and they were far more likely to remain in the care system long term (Thorpe and Bilson, 1987). More recent research has found that the leaving care curve still exists but the time period before a child's chances of returning home decrease markedly is now closer to a year rather than six weeks: Sinclair and colleagues (2007) found that a fifth of children leave care in the first four weeks after entry into care. By contrast, of those children who have already been in care for a year only one-fifth will leave in the entire subsequent year.

As Biehal (2006) points out, however, it is not the time in care in and of itself which is likely to be the decisive factor in a child successfully returning home; rather, those children who leave care quickly tend to have less complex difficulties and/or home circumstances compared to those children who stay in care for longer. For example, Thoburn (2009b) reports that children who return quickly are more likely to have entered care via a voluntary admission by parental request following a family crisis or emergency. As a result it is important to note that the leaving care curve should not be interpreted to mean that a child whose home circumstances remain very difficult should be returned to parental care quickly

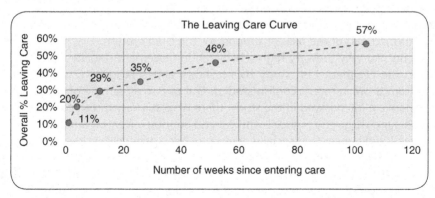

Figure 5.1 The leaving care curve based on data from Sinclair and colleagues (2007, pp. 88–89): likelihood of return to parental care reduces over time

simply in order to achieve reunification. On the contrary, the evidence suggests that unless there has been a change in circumstances which addresses the concerns which led a child to enter care in the first place, reunification will be unlikely to succeed (Biehal, 2006).

Successful reunification practice

Decisions about reunification are not an exact science but a judgement call. At best they will be based on weighing up the available information on what a child wants, what birth parents wish and whether it appears those parents can sufficiently meet the needs and promote the welfare of that child. In assessing the possibility of a child's return home, it is also useful to be aware that there are some indicators that the child's return home will work well.

The first of these is that there has been a change in family membership – a parent has ended or begun a relationship since their child came into care – or the child is returning to the care of a different parent to previously (Wade et al., 2011; Farmer and Wijedasa, 2013). When the child's current foster carers become actively involved in the return process and support the parents, including by offering to provide respite care for the child after their return home, this increases the chance of a child returning (Thoburn, 2009b), and of that return being successful (Farmer, 2014). Children's expressed wishes about their future care, as well as their behaviour in and around contact should give some indicators regarding their feelings about a possible return to parental care, while the quality of contact itself should provide some insight into the current nature of a parent–child relationship (Cleaver, 2000): good-quality contact and the child and parent(s) both being motivated and positive about the return increase its chances of success (Cleaver, 2000; Farmer and Wijedasa, 2013).

Adequate social work preparation for returns and support during reunification are also – unsurprisingly – associated with more successful returns (Lutman and Farmer, 2012; Farmer and Wijedasa, 2013). Wade and colleagues (2011) found that where children return to parental care on a Care Order (s.31 as a 'placement with parents') social work services are more likely to provide the support to families which formed part of the plan of support for the child's return.

It is unclear why the very high rehabilitation placement stability rates (95 per cent) in the Northern Irish study by McSherry and colleagues (2013) differ so much from those in recent English studies. Out of a small sample of 11 birth parents who were interviewed in the study, there were still very mixed parental views on both support given by social workers and support given by family members. However, it did appear that social workers had been generally successful in linking families into other non-social work support services post-return. Farmer and Wijedasa (2013) also found that where at least one other agency or professional, other than a social worker, was involved in monitoring and supporting children's progress, greater post-return stability was more likely. It might be surmised that birth parents are very wary of social work services post-return – given they are the agency responsible for removing children from parental care – and therefore that the involvement of other support agencies may better facilitate parents to work with supports for their care of their child.

Finally, taking returns slowly and practitioners continuing to assess the feasibility of a return after a decision has initially been made are important so that early emerging issues can be identified. Reunification decisions can be seen as one-off events, taken at a formal social work meeting – once this decision has been made it may appear set in stone, particularly given the likely emotions involved for children and parents on hearing such a decision. However, social workers viewing returns as a process rather than an event and being prepared to change their mind about a child returning where new evidence emerges are important. If there are clear early indications that the reunification plan is not working, reassessing the feasibility of reunification at that point can avoid future return breakdowns (Thoburn, 2009b; Wade et al., 2011).

Practice Pointer 5.2

Social workers have a role in assessing whether reunification should happen. They also have a role in supporting birth parents, and sometimes looked after children, to make changes which will allow reunification to happen. What kind of support do you think social workers can provide to birth parents and children to make reunification more likely?

Circumstances associated with unsuccessful reunification

Though reunification decisions should be taken in a measured way, it appears they are often rushed. Farmer's (2014) study of 180 children who returned home found that external pressures affected most return decisions: in 28 per cent of cases children returned under pressure from children, parents or courts; 27 per cent of returns followed placement breakdowns; and 9 per cent occurred after a looked after child was abused in care. The fact that there was external pressure does not automatically mean the reunifications should not have happened – for example, parental pressure for a child's return may indicate a motivation to care for their child, which has been found to be positively associated with the likelihood of a successful return (Cleaver, 2000).

However, social workers do need to consider their own assessment of whether return is the right option for a child at that point. It appears that this often does not happen. Farmer (2014) found that 43 per cent of children returned home without in-depth assessment and the provision of support services was less likely without such an assessment. She also found that professionals had concerns about children's return in over a third of cases, and social workers themselves had concerns in over a quarter of them. It may be impossible to entirely avoid all unplanned returns. For example, if a young person is repeatedly 'voting with their feet' and running away from their placement to the parental home, this may mean that a return home happens if it is safe for that young person, even if it is not an ideal move. Where such a move does happen then a package of support for that young person in the family home needs to be put in place quickly (Wade et al., 2011). A pressured return, without assessment and proper support, is very likely to break down (Farmer, 2014).

Practice Pointer 5.3

Naomi is 15 and in a foster placement described as long term, but which Naomi has repeatedly said she does not want to be in. Instead she wants to go back to her mum's. She absconds from her foster placement regularly, some of these times appearing at her mum's flat. Her mum usually sends her back to her foster placement. However, on the latest occasion Naomi's mum says she is running away so often she may as well come back to stay at home, and Naomi agrees, refusing to return to her foster placement. You are Naomi's social worker. What are your thoughts on how to respond?

A child's increasing age at time of the return (Farmer, 2009) and whether the child has emotional or behavioural problems (Lutman and Farmer, 2012) make reunification breakdown more likely – although it should be noted these two factors make any placement more likely to break down. Where children have been subject to parental neglect it seems that return outcomes are particularly poor (Wade et al., 2011; Lutman and Farmer, 2012) and where a child accepts the need to be in care and/or shows no desire to be returned to parental care, successful rehabilitation is also, unsurprisingly, less likely (Cleaver, 2000; Wade et al., 2011). Reunification to families where there has already been one return breakdown is both less likely to occur (Sinclair et al., 2007) and less likely to last (Farmer and Wijedasa, 2013). Finally, there is evidence that poverty, parental isolation and social deprivation are linked to an increased risk of a return breakdown (Farmer, 2009). While individual-level social work practice cannot address all of these social factors, the finding suggests that social workers should consider what social support is available to a parent as part of the assessment of return. It also shines a light on the need for social workers to support parents in respect of matters like benefits and income maximisation as a part of the planning for a child's return.

Is a reunification breakdown always a 'bad' outcome?

This may seem a strange question to ask. However, US research (Fein et al., 1983, in Thoburn, 2009b) suggested that children who had returned to parental care and then experienced return breakdowns went on to settle into long-term foster or adoptive placements better and subsequently fared well – in other words the attempted return and its breakdown appeared to allow children to invest in committing to a substitute care placement. However, this finding is not mirrored by the most recent UK research which rather suggests that children who return to care after reunification breakdown are more likely to have unstable placement pathways, and generally fare worse, than those children who stayed in care throughout (Sinclair et al., 2007; Wade et al., 2011). This is, in part, likely to be connected to the child's increasing age at re-entry into care. Lutman and Farmer (2012) found 58 per cent of those reunified at less than three years of age found a permanent placement if the return broke down, compared to only 31 per cent of 3 to 6 year olds and 21 per cent of 6 to 12 year olds.

Having said that, it may be necessary to 'test out' reunification with children who desperately want to return home and cannot commit to their care placement as a result. This may allow that the child's 'idealised picture of a parent can be tested against the reality' (Farmer, 2009, p. 85) and, by implication, facilitate the child to settle in a substitute care placement if the return breaks down. Such an approach may sound quite clinical and detached but reflects a reality that social workers are faced with when children cannot settle in substitute care due to strong birth family loyalties (Farmer and Parker, 1991). Even though children and parents may both wish a return to happen, approving a return in such circumstances should be done cautiously; it is imperative that social workers are clear that the reality children are being returned to is one that can meet their needs, even if there are ongoing difficulties. Where it is believed that there is a good chance of a return breaking down, consideration should also be given to keeping a child's care placement open so they can return to it if the return breaks down quickly.

Implications for practice

As noted in Chapter 4, one of the drivers for reunification was concerns about the impact of growing up in long-term state care. More recent research has led to some questions about this presumption because of the poor outcomes for children who are reunified and because recent findings suggest children in care tend to do better. Some caution is needed in interpreting this evidence as an argument against reunification more broadly: firstly, because the returns that happen very quickly, and are therefore likely to be the least problematic, have not tended to be included in the recent research as their focus has been on those returns which are more complex; secondly, there are ethical and legal imperatives supporting reunification – it is broadly accepted that children should live with their birth families where it is possible and consistent with their welfare.

Even where research indicates there is an increased risk of a return breaking down, it is important to remember that the research only suggests that such returns *tend to* produce poorer outcomes, and not that they always will. Detailed individual assessment of a family, including bringing practice wisdom to bear on whether and how a child's return may be successful, as well as agency policies, legal duties and values are also important sources of knowledge when making such complex decisions (Hill, 2009). However, research evidence does usefully identify child and family circumstances where there are increased chances of a return breaking down, and thereby situations where more careful and detailed assessment of the possibilities of return, and the supports required for a successful return, are required.

Family Group Conferences to support reunification and kinship care

Family Group Conferences (FGCs) were introduced in Chapter 2. Their use to support reunification in the UK has been suggested (Wilkins and Farmer, 2015) and there is evidence from the UK and USA that FGCs can aid permanence for a child by engaging their wider family network in supporting a reunification plan, or by helping to identify family and friends carers who might care for them where a return to parental care is not feasible (Wang et al., 2012; Harwin et al., 2014). FGCs have also been used in the USA to find family links for children who are already in the care system and who have no live birth family links. The Family Rights Group is currently piloting a similar initiative in the UK (see the list of online resources at the end of this chapter). Over ten years ago, Scottish Government guidance (2007) suggested that FGCs should be routinely used in Scotland when a child was likely to come into care and there was consideration of a kinship care placement, or when a child in kinship care needed a plan for their long-term care. However, though the use of FGCs in Scotland has grown, as elsewhere in the UK, this routine use of FGCs has not been put into practice.

Practice Pointer 5.4

Why might FGCs help support reunification?

Contact

'Contact' refers to direct and indirect communication between a child in care, their birth family and their wider family and friendship networks. There are three core purposes of contact: supporting family connection and a child's identity; assessing family relationships; and therapeutic aims – see Figure 5.2 (Cleaver, 2000; Sen, 2010).

Contact is important for a child's *Connection and Identity*. The maintenance, promotion and re-establishment of family and friends relationships can be hugely important for a child's sense of self, their psychological well-being and for maintaining live links with the family and community from which they came. This is not

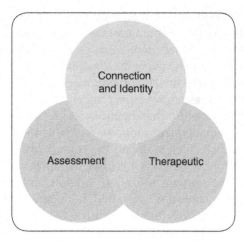

Figure 5.2 The purposes of contact

universally true for all looked after and adopted children; in some cases children may wish to have no contact with some or all of their birth family members – for example, in the case of some looked after and adopted children in permanent placements where there have been previous complex issues of abuse within the birth family. However, these cases tend to be relatively rare and most looked after and adopted children will want to at least know more of their birth families and have the possibility of direct contact with at least some birth family members. The maintenance of relationships with birth family members, and particularly birth parents, is often, understandably, the focus of contact. However, other prior relationships can also be important, including friends from their home community and friends, carers and other co-placed children from previous placements. Though it's important to distinguish between 'family and friends networks' and networks of professionals who have worked with a child, some professionals can build very significant relationships with a looked after child and can be important figures for a child to maintain some connection with (Sen and Broadhurst, 2011).

The *Assessment* purpose of contact is most emphasised where there is an ongoing possibility of a child returning to full-time parental care. Where that is the case contact between children and their birth parents is likely to be, at least partially, supervised by a social worker or contact worker, and feedback from contact sessions will form part of the assessment of reunification; parental motivation to attend contact; a parent's ability to respond to their child's needs in the contact session; and the child's reaction before, during and after the contact session are all used as – admittedly imperfect – indicators of the quality of the relationship between a child and their parent. Where a decision has been made that a child will be living in a permanent substitute placement, though there may be ongoing monitoring of contact sessions, the assessment function will be less pronounced, given that a decision about the child's future care has been made.

The *Therapeutic* purpose of contact is often given the least attention but can also be the most important (Cleaver, 2000). This consists of using contact as a means of restoring and repairing relationships including for the child's parents to give them important information about past events when the child was in parental care in an appropriate way, to let them know of significant developments in the birth family and to provide reassurance to the child about their family's ongoing commitment to them despite the child being placed outside their care. Though there may sometimes be a restorative aspect merely to a child seeing their parents, it is unlikely that contact can be therapeutic in all of the ways suggested above without professionals preparing and supporting parents to manage the discussion of difficult topics with their children during the contact session.

During supervised contact sessions it is likely that all three purposes of contact will overlap, though one purpose is likely to predominate. Which purpose predominates will affect how contact is supervised. For example, where an *Assessment* purpose predominates it is likely that all contact will be closely supervised and contact supervisors will take a largely observational role. Where *Connection and Identity* aims predominate it is likely that not all of the contact will be closely supervised and the supervision of contact, where it does occur, may be less formal. Where *Therapeutic* aims of contact predominate the contact supervisor may take a more proactive role, supporting parents and a child to have, potentially very challenging, conversations about the child's previous, current and future care.

Types of contact

Contact between children in care and their family and friends networks can be 'direct' in terms of face-to-face meetings, or 'indirect' via letter, phone, e-mail and so on. The advent of digital communication (online messaging and communication platforms and mobile phones) has started to dissolve some of the distinctions between face-to-face and indirect contact, but has not done so entirely. In most short- and long-term foster, kinship and residential placements it is usual for there to be at least some face-to-face contact, but this will be less frequent in long-term foster placements than in short-term ones. Evidence on contact in special guardianship arrangements is still emerging but it seems that some element of direct contact has been occurring in most of these (Wade et al., 2014). Though there have been increasing moves towards having some form of direct contact in adoptive placements (Neil et al., 2014) the main form of contact post-adoption tends to be indirect 'letterbox contact' – letters sent between the adoptive family and birth parents a few times a year (Sen and Broadhurst, 2011).

It should be noted that research suggests that social work agencies often overlook sibling contact – where siblings are in care but in different placements – failing to give it due importance (Kosonen, 1996; Herrick and Piccus, 2005; Sinclair, 2005). Though statutory guidance suggests siblings should be kept together in the same placement where they are in care and it is consistent with their welfare, siblings may be split where their needs dictate this. For example, there may have been abuse between siblings or their needs may be so extensive that it would be difficult for one carer to meet them together.

Separation can also happen where siblings enter care at different points in time, where they cannot be found a placement together due to placement shortages and where some siblings remain at home while others are in care placements.

Practice Pointer 5.5

What do you think are the potential negative and positive consequences of separating a sibling group in care?

Though sibling contact is generally viewed less contentiously than parental contact (Sen and McCormack, 2011), most separated siblings want more sibling contact than they actually get (Morgan, 2009a; Biehal et al., 2010), with UK studies suggesting that only around half of siblings in long-term care enjoy regular contact (Rushton et al., 2001; Moyers et al., 2005) while a Swedish study of sibling contact in foster and residential care found 40 per cent of children had contact less than monthly (Lundström and Sallnäs, 2012). Studies of adults formerly in care suggests that the maintenance of sibling links can be a highly important source of social support as young people leave care and transition into adulthood. It is suggested that social workers can improve sibling links in care by having – or gaining – an awareness of a child's family and sibling network, proactively planning for sibling contact when children are split, holding open the prospect of reuniting siblings in the same placement where it is in their welfare interests and holding open possibilities for contact even after a period of non-contact (Kosonen, 1996; Herrick and Piccus, 2005). Intervention programmes focused on improving sibling relationships in care have been developed in the USA (McBeath et al., 2014). Though they are still in their infancy, their existence arises from recognition that where sibling relationships are difficult or damaged it will take proactive social work involvement to restore them.

Debates about contact

Debates about the merits and drawbacks of contact are emotive and tend to be influenced by value positions on children's rights, child welfare, family rights and the role of the state that link back to the value positions outlined by Fox Harding (1991), explored in Chapter 1 (see, e.g., Quinton et al., 1997; Ryburn, 1998; Dale, 2013). The Children Act 1989 resulted in a significant increase in the number of children seeing a birth family member regularly (Cleaver, 2000; Sinclair, 2005). Prior to the 1989 Act, there had been concern that when children were taken into care parents had very limited rights in respect of, not only contact, but knowledge of where their child was residing. Research also identified that parents were often discouraged from visiting children or practical barriers such as distance made it difficult for them to do so (Millham et al., 1986). At that time it seemed that evidence suggested that contact for children in care:

1. Increased chances of reunification to parental care.

2. Supported placement stability.

3. Promoted children's development.

A review of the evidence by Quinton and colleagues (1997) forced a re-think by highlighting that there was inconclusive evidence on all of these three things. There is a connection between the amount of contact a child has with their parents and the likelihood of their reunification (Cleaver, 2000), but little evidence to suggest that contact is itself the cause of reunification – families where relationships are less problematic and where there are fewer child protection concerns are more likely to see each other more often, and are also likely to be reunified more quickly – it is not the contact itself which 'leads to' the reunification. Equally, while contact can be associated with greater placement stability (Berridge and Cleaver, 1987), poor-quality contact with birth family members, especially when unsupervised, is linked to placement breakdown (Sinclair et al., 2005a; Moyers et al., 2005). Finally, there is no research which conclusively shows that any type of contact with birth family members supports the development of children in care (Quinton et al., 1997; Neil et al., 2014).

There are, however, powerful legal and ethical imperatives supporting contact: UK legislation, the United Nations Convention on the Rights of the Child (UNCRC) (1989) Article 9, and the Human Rights Act 1998 Article 5 all currently give impetus and importance to maintaining family links. Local authorities have a duty to endeavour to promote contact between children in care and their family and friends networks unless it is not consistent with the promotion of welfare. In the wording of the Children Act 1989 (schedule 2, para 15) family and friends are defined as any parent of the child, anyone who is not a parent but who has parental responsibility for them (for example, a special guardian), and any relative, friend and other people connected with the child.

A strong imperative for contact is provided by the fact that many children in care, although not all, tend to miss their birth families and wish for significant levels of direct contact (Morgan, 2005, 2009a). There is a complexity to this finding in that children in care often wish for more contact than they get but can also be very distressed by it (Sinclair et al., 2005a). Parents generally also want more contact than they get, though many find supervised contact difficult and often resent it (Cleaver, 2000; Freeman and Hunt, 2000; Malet et al., 2010). Some parents also fail to attend arranged contact sessions, or engage in negative behaviours during contact (for example, saying or doing things which distress the child or undermine their care placement), which children's carers are then often faced with managing the consequences of (Cleaver, 2000; Triseliotis et al., 2002; Sen, 2010; Larkins et al., 2013). At worst contact can be a conduit for the re-abuse of children by some family members (Sinclair et al., 2005b; Moyers et al., 2005).

Practice Pointer 5.6

What reasons can you identify as to why birth parents may fail to attend arranged contact sessions with their children? What could a social worker do to help prevent this from happening?

More positive findings on family satisfaction with contact were found by Larkins and colleagues (2013) as part of a wider evaluation study of new Social Work Practice pilots. Most children reported being consulted about contact and felt they had the right amount of contact with the family members they wanted to see. Parents, while having more mixed views overall, also reported positively on their involvement in contact decisions and efforts to support contact. Proactive social work support for practical and emotional issues connected to contact was noted and appreciated by both. This may suggest that there has been some positive development in social work practice around managing contact in recent years.

The core message arising from this mixed picture is that there are strong imperatives supporting the maintenance and promotion of contact between children in care and their family and friends networks. However, contact is not universally positive for all children and therefore the type, frequency and manner of contact requires individual assessment of children's circumstances allied with monitoring, supervision and support for children, parents and carers to ensure it is working in children's best interests (Mackaskill, 2002; Sen and Broadhurst, 2011; Boyle, 2017).

Issues regarding contact in non-permanent placements

Given the 26-week limit on care proceedings introduced by the Children and Family Act 2014 it is likely that the assessment purposes of contact are now pre-eminent in cases where care proceedings are ongoing. If contact is still intended to serve all the three purposes set out above in Figure 5.2, it is important that practitioners think about how contact sessions can be used to sustain and repair relationships. That will require proactive work with children and, most of all, parents.

Research in Australia (Humphreys and Kiraly, 2009) and on foster to adopt placements in England (Kenrick, 2009, 2010) has raised questions about the impact of high-frequency contact with parents (five days or more per week) on young children due to the long travel involved and concerns that the separation from their carers negatively impacts on a child's developing attachment to the carers. It is important to note that the concerns raised in these studies principally came from children's foster carers and neither the children's viewpoints (due to age) nor the birth parents' perspectives were represented (Dale, 2013). This does not invalidate the concerns, but it needs to be recognised that their views come from a particular perspective. Indeed, concerns were raised by a prominent UK child welfare researcher that birth parents' perspectives of contact are poorly recognised within current social work practice (Triseliotis, 2010).

Moves to reduce contact while rehabilitation is a live consideration are questionable given this may imply the local authority has already determined to seek a permanent placement for a child outside the birth family (Dale, 2013). In respect of long travelling times to and from contact sessions, the Children Act 1989 suggests that children should be placed close to their home area where possible. Children may, however, be placed at distance due to a shortage of appropriate local placements. Though this situation is hardly parents' fault, the impact on children of frequent long journeys to and from contact does need to be considered. There is little research which points conclusively towards what balance there should be between the frequency and duration of contact and careful assessment of an individual child's circumstances is needed, taking into account the complex trade-offs between frequency, duration and quality of contact for that child (Miron et al., 2013).

Contact in permanent placements

Where children have moved to a permanent substitute placement there will normally be a reduction in the frequency of contact with a child's birth parents as the child's relationship with their long-term carers and substitute family becomes the primary focus. The possible exception to this may be where children move to long-term kinship placements and there are close, and unproblematic, relationships between the child's parents and kinship carers. In permanent placement the primary purpose of contact is maintaining *Connection and Identity* (see Figure 5.2) to support a child's links to, and understanding of, their birth family culture, family history and personal identity (Neil and Howe, 2004).

Some children in permanent placement will want more contact with their birth family than they can emotionally manage (Mackaskill, 2002; Sinclair et al., 2005b; Biehal et al., 2010). Poor-quality and problematic contact in long-term placement is linked to greater likelihood of placement disruption (Mackaskill, 2002; Moyers et al., 2005). Safe contact with one family member can also bring a child into more problematic contact with other birth family members, so arrangements for contact (whether it is supervised or not, for example) and which family members will be attending contact need to be agreed explicitly in advance of contact sessions and regularly reviewed to see that they are working well in children's interests.

Practice Pointer 5.7

What reasons are there for and against significantly reducing the frequency of birth family contact when a child moves to a permanent substitute placement?

A study of teenagers in long-term foster care and their contact with birth family members revealed a range of difficulties – including contact not happening, leading to bitter disappointment, negative pre-care family dynamics reoccurring in contact and threats to young people's safety and well-being during contact (Moyers et al., 2005). Young people were also often left to manage such contact by themselves on the basis that they were older, and the authors found greater social work involvement was needed to help young people manage these contact arrangements. Positively it was found that easily implementable changes, such as regular communication between social workers and carers about contact, and relatively small changes to the contact arrangements around duration, frequency and which family members should attend, could make considerable differences to its improvement (Moyers et al., 2005).

It should also be acknowledged that children can be highly distressed by an absence of contact with parents (Schofield et al., 2000) and siblings (Mackaskill, 2002). The study of children in long-term placements in Northern Ireland (McSherry et al., 2013) used the concept of 'ambiguous loss' to explore children's feelings where there was no contact with birth family members but the birth family members remained psychologically present in children's lives. Some children were happy with this situation, but others yearned for contact – including one adopted girl whose adopted parents were oblivious to these wishes and had not yet passed on letters and presents from her birth father, believing she had shown no interest in her birth family.

An emerging area of knowledge is that of contact under special guardianship arrangements. Wade and colleagues (2014) found that levels of contact were higher than in adoption, as was to be expected, but three to six years after the Special Guardianship Order (SGO) was made over half of birth fathers and over a quarter of mothers had no direct contact with their children. Of the contact that did exist, guardians also only rated contact with mothers as positive in one half of the cases. Where there was higher frequency this tended to indicate contact was viewed more positively for the child. However, higher frequency contact also seemed to prompt more divided loyalties for children between their guardianship and parental families. Guardians and social workers therefore need to be aware of the possibility that such difficulties may arise and children may need support to negotiate them (Wade et al., 2014).

Contact in adoptive placements will typically be less frequent than in other permanent placements. This difference can be traced back to the historical usage of adoption as a 'clean break' with a child's birth family past (Triseliotis et al., 1997). There have been increasing, if gradual, moves over the last 30 years towards direct birth parental contact after adoption (Neil and Howe, 2004). However, it has been argued that it is also important to think beyond levels and types of contact in adoption, or 'structural openness', to 'communicative openness' (Brodzinsky, 2006). Communicative openness is defined as adopters' broader openness to discussing the experience of adoption within their family, including recognition of their adopted child's connections to their birth family as well as their own.

The research by Neil and colleagues (2014) was the first major longitudinal UK study to explore post-adoption contact. It demonstrated that post-adoption direct contact can work well, with the reliability of contact a more important factor than its frequency in terms of whether the contact endured. It was found that young people sometimes initiated increases in contact during adolescence and while around half of them were experiencing difficulties in later childhood or early adulthood the difficulties were found to be unrelated to birth family contact. The research also found there were also benefits which both birth parents and adoptive parents derived from the direct contact. There is one important characteristic of the study sample which should be noted in taking these findings forward to practice, however: the children in the study were adopted at a young age and links to their birth families were generally weak at this point, meaning that at the outset there were not questions about children's divided loyalties which might have posed greater challenges for adopters.

Contact via mobile phones and the Internet

Digital media have become increasingly prevalent as a means of communication in all of our lives over the last 20 years and are an increasingly integral part of the lives of children in care (Neil et al., 2014; Sen, 2015). Sonia Livingstone's work (2008, 2009) has adapted the framework of 'risks' and 'opportunities' to help classify the benefits and drawbacks of Internet use for children, the primary risks being identified as online grooming, online abuse/bullying, accessing inappropriate content and overuse of the Internet; the primary opportunities being social, recreational and learning ones.

Practice Pointer 5.8

Are the 'risks' and 'opportunities' of mobile phone and Internet use different for children in care than for other children, or not? What assumptions can you identify underpinning your views?

There has been increasing concern on the part of professionals, foster carers and adoptive parents that children's digital media usage can facilitate unmediated contact between them and birth family members. Unsolicited, unexpected contact from birth parents with children who have been adopted has been a particular cause of concern (Fursland, 2010) but there has also been some concern over unmediated contact via new technology between children in foster care and residential care and their birth families (Fursland, 2011; Macdonald et al., 2016). Due to the difficulties that brought them into care it is certainly reasonable to argue that children in care face more 'risks' than children in the general population.

However, by the same token the 'opportunities' afforded through their digital engagement offer the same, if not greater opportunities, than their peers. As such, it is important for professionals to bear both opportunities and risk in mind when approaching looked after children's use of digital technology (Ballantyne et al., 2010; Sen, 2015; Simpson, 2016).

Fursland's (2010, 2011) practice guides are helpful tools for practitioners and carers seeking to respond to the impact of digital media on looked after and adopted children. However, the anecdotal examples recounted largely focus on negative portrayals of contact with birth parents and birth family via the Internet. The research base suggests a more nuanced picture. Neil and colleagues (2014) found that contact via social media by birth family members with adoptees could indeed be problematic but was also manageable where adopters were able to engage and communicate openly with their child around both their birth family and social media use.

Greenhow and colleagues' (2017) research on digital contact in adoption found that there were opportunities offered through such contact in terms of children's connection with birth family members and identity, but there were also examples where online birth family contact, and the behaviour of some birth family members, impacted negatively on children in ways they were ill-equipped to handle. Macdonald and colleagues' (2016) study of contact via mobile phones in foster and residential care found that their use for contact with birth family members often transgressed agreed contact plans; they also noted the lack of explicit attention given to addressing contact via digital media in children's contact plans in the first place. Carers in the study noted examples of where contact via mobiles had caused some difficulties – for example, where some parents failed to return texts or calls leading to feelings of rejection on children's part. However the benefits of children's mobile use was also acknowledged – for example, it could provide carers with reassurance about where children were at a given time and that they were safe.

Whatever misgivings practitioners may have about the impact of looked after children's use of mobile phones and the Internet, there is an inevitability about it given their modern-day ubiquity. While carers providing some oversight of children's online activities is uncontroversial, asking them to monitor all looked after children's digital communication is not only impractical but also throws up questions about the legitimate boundaries of intrusion into children's private space given that much of children's social worlds are now facilitated through such media (Livingstone, 2008, 2009).

Practice Pointer 5.9

A young person, aged 13, is in foster care and has a Facebook account. Is it acceptable for their carer to insist on seeing their account? Consider how this may be similar to or different from a carer insisting on seeing a private paper diary which the young person is keeping.

The only realistic option is to support carers, adoptive parents and – most of all – children themselves to manage the risks and opportunities arising from the use of digital technology through open discussion, rather than trying to prevent its use or monitor every instance of it (Sen, 2015; Simpson, 2016; MacDonald et al., 2016).

Key messages for practice

- Reunification outcomes are poor for children judged by return breakdown rates and children's further experience of maltreatment. Research shows that there is a large variation in the proportion of 'successful' returns between local authorities, suggesting that local practice and procedure makes a difference to reunification working well.

- Increasing the chances of positive reunification requires practitioners to undertake individualised assessment of what has changed within the birth parental home to address the original issues of concern. Children and parents' motivation for the return, taking returns gradually and reviewing ongoing progress towards reunification are all important parts of the assessment process. Planning for post-return support, ensuring that this support is then put in place and involving non-social work agencies in providing post-return support to parents are all important parts of post-return practice.

- Contact between looked after children and their birth family is a contested and emotive issue. Both birth family and children in care tend to want greater levels of contact and it can be a benefit for looked after children. However, poorly managed and poor-quality contact is likely to have a negative impact which can sometimes undermine a child's placement stability. Individualised assessment of the levels of contact a child should have are required, bearing in mind legal and ethical frameworks which suggest that relationships between children and their birth families should ordinarily be encouraged and supported.

- Internet and mobile phone use by children in care can give rise to significant concerns for adoptive parents, carers and professionals. There are real risks to such use but also opportunities and practitioners' focus should be on supporting parents, carers and children to manage such use through open communication in a way that maximises opportunity and minimises risk.

Suggested reading

Boyle, C. (2017) '"What is the impact of birth family contact on children in adoption and long-term foster care ?" A systematic review', *Child and Family Social Work, 22*: 22–33, and Sen, R. and Broadhurst, K. (2011) 'Contact between children in out-of-home placements and their family and friends networks: a research review', *Child and Family Social Work, 16* (3): 298–309 – Two research reviews which provide detailed consideration of the evidence base around contact for children in care.

Simpson, J. (2016) 'A divergence of opinion: how those involved in child and family social work are responding to the challenges of the Internet and social media', *Child and Family Social Work, 21* (1): 94–102 – A useful summary of the differing, polarised, positions which professionals have so far adopted around children's digital media usage.

Online resources

Family Rights Group is a charity which promotes and supports the use of FGCs in the UK. They are currently involved in establishing Lifelong Links, which is a new approach in the UK that aims to build lasting relationships for children in care. The Lifelong Links model uses online tools and face-to-face techniques for professionals to search for and find family members and other adults who care about the child. This network is then convened at an FGC to make a lifelong support plan with and for the young person, which then becomes part of their care plan. This work is available at: www.frg.org.uk/involving-families/family-group-conferences

Wilkins, M. and Farmer, E. (2015) *Reunification: An Evidence Informed Framework for Return Home Practice*. London: NSPCC – A practice reunification framework co-authored by a leading researcher on reunification in the UK. Available at: www.nspcc.org.uk/services-and-resources/research-and-resources/2015/reunification-framework-return-home-practice/

CHAPTER 6

FOSTER CARE AND KINSHIP CARE

Chapter Overview

Foster care is by some margin the most used placement for children in care and it fulfils a variety of roles. This chapter considers the different types of roles that foster care plays in the care system. It also considers kinship care, as a particular kind of foster care provided by family or friends carers. The chapter then provides an overview of the assessment process for foster carers, what good fostering consists of, meeting children's wishes and needs in foster care and what support foster carers require to fulfil their role effectively. The chapter finishes by considering the use of (SGOs) and Child Arrangement Orders (CAOs) as an alternative to long-term foster care in England and Wales, focusing on emerging evidence about the use of SGOs.

Foster care in context

The use of foster care has grown as a placement choice over the last 40 years and is now by far the most frequently used placement type. However, the growth in its use has not been uniform. The immediate post-war period saw significant growth in the foster care sector. However, in the late 1960s and early 1970s evidence that placement disruption rates were as high as 50 per cent in long-term placements (Parker, 1966; George, 1970), allied with increasing numbers of children coming into care overall, saw the increasing use of residential child care. This was then followed from the late 1970s onwards by a strong swing back in favour of using foster care. Despite the increasing turn towards foster care in the 1980s, there were questions about its future direction in the early 1990s (Kelly, 2000). These arose from the introduction of the Children Act 1989, which primarily conceptualised foster care as a short-term support for birth family care rather than a long-term substitute for it; debates around moves to 'professionalise' foster care; and, lastly, an increasing emphasis on the achievement of permanence via adoption. However, in fact, the use of both short-term and long-term foster care increased. Research in the late 1990s and early 2000s has highlighted the variety of care provided to looked after children in foster care (Sinclair, 2005). And, the viability of long-term foster care as a permanence option has been strengthened by the introduction of the *Staying Put* policy in 2014. Though there are still questions about the use of foster care these are no longer about whether it will continue to be used as a placement option – it is now hard to envisage how the care system could operate in the UK without it; rather, they are around how its exact role as a permanence option fits alongside other, more legally permanent, options outside the care system, in particular adoption and special guardianship (Schofield, 2009).

Types of foster care

The large number of children in foster placements, in very different circumstances, means that the functions and purposes of foster care are varied. In order to explore some of these differences the main types of foster care are set out below – they are based around ways in which academics have classified fostering but it is worth noting that local authorities and fostering agencies will employ their own classifications which might be slightly different. It is also worth noting that the categories are not exclusive and some foster carers will fit across more than one of the categories set out below.

Respite care

Under this category are forms of short-term care primarily provided as a planned package of support to parents or main carers to offer a break from caring responsibilities. Respite care includes:

- Short Break Care for children with disabilities living with their families which all local authorities have a duty to provide for disabled children in their area under s.25 of the Children and Young Persons Act 2008. Local authorities also have a statutory duty to publicise these services.

- Support Care for children living with their parents where there are family difficulties or stresses in order to support children to remain in parental care.

- Respite Care for foster carers for foster children on placement with them, usually provided by other foster carers.

Although all the respite care is provided by formally approved carers, not all of it is technically 'foster care', in that a local authority can provide Short Break Care and Support Care under either its general duties to promote child welfare under s.17(6) or its duties to provide accommodation to children who need it under s.20(4) of the 1989 Act. Where a child is provided with respite under s.17 they are not legally 'looked after', whereas if they are cared for under s.20 they are, and the 2010 Care Planning Regulations apply in full or in part depending on the length of the child's stay and whether care is provided in a single or multiple respite placement settings (DCSF, 2010b).

Short-term foster care

This category consists of:

- Emergency fostering where children are unable to remain with their parents at very short notice due to unforeseen family crises of whatever nature. Placements will normally only last a few days.

- Planned short-term foster care, where children may reside to allow further assessment of future longer-term options for their care, whether that be a return to birth parents or an alternative long term placement. Berridge and Cleaver (1987) defined short-term care as lasting up to eight weeks while Triseliotis and colleagues (1995b) defined it as up to 12 weeks and also distinguished between 'short-term' foster care and 'medium-term' foster care. More recently, however, the length of short-term foster placements has increased. Sinclair and colleagues (2004) found that short-stay foster care averaged 12 months, with a third of carers registered as both short-term and long-term foster carers. This suggests that the definition of short-term foster care has become more elastic over time, and the boundaries between short-term, medium-term and, sometimes, longer-term foster care have thinned. The introduction of foster to adopt placements in the late 1990s, whereby prospective adopters are also approved as short-term foster carers for a child (Borthwick and Donnelly, 2013), has further expanded the range of short-term foster care.

Specialist foster placements

Hill and colleagues (1999 [1993], p. 36) remarked that the development of specialist fostering in the UK was 'one of the child care success stories of the 1980s'. In this category are placements for children with particularly high levels of need, including placements for children with severe disabilities, children with emotional and behavioural difficulties, children who have been charged with, or convicted of, serious criminal offences, and specialist placements for parents (usually young parents) and children together which typically have both an assessment and support role where the viability of the parent assuming long-term care of their child is under consideration. The most well-developed type of foster care within this category is 'treatment foster care' – a time-limited, task-orientated placement, for young people engaged in offending behaviour and/or with substantial emotional and behavioural difficulties. Key features of treatment foster care are that it is:

- Provided to young people with a higher level of behavioural or emotional difficulties who might typically otherwise have been placed in some form of residential care.

- Focused on achieving particular tasks – for example, behavioural change in young people – rather than general care.

- Provided in time-limited placements which offer tailored individualised programmes of work with a young person.

- Involves greater levels of remuneration and support for carers – for example, specialist training and more intensive foster agency support and supervision.

Sinclair and colleagues (2005a) concluded that the 'treatment' role of foster care can, and should, be increased. A version of treatment foster care was used by

National Children Homes (NCH) in Scotland as an alternative to young people going into secure care (Walker et al., 2002). The treatment programme included salary-level remuneration and specialist training for carers, 24-hour support for carers, automatic provision of eight weeks respite care per year and educational support and tailored individual programmes for young people. It was notable that no carer left the scheme in the first three years it operated. The 'end' outcomes were mixed in that 14 of the first 20 foster placements broke down prematurely and broader outcomes were similar to those for young people who entered secure care. However, the foster care programme also achieved similar outcomes without the high costs of secure care and allowed young people to retain their liberty. Moreover, where there were benefits, progress was very stark in terms of young people's increased self-esteem, social networks and social support. Unsurprisingly, those who remained in placement longer showed greater progress, with the greatest benefit shown by young people who had been in placement for over a year (Walker et al., 2002).

Practice Pointer 6.1

'Foster care can achieve the same outcomes as secure care at less expense and without locking young people away, therefore it should always be preferred to secure care.' What do you think are the pros and cons to this proposition?

More recently there has been focus on Multidimensional Treatment Foster Care (MTFC), an approach adapted from the USA which has now been piloted in 18 local authorities with government funding (Biehal et al., 2012). It is part of the suite of 'evidence-based' interventions which the government are promoting via the National Implementation Service (NIS, 2017). MTFC is influenced by social learning theory and systems theory and combines individual and family therapy, social skills training and tailored educational support (Biehal et al., 2012). It has had some impressive impacts in the USA: in one evaluation young people receiving MTFC spent 60 per cent less time in prison after a year, absconded less and were involved in less problematic drug use (Fisher and Chamberlain, 2000; Chamberlain, 2003). A systematic review which evaluated the research evidence from a number of different evaluations of MTFC found evidence of its promise in reducing anti-social behaviour, criminality and time spent in incarceration, but also emphasised caution as much of the evidence was US-specific and the programme's developers had also been involved in the evaluations (Macdonald and Turner, 2009).

Biehal and colleagues were subsequently involved in two evaluations of MTFC in England. The first of these (Biehal et al., 2011) involved MTFC for young offenders who would otherwise be placed in custodial settings. It showed impressive results initially: one year after first entering placement those receiving MTFC had lower reconviction rates, greater educational engagement and were more likely to be living in community settings. However, once these young people left their MTFC placements there was a marked deterioration in their circumstances resulting in no significant difference in final reconviction rates between the groups of young people who had MTFC and the groups who did not (Biehal et al., 2011).

The second evaluation (Biehal et al., 2012) looked at the use of MTFC with teenagers who were already in the care system in foster placement with emotional and behavioural problems, educational difficulties and risk of repeat placement breakdown. They moved to specialised MTFC placements and their progress was compared to young people who did not move to them. The results were disappointing: those receiving MTFC did not demonstrate significantly better outcomes overall, including in school performance and offending behaviour (Biehal et al., 2012). The research did find the MTFC had a disproportionately beneficial effect on young people exhibiting anti-social behaviour and the most significant gains were made while young people were still in their placements.

Overall, the current UK evidence base suggests that MTFC has great promise but some of the high expectations surrounding the potential outcomes MTFC might achieve with young people have so far not been borne out (Walker et al., 2002; Biehal et al., 2011, 2012). The evidence suggests that the longer treatment placements last the more beneficial the gains for young people, leading to the question of how the treatment gains may be sustained once young people leave their treatment placement. Indeed, Biehal and colleagues (2012) suggest that rather than prolonged, and costly, use of specialised MTFC placements, it may be better to train existing foster carers in MTFC.

Practice Pointer 6.2

The current evidence base suggests MTFC can have a considerable positive impact on a young person while in their placement, but this positive impact dissipates once they have left the placement. Why do you think this might be? What might be done to address it?

Long-term foster care

These are foster placements which are intended to provide a stable base to children over a number of years, and in many cases are intended to last until a young person is ready to leave care, and sometimes beyond. Although there has been increasing focus given to reducing the number of placements which children in the care system experience it is most likely that children will move into long-term foster care from a 'short-term' or 'medium-term' foster placement (Sinclair et al., 2007). However, a small minority of children will stay with the same foster carer throughout their time in care, and in some cases be adopted by previous foster carers (Sinclair et al., 2005a, 2005b; Biehal et al., 2010). In a study of permanence planning in foster care in England and Wales, Schofield and colleagues (2008) found that there were nuanced differences in definitions of long-term foster care across local authorities. Notably, some authorities had a dual system of 'long-term' and 'permanent' foster care – with long-term usually meaning the plan for the child was to stay until independence, while 'permanent' foster care carried an additional expectation that the child would remain in the family beyond 18 – whereas other authorities merged both functions under the single label of 'long-term foster care'.

Since that study was completed the government has issued new secondary legislation in England (DfE, 2015a) which amends the Care Planning, Placement and Case Review (England) Regulations 2010 to legally define a 'long term foster placement' as:

- One where there is a 'plan for permanence', defined as a long-term plan for the child's upbringing.

- The permanence plan is for the child to remain in foster care.

- The foster carer has agreed care for the child until that child ceases to be looked after.

- And this arrangement has been confirmed with the child, foster carer and birth parents by the responsible local authority.

It is worth noting that this recent re-definition excludes a number of foster placements from being formally labelled as 'long-term' which previously may have been considered as such. Most obviously the re-definition rules out including as 'long-term' those foster placements for young people who need a stable place-ment beyond the short-term, perhaps for a number of years, but who do not want to be in foster care throughout their childhood, and for whom a future return home has not therefore definitively been ruled out.

Kinship care

As noted in Chapter 1, close relatives may provide care to children who are not looked after through a private arrangement directly agreed with the child's parents. However, the focus here is exclusively on kinship carers providing place-ments for a child who is formally 'looked after'.

Kinship carers *are* foster carers. Like other foster carers, they must legally be assessed and approved by a fostering panel as foster carers to care for a child in their network who is looked after, and as such are sometimes referred to as 'family foster carers' in distinction to 'unrelated foster carers'. At different points during the last 30 years it has been envisaged that there would be an increasing number of kinship foster carers. However, the proportion of looked after children in kinship placements has remained broadly static in England during that period, with between 10 and 12 per cent of looked after children in kinship placements from

2009 to 2017 (Brown and Sen, 2014; DfE, 2017a, 2017c). It should, however, be noted that considerably greater proportions of looked after children are in kinship care in other countries in the UK: 2014 statistics show that while there were only 11 per cent of looked after children in kinship care in England, 15 per cent of looked after children were in kinship care in Wales, 26 per cent in Scotland and 32 per cent in Northern Ireland (McGhee et al., 2017). However, Sinclair and colleagues (2007) found the proportion of kinship care placements varied between authorities in England from 6 to 32 per cent, suggesting that local practice makes a considerable difference as to how much this placement type is used. Although there is statutory and policy guidance to suggest that kinship care should be preferred to other types of substitute care where it is consistent with a child's wishes and welfare, social workers can be reluctant to prefer kinship care to unrelated foster care (Hunt, 2009) which may help explain the relatively modest proportions of looked after children currently in kinship care arrangements in England.

It seems that the majority of kinship placements still occur when kin carers themselves come forward to offer care rather than through the initiation of social workers (Hunt et al., 2008; Farmer and Moyers, 2008). Kinship foster placements are more likely to be offered on a longer-term basis than unrelated foster care (Sinclair et al., 2007) and it also seems to be the case that kinship carers are far more likely than unrelated foster carers to apply for an SGO thereby offering a looked after child permanence outside the looked after system (Wade et al., 2014; see section below).

Practice Pointer 6.3

Why do you think some social workers appear reluctant to use kinship foster carers in preference to unrelated foster carers?

Recruiting and assessing foster carers

Given the shortage of foster carers, recruitment of new foster carers – as well as retention of current ones – is an important role that family placement social workers have. The growth of independent foster agencies (IFAs), some set up and run by previous local authority social workers, has increased competition for carers (Sellick and Connolly, 2002). Though local authorities can subsequently 'purchase' foster placements for children in their care from IFAs these tend to be a lot more expensive than if the placement were an 'in-house' one provided by local authority carers.

Recruitment activities can range from staffing recruitment stalls at community events, responding to initial enquiries and helping devise the wording and content of local recruitment campaigns. The evidence suggests that rolling recruitment strategies are better than one-off campaigns but targeted drives to attract carers from particular social backgrounds (for example, BME and LGBT carers) can be effective (Wilson et al., 2004). The importance of responding to enquiries about fostering in a timely period is highlighted (Wilson et al., 2004) – my own experience being that IFAs have traditionally been far better at doing this than local authorities. Finally, it has been identified that word-of-mouth recruitment by current foster carers, who can talk about the rewards and positive experiences of the role within their own networks, can be an important strategy (Sinclair, 2005).

A fostering service is required to carry out an assessment of anyone who applies to be a foster carer and anyone assessed as suitable to foster must be approved by a fostering panel (DfE, 2011c, 2013b). Fostering panels will be comprised of several agency representatives and, normally also, independent members with expertise around looked after children and fostering. The exact composition will differ from panel to panel but in England *The Fostering Services (England) Regulations 2011* (DfE, 2011c) stipulate that the Chair of a given fostering panel must be independent of the fostering service provider. At a fostering panel, the family placement social worker who has completed the assessment of the foster carers using a Form F assessment, otherwise known as a Prospective Foster Carer Report – a structured assessment tool for assessing prospective carers devised by CoramBAAF – will present their assessment to the panel and address any questions arising from this. The panel will then invite the prospective foster carers in for discussion of the assessment, with a decision as to their approval usually made on the same day. Fostering panels are also responsible for reviewing and, where there are concerns, terminating foster carers' approval.

Under Regulation 26 of the Fostering Services Regulations (DfE, 2011c) the assessment of foster carers is now a two-phase process, with the first phase – sometimes called a viability assessment – intended to quickly rule out those who appear clearly unsuitable before the more detailed second phase of the assessment. Stage one consists of gathering background information on the applicant's household composition, health, family circumstances, previous history of fostering and fostering applications. Two references and enhanced Disclosure and Barring checks on all adults in the household may be obtained at this point. Where an applicant moves to stage two, guidance specifies the assessment should cover details of the applicant's personality; their religious beliefs, racial, cultural and linguistic background and capacity to care for children of different backgrounds and beliefs; present and past employment, income and interests; and skills, competence and potential related to caring.

The detail of stage two of the assessment process will vary according to the type of fostering which the person is applying to do and the age of the children which the applicant wishes to foster. Kinships carers are likely to be seeking to be approved only as a foster carer for a particular child in their network, rather than as a carer for any child whom the local authority may place with them, and the process should reflect this. It is not unusual for children to come into care at short notice and the timescales mean that there is often not time to fully assess and approve new kinship carers who wish to put themselves forwards as potential carers on learning that a child in their network is likely to come into care (Aldgate and MacIntosh, 2006; Hunt et al., 2008). As a result a 'Connected Person' (someone who is a family member, friend or who has a prior relationship with the child such as a teacher) can be temporarily approved as a Connected Person foster carer in urgent situations where an immediate placement is needed (DCSF, 2010a). The temporary approval is for up to 16 weeks and the local authority must be satisfied both that the placement is the most suitable way of promoting the child's welfare and that the child's placement there cannot wait until the full approval process has been completed.

Practice Pointer 6.4

What arguments can you identify for and against approving prospective foster carers quickly?

Good foster caring

Sinclair and colleagues (2007) found that the care provided to looked after children was the most important variable in outcomes for looked after children and there is clear evidence of what – in broad terms – good foster care consists of. An 'authoritative' parenting style rather than an 'authoritarian' or 'permissive' style of parenting (Baumrind, 1967) has been found to be the most effective in the general parenting of children, and there is evidence that such an approach is also the most effective in foster care. Research has found carers who are more successful are:

- More caring, accepting and encouraging, and can see events from the child's perspective (Sinclair et al., 2005a).

- Good at communicating clear expectations of and boundaries on behaviour and are not easily deterred when a child fails to respond as they wish (ibid.; Farmer and Moyers, 2008).

- Able to develop shared understandings with children about levels of autonomy, particularly for older children (Sinclair et al., 2005a).

- Able to challenge children's behaviour without undermining their self-esteem (Berridge, 1997). For example, Walker and colleagues' (2002) study of fostering as an alternative to secure care illustrated how more successful carers managed to identify strengths in young people by reframing young people's rule-breaking in more positive ways: '[W]hen one girl stayed out to 2am, her carers praised her for coming home at all, seeing this an improvement compared with her usual pattern of running off' (p. 126).

Schofield and Beek (2014) developed their attachment theory-influenced 'Secure Base Model' from a longitudinal study of long-term foster care. It lists five dimensions of caregiving, linked to five needs that children in long-term fostering (and adoption) have:

1. *Availability* – linked to supporting the child to develop trust.

2. *Sensitivity* – linked to supporting the child to manage their own feelings.

3. *Conveying acceptance* – linked to building the child's self-esteem.

4. *Co-operating with the child* – linked to building the child's sense of self-efficacy.

5. *Family membership* – linked to supporting the child's sense of belonging within the family and positively managing feelings and relationships with their birth family.

Carers' ability to support children's schooling and out-of-school interests is also important. The first is clearly important in and of itself in terms of children's educational development, but some research also suggests links between children being settled at school and placement stability (Gilligan, 2000; Farmer et al., 2004; Sinclair et al., 2005b).

Meeting children's wishes and needs in foster care

We have a fair idea from research about what children in foster care say they want from foster carers and social workers. They are generally positive about it as a place to live and would prefer to stay in foster care than another placement (Morgan, 2005; Sinclair, 2005). A fairly frequent complaint, however, surrounds a lack of involvement and consultation in decisions. This can range from smaller decisions about their care within the foster home to decisions about contact with birth family, about their overall care plan and, particularly, about their moves into foster care, and to specific foster families (Farmer et al., 2004; Morgan, 2005; Sinclair, 2005; Goodyer, 2011).

Secondly, some of the bureaucratic rules surrounding fostering, which single out foster children as different, can frustrate or embarrass foster children (Goodyer, 2011). Foster children have noted that they particularly dislike what they see as stigmatising processes that mark them out as negatively different, and which undermine their wish to be seen as 'ordinary' and similar to their peers (Sinclair, 2005). For example, meetings about them held in school and requirements that permission be sought from the local authority for basic things like school trips and overnight stays tend to be disliked (Sinclair, 2005; Broad, 2008). Within the foster placement, foster children have expressed that having their own belongings, their own room and a more general sense that they are wanted and belong in the placement are very important to them (Pithouse and Rees, 2015).

Overall, foster children usually want to feel like they are part of the foster family and given opportunities to develop, while having their birth family origins, and wishes around their care, respected at the same time (Sinclair, 2005; Broad, 2008).

Being part of the family implies that children enjoy placement stability. The accounts of children in care and adults who have been in care do illustrate that a large number of placement moves, and particularly placement breakdowns, can be highly damaging (Triseliotis, 2002b; Sinclair, 2005; Randle, 2013). As noted, one of the current dilemmas of foster care is that while its diversity and ability to provide a range of care is one of its strengths, its track record of providing permanence for those staying in it is relatively poor. This dilemma is neatly summed up by Sinclair and colleagues (2005a, p. 264) when they write:

> Viewed as an isolated experience foster care is often impressive. Viewed as part of a career it too often offers a truncated, tantalising and disrupted experience of family life followed by stressful and ill supported moves to birth family, residential care or independent living.

Supporting foster placement stability

Over the last 20 years there have been moves to reduce the numbers of placements children in care have, and indeed local authorities must submit returns to government on the proportions of children who have had three or more placements. However, two studies of the care system, largely based on fostering, sound a note of caution about local authorities rigidly trying to meet performance indicators on placement stability (Sinclair et al., 2005b, 2007); they found evidence that some younger children were being kept in placements where they were clearly unhappy and/or which were not meeting their needs.

Sinclair and colleagues (2007) recommend that there should be greater flexibility in short-term placements, allowing them to become longer-term ones where it suits children's circumstances, and that there should be better support for children where they do need to make a placement move. Another potential systemic change is the better matching of placements. Though there is a lack of clarity over exactly how agencies can make a good 'match' in adoption, there is at least significant consideration of its importance in the adoption planning process (Quinton, 2012). This is less the case in fostering placements but research suggests that it should not be. Placements are more likely to be successful where there is 'chemistry' between the carer and child, the child wants to be in the placement (Sinclair et al., 2005a). Farmer and colleagues' (2004) study of teenagers in foster care also found that where carers were content with the placement at the outset it was more likely to endure, and that where carers had a definite gender preference for the child they wished to foster and the preference was ignored, placements were more likely to disrupt.

The difficulty here is that there is frequently a lack of choice of foster placements due to placement shortages, thereby removing the possibility of matching a child to a placement. The statement 20 years ago that 'Too often, social workers in the field are forced to set the priority of finding a child an empty bed above any hope of finding a placement that will meet a child's needs' (DOH, 1998a, p. 22) holds true today. In one estimate an additional 7,000 foster carers are currently needed in the UK (The Fostering Network, 2017). Addressing this shortage is likely to require significant recruitment efforts to increase the pool and variety of foster placements as well as improvements to the attractiveness of the overall package of training, support and remuneration given to foster carers (Kirton et al., 2007).

Practice Pointer 6.5

What support do you think might be effective in maintaining a placement which is at risk of disrupting? What factors might help a social worker decide if it is in fact better for a child to move to a new placement when there are difficulties within their current placement?

Supporting foster carers

We likewise have a fair idea of what, in general terms, foster carers want from social workers. They want social workers who are reliable, respect their views, keep them informed regarding the child's care and care planning, have an awareness of their other commitments and are generally supportive and warm (Sinclair et al., 2004; Farmer et al., 2004). Recognising the significance of carers' birth children with a foster placement is important. They will have an influence on the success of the foster placement and fostering will also impact on them. Foster carers tend to be of the view that fostering also benefits their own children. This view is supported by the first-hand accounts of some birth children who have expressed the satisfaction they gain from supporting foster siblings (Pithouse and Rees, 2015). Some fostering agencies do now provide tailored support to 'foster siblings' or seek to involve them in parts of foster carers' training, recognising their importance within the placement.

The importance of social work support to carers is highlighted in two studies. A Scottish study of foster carers who had left fostering found a lack of social work/ agency support was the most common cause for ceasing (Triseliotis et al., 2002), while an English study (Sinclair et al., 2004) reached a similar finding and also found carers were far more likely to cease fostering after a placement disruption. Interestingly, however, a few studies (Quinton et al., 1998; Sinclair et al., 2005b) have found no link between the level of social work support provided to placements and the likelihood of a placement disruption. This may have been because greater social work involvement was provided when placements were already in crisis and liable to break down. It may, however, also suggest that placement support needs to be more purposive and intensive to prevent disruption once difficulties have started to emerge.

Training has been identified as an important support for carers and placements. Earlier research had identified a link between an absence of training, including basic preparatory support for the placement, and greater levels of placement breakdown (Berridge and Cleaver, 1987; Triseliotis et al., 1995). Subsequently, however, Sinclair and colleagues (2005b) found no link between the amount of training a carer had done and placement outcomes, while a training course for carers in behaviour management strategies (Macdonald and Turner, 2005) also showed no effect on placement outcomes, despite the training being well received by carers. Other studies have, however, reported some limited impact of training on outcomes (Cleaver, 2000; Famer and Moyers, 2008). The takeaway lesson should not be that providing training to foster carers is futile – for one reason we know that carers tend to value training and it is one means through which they feel their fostering agency is valuing and supporting them (Triseliotis et al., 2002; Sinclair et al., 2004). The findings may, however, suggest that foster carer training programmes aiming to change actual caring practices need to be supported beyond the delivery of the course if they are to have an impact.

Supporting kinship carers

Much of the above section also applies to kinship foster carers; however, previous research has identified that kin carers are less well supported by social workers than unrelated carers. Kinship carers are less likely to be allocated a family placement social worker to support them or have access to child care help and respite care (Brown and Sen, 2014).

There is evidence that contact and relationships with birth parents are likely to be challenging in the majority of kinship foster placements, yet kin carers are usually left to manage contacts unsupported (Farmer and Moyers, 2008; Hunt et al., 2008), in distinction to unrelated foster carers where a majority wish, and receive, extensive support in managing contact arrangements (Sen and McCormack, 2011; Austerberry et al., 2013). This may suggest a 'dump and run' mentality on the part of social workers towards kinship care. In a minority of cases less support may be provided because kinship carers wish to be left to get on with caring, with minimal social work involvement; however, the evidence suggests most kin carers want more support and do not get it (Brown and Sen, 2014).

Social workers may themselves need training and support around effective working with kinship carers given they are less likely to have worked with them, and local authority systems around practice with kin carers are less well developed (Doolan et al., 2004; Aldgate and McInstosh, 2006). Case law in 2002 and 2013 England has established that it is illegal for local authorities to, as a matter of policy, pay kinship foster carers smaller allowances (given to meet the needs of the fostered child) and lower fees (given to remunerate the carer for their services) (see Family Law Week, 2013); however there is still anecdotal evidence that kinship carers tend to be less well financially supported systemically. This is important as kinship carers are more likely to struggle with poverty, overcrowding, juggling work and caring commitments, ill health and lone caring than unrelated carers (Brown and Sen, 2014).

Practice Pointer 6.6

What key differences do you think there might be between supporting a kinship foster carer and supporting an unrelated foster carer?

SGOs and CAOs as alternatives to long-term fostering

As noted the role of long-term fostering now sits alongside the option of special guardianship for children who are in long-term family-based care. SGOs were introduced in England and Wales by the Adoption and Children Act 2002 and came into force in 2005. CAOs replaced Residence Orders in England and Wales in 2014. Foster carers, extended birth family and others with whom the child has resided for an extended period can apply for a CAO or an SGO where the intention of the applicant is to provide long-term care for a child – although the eligibility criteria for application differ according to whether the applicant is a foster carer, birth family member or unrelated carer and whether or not the applicant is applying with local authority consent (see Child Law Advice, 2017). Applications can be made for CAOs and SGOs for children who are not looked after; however, the focus here is only on those made for children in the care system. An SGO gives special guardians the right to exercise most parental rights in exclusivity to anyone else, is harder to challenge through the courts and therefore may be said to give greater legal permanence to a child and their primary carers than a CAO – see Box 6.1.

Box 6.1 Key legal similarities and differences between SGOs and CAOs

Key Similarities
Both CAOs and SGOs ordinarily last until a young person is 18, unless they are successfully challenged in court. Where a child is looked after and a CAO or SGO is sought, a local authority social worker must prepare a report for court which should include information about the child's situation and views, the background and suitability of the applicant(s), their current and past relationship with the child, the prospective carers' understanding of the child's needs, the child's birth family's circumstances and views, the merits of a CAO/SGO and recommendations regarding the granting of the CAO/SGO and subsequent birth family contact. On successful application both terminate any Care Order which related to the child, and the child therefore ceases to be 'looked after'.

Key Differences
Neither CAOs nor SGOs remove a birth parent's parental responsibility (PR). However, unlike CAOs, SGOs allow special guardians to exercise their parental authority to the exclusion of others with PR. As a result special guardians can override any birth

▶

parental objections to their decisions about the child, with the exception of decisions to change the child's name, consent to the child's adoption or take the child out of the UK for more than three months. Secondly, while both CAOs and SGOs can be challenged in court, CAOs can be directly challenged, whereas in most cases a birth parent or other relative must first acquire the leave of court before seeking to vary an SGO. To be granted such leave they must prove there has been a significant change in circumstances. Overall, SGOs are less easily challengeable and therefore are more 'permanent' than CAOs. The placement arrangement underpinning an SGO is expected to last until a child reaches 18 at least. This is not always the expectation when a court grants a CAO.

In recent years SGOs have become increasingly popular as a route out of the care system (see Table 6.1). The use of special guardianship has increased very significantly since they were introduced in 2005 and continued to increase yearly. Selwyn and colleagues (2014) note that it was expected that the rise of SGOs would see a reduction in the use of Residence Orders/CAOs but, so far, while there is evidence of SGOs increasing, the use of CAOs has not reduced by nearly as much, meaning that more children than before are entering legally permanent placements. The statistics also show that while the granting of SGOs has been increasing overall, the greatest increase has been in those granted to applicants who were *not* previously the child's foster carers.

Wade and colleagues (2010) suggest that children with high-level needs requiring significant ongoing support, older children in settled foster and kinship placements, asylum seeking children and children living in family and friends placements might all benefit from special guardianship. While it was envisaged that foster carers and family and friends carers might be the principal applicants

Table 6.1 Children ceasing care via SGOs and Residence Orders/CAOs 2012–2017 (DfE, 2017a, 2017c). The percentages given indicate the proportion of total numbers in care/the proportion of children leaving care

Year	2012	2013	2014	2015	2016	2017
Total numbers looked after	67,070	68,060	68,810	69,480	70,440	72,670
Total numbers ceasing to be looked after	27,510	28,650	30,590	31,330	31,830	31,250
Residence Order or CAO	1,310 (2%/5%)	1,670 (2%/6%)	1,710 (2%/6%)	1,030 (1%/3%)	1,120 (2%/4%)	1,200 (2%/4%)
SGO made to former foster carers	1,340 (2%/5%)	1,600 (2%/6%)	1,750 (3%/6%)	1,660 (2%/5%)	1,950 (3%/6%)	1,970 (3%/6%)
SGO made to carers other than former foster carers	810 (1%/3%)	1,180 (2%/4%)	1,610 (2%/5%)	1,900 (3%/6%)	1,880 (3%/6%)	1,720 (2%/6%)

for an SGO, the legislation leaves it open for anyone with an 'interest' in the child to apply, though there are different criteria according to who applies. It should also be noted that not all SGO applications will relate to looked after children – they may also include applications for children who are cared for by extended family, who have never been looked after or who have been cared for in private fostering arrangements (these children are not included in the statistics in Table 6.1).

Wade and colleagues (2010) also found that 86 per cent of SGOs included in their study were granted to relatives, the majority of whom were grandparents, with just 13 per cent granted to foster carers, suggesting that the use of SGOs as a legal route to permanency for children in long-term foster care may initially have been limited. Early results from a further study by Wade and colleagues (2014) seemed to confirm this finding, with only 15 per cent of special guardians for looked after children being *unrelated* foster carers. More recent government figures, however, show approximately half of SGOs for looked after children were granted to former foster carers. It is not entirely clear why there should be such a difference, but it may be that a number of the 'former foster carers' in the DfE statistics were also kinship carers and therefore both former foster carers *and* related to the child.

Though the overall evidence is that special guardian arrangements are tending to provide lasting placements for children, some concerns have also been expressed. Comparing disruption rates after orders have been granted, Selwyn and colleagues (2014) report disruption rates over five years as 0.7 per cent for adoption, 5.7 per cent for SGOs and 14.7 per cent for Residence Orders. A similar rate of disruption for SGOs (6 per cent over five years) was also found in a study by Wade and colleagues (2014). These disruption rates are all low compared to movement within the care system (Sinclair et al., 2007) but may reflect that children with greater difficulties, or those entering care at an older age, are more likely to remain in the looked after system. Selwyn and colleagues (2014) also note that two-thirds of SGOs and Residence Orders disrupted quickly, unlike adoptions, a finding they were unable to explain.

An earlier study into the first use of SGOs with 120 children (around two-thirds of whom were looked after before the SGO) also positively reported that the vast majority (80 per cent) of carers and social workers believed SGO placements had progressed well (Wade et al., 2010). Special guardians reported that the SGO gave them the secure power to make the decisions they needed to for the child in their care while retaining some links with the child's birth parents. The process was not, however, without its personal costs – some special guardians had given up employment due to taking on the long-term caring responsibilities associated with SGOs, and some had also found managing birth family contact very stressful. A government report into the use of SGOs (Bowyer et al., 2015), commissioned before the publication of the most recent regulations on special guardianship (DfE, 2016), highlighted some issues around SGO use. These included concerns about the lack of thoroughness of SGO assessments; questions about whether the use of SGOs for babies and infants went against the original idea of SGOs as an arrangement for older children in settled substitute care relationships; and concerns about the lack of post-order support for special guardians. The subsequent regulations (DfE, 2016) consequently extended the requirements for what local authority assessment of potential special guardians should include.

Practice Pointer 6.7

Compare what you think are the key advantages and disadvantages of long-term foster care and special guardianship from the point of view of:

- Children in those arrangements
- Birth parents
- The children's carers.

Support for special guardians

While local authorities have a duty, if requested, to undertake a needs assessment of prospective special guardians' needs for financial and other post-order support, the provision of such support is discretionary (Wade et al., 2014). Local authorities may agree to provide financial and other support to a special guardian to support moves to permanence outside the care system for a looked after child – though written agreements pre-order may be important to establish entitlements post-order (Wade et al., 2014). Former foster carers will no longer be entitled to the fostering allowance previously provided by the local authority for the child, nor will they usually receive the same level of social work support. Wade and colleagues (2010) found that although 90 per cent of special guardians were receiving an allowance post-order, most former foster carers were financially worse off. Similarly, Wade and colleagues (2014) found that 80 per cent of special guardians did in fact get some support post-order, but that it was less than that normally provided for foster carers; they recommend that support for special guardians should be increased. For some special guardians, the lack of social work involvement may be an attraction – allowing family life to progress without the need for the bureaucratic processes of oversight associated with a child's looked after status. However, there may also be a concern that they will be left to deal with any difficulties relating to a child without the financial and practical support that goes alongside fostering.

Key messages for practice

- Most children in care will be in foster care of some sort and its use has grown over recent years. The range of types and functions of fostering is impressively varied but one of the concerns raised in research and policy over the last 20 years has been the relative lack of permanence within long-term foster care.

- We know a good deal about what effective foster care consists of and what children want from foster carer and foster carers; we are less clear about how to achieve this uniformly.

- Kinship is a type of foster care – carers must be approved by a fostering agency and panel, though the assessment process should take account of the fact that kin carers are only seeking to be approved as carers for a particular child (or particular children) in their network rather than as a carer for any child who may be placed with them as in unrelated foster care. Evidence suggests that kinship carers tend to be more poorly supported by social work services than unrelated foster carers.

- Special Guardianship Orders (SGOs) and Child Arrangement Orders (CAOs) are two alternatives to long-term fostering. They share some features but SGOs are more legally secure. They have become increasingly popular in recent years. It seems that kinship carers, rather than unrelated foster carers, are more likely to take them. The stability of SGOs post-order appears to be reasonably strong, suggesting they are proving to be an effective route to permanence. However, while local authorities have improved post-order support to special guardians over recent years, research suggests that many guardians are financially worse off after the granting of an SGO.

Suggested reading

Goodyer, A. (2011) *Child-Centred Foster Care: A Rights-Based Model for Practice*. London: Jessica Kingsley – Based on a doctoral study of children in foster care, this engaging study provides a strong argument for the benefits of applying a sociological understanding of childhood to practice with children in foster care.

Sinclair, I. (2005) *Fostering Now: Messages from Research*. London: Jessica Kingsley – Although the research data on which this is based are now starting to date, this summary still provides an excellent overview of the key findings from large-scale studies of fostering in England and Scotland in the 1990s and early 2000s.

Online resources

The Fostering Network – Website of major, UK-wide, fostering charity, providing a range of information about foster care: www.thefosteringnetwork.org.uk

The Kinship Care Guide for England, First Edition – Accessible guide written for kinship carers produced by two charities, Grandparents Plus and Mentor: http://mentoruk.org. uk/wp-content/uploads/sites/3/2017/11/Kinship-Care-Guide-LICENSED-COPY.pdf

CHAPTER 7

ADOPTION

Chapter Overview

Adoption has a long ancestry but as a legal mechanism for transferring parental rights from birth parents to adopters it is less than 100 years old in the UK. This chapter outlines the changing character of adoption since this time, describing successive government initiatives to increase the number of adoptions from care since the 1990s, the mixed impact this has had on adoption numbers, and debates around the use of adoption. The chapter goes on to consider the assessment and matching of prospective adopters, support for adopters, children's views of adoption, adoption by LGBT parents, the debates around 'transracial' adoption and the adoption of disabled children. The chapter concludes by considering the perspectives and needs of birth parents whose children are adopted.

Adoption in context

Adoption has, in some form, a very long heritage. With a playful merging of the old with the new Triseliotis and colleagues (1997, p. 3) note that the first recorded adoption in Western literature is that of Moses, 'a transcultural and possibly transracial adoption in which an infant of a subjugated people was adopted by a woman of the ruling class – possibly a single parent.' However, as a legal remedy which invests parental rights in adults who are not the biological parents of the child, it is a relatively recent phenomenon dating to the mid-nineteenth century in the USA and to 1926 in English law (1930 in Scotland). In the UK bestowing parental responsibilities (PR) on adoptive parents for a child adopted from care can only be achieved by removing them from the child's birth parents, although since the Adoption and Children Act 2002 a step-parent can now in England and Wales apply to become the parent of a child without removing the parental rights of one of the biological parents.

The changing character of adoption

Four phases of modern adoption practice have been identified. In the first phase, from 1926 to 1945, adoption was largely restricted to the working class due to stigma about illegitimate children, fears about inherited 'bad blood' and class divisions based on biological kinship (Triseliotis et al., 1997).

After World War II adoption came to be seen as a solution to infertility in the UK and its popularity among the white middle-class population grew. The initial focus was on the adoption of young, predominantly white, children and three-quarters of those children placed for adoption by the late 1960s were under the age of one. For this reason Triseliotis and colleagues (1997) characterise the overarching ethos at this time as that of 'A child for a home' – adoption primarily in order to satisfy the needs of the adopters. The numbers of adoptions peaked in England, Wales and Scotland in 1968, at a combined total of 27,500 (Triseliotis et al., 1997; Selman, 2004). The majority of these adoptions were of children born outside of marriage (Selman, 2004).

Better contraception, the legalisation of abortion in 1967,[1] reduced social stigma around children born outside marriage and greater financial support given to single parents all resulted in a dramatic fall in the number of babies 'voluntarily' relinquished by single mothers. Adoptions had fallen to 15,000 by 1977 (Triseliotis et al., 1997) and the practice of adoption began to change with an increased focus on adoption for children in the care system who had, until that point, been seen as hard or impossible to adopt – older children, Black Minority Ethnic (BME) children, children with disabilities and larger sibling groups (Rowe and Lambert, 1973). In this way, the ethos behind adoption was transformed into that of 'A home for a child', with the needs of the child, rather than those of the adoptive parents, placed centre stage (Triseliotis et al., 1997).

Adoption also changed from the late 1970s in that non-consensual adoption became widely practised, where children were placed for adoption without the consent of their birth parents (Clapton and Clifton, 2016). From the 1980s increasing proportions of those entering care have also experienced maltreatment. As a result children who are adopted are likely to have a greater level of need, which for some children will require additional support throughout childhood, and potentially beyond. As a result the nature of the long-term care provided to such children explicitly encompasses a restorative dimension, as previously, but it is not assumed this will lead to full developmental recovery. Quinton (2012) terms the latest period in adoption practice as 'A family for developmental recovery'. The 'home for a child' and 'family for developmental recovery' framings of adoption may suggest that adopters' motivations are primarily altruistic. However, research suggests their motivations remain a mixture of meeting children's needs and their own, with infertility the primary reason why adopters seek to adopt (Parker, 1999). The period since the early 1980s has also seen a move to greater 'openness' in adoption – an expectation that adopters will talk openly to the child about birth family roots and past, and in some cases facilitate direct contact between adopted children and their birth families, as discussed in Chapter 5.

Practice Pointer 7.1

What do you think are the differences between adoption and other kinds of permanent family-based substitute care for looked after children (Child Arrangement Order (CAO), Special Guardianship Orders (SGOs) and long-term fostering) in terms of children's daily lived experiences?

Policy initiatives to increase adoption

Since the mid-1990s successive governments of different political complexion have aimed to increase the numbers of children adopted from care. In one of the last policy initiatives of the Conservative government in 1996, Prime Minister John Major pledged to speed up adoption and introduced a draft adoption bill which never made it to the statute books due to the 1997 general election. However, the mantle was taken up by the first New Labour government which succeeded it, with Tony Blair personally championing efforts to increase the numbers adopted from care (PIU, 2000). The government raised concerns about what it viewed as the low numbers of children adopted from care, delays in permanence planning for children and variations in local authority use of both adoption and support for adopters (PIU, 2000). Under this and subsequent New Labour governments there followed a series of initiatives to increase and support adoption from care, including reform of adoption law via the Adoption and Children Act 2002 in England and Wales; a target of increasing the number of adoptions from care by 40–50 per cent by 2004/5; the establishment of a National Adoption Register in England and Wales in 2001 to promote the linking of prospective adopters with children for whom adoption was being sought; ring-fenced funding to local authorities to support adoption services; and performance indicators and targets to gauge local authority performance on adoption (DOH, 2000b; Thomas, 2013; Brammer, 2015).

The government's target for increasing the number of children adopted from care was almost achieved, with an increase of 38 per cent by 2004/5; however, the numbers and proportions of children adopted from care plateaued after 2005 (see the section 'How many children are adopted today?' and Table 7.1 for details). When the Liberal Democrat–Conservative coalition came to power in 2010, there was a further concerted push for the greater use of adoption spearheaded by David Cameron. Sir Martin Narey was appointed as a ministerial adviser on adoption and around the time of his appointment had authored a report in *The Times* which highlighted delays in the adoption process and variation in the use of adoption between local authorities. This argued for a 'dramatic increase' in the use of adoption as well as calling for the earlier removal from parental are of some children who were experiencing neglect (Narey, 2011). The coalition and the Conservative majority governments which succeeded it from 2015 subsequently introduced a range of measures to both increase the numbers of children adopted from care and speed up the process of adoption. These have included:

- The *Action Plan for Adoption* (DfE, 2011a) which produced a performance scorecard to allow comparison of how quickly local authorities place children for adoption and respond to prospective adopters.

- Providing £150 million of funding to local authorities and £16 million to voluntary adoption agencies to increase the number of adopters (DfE, 2013a).

- Reforms via the Children and Families Act 2014 which include the requirement for local authorities in England to consider placing children in foster to adopt placements if no suitable friends and family are available (see Chapter 4); and giving prospective approved adopters direct access to the Adoption Register to see details of children for whom adoption is planned.

Northern Ireland and Scotland

The above-mentioned adoption legislation and policy refer to England and Wales only. In Scotland, while the policy discourse has been less pronounced on the need for increased adoption, moves to promote permanence for children in care were enshrined in the Adoption and Children (Scotland) Act 2007, which also sought to improve adoption services, alongside the introduction of Permanence Orders which may be used where there is a plan for adoption. In Northern Ireland the adoption law currently in place is the Adoption (Northern Ireland) Order 1987 which was itself based on the Adoption Act 1976 in England and Wales and is therefore dated. Given the changes in adoption practice and policy, and the legislative changes in the other three countries in the UK, there has been discussion of new adoption legislation for several years. A draft Adoption and Children (Northern Ireland) Bill was produced in early 2017, with consultations ending in April of that the same year; however, at the time of writing the Northern Irish government is suspended and it is not clear when the draft adoption legislation might be progressed.

How many children are adopted today?

There are other types of adoption in the UK every year other than adoptions from care. In 2012, for example, 5,206 children were adopted; 3,470 of these were from care; the remaining 1,736 were either step-parent or international adoptions (Office of National Statistics, 2012 cited in Ward and Smeeton, 2017). Table 7.1 provides details of the numbers of children adopted from care in England. It also presents figures on the children placed for adoption but who are not yet adopted – these children will be placed with their prospective adopters via placement orders under s.19 or s.21 of the Adoption and Care Act 2002.

Table 7.1 Adoptions from care in England 2012–2017

Year	2012	2013	2014	2015	2016	2017
Placed for adoption	2,910	3,620	3,940	3,590	3,160	2,520
As %age of children in care overall	4%	5%	6%	5%	4%	3%
Adopted unopposed	1,910	2,150	2,660	2,850	2,430	2,180
Adopted opposed	1,560	1,860	2,400	2,500	2,270	2,170
Total adopted	3,470	4,010	5,060	5,350	4,690	4,350
As %age of children leaving care	13%	14%	17%	17%	15%	14%
As %age of children in care overall	5%	6%	7%	8%	7%	6%

Source: DfE (2017a, 2017c)

Practice Pointer 7.2

Table 7.1 suggests there has been fluctuating use of adoption between 2012 and 2017 in England. What practice factors might underlie this fluctuating use?

The proportion of children in care who were adopted in England increased marginally but notably in the 2000s compared to the 1980s and 1990s. In 1987 there were 2,038 adoptions (3 per cent of those in care); in 1995, 2,000 adoptions (4 per cent of those in care); with the proportion adopted remaining largely steady at 4 per cent of those children in the care system throughout most of the 1990s (Triseliotis, 2002a [1998–99]). For each year in the 2000s, other than the year 2000, there were over 3,000 children adopted from care each year, with the proportion adopted from care this represented increasing to over 5 per cent of all looked after children (DfE, 2017c).

Following government reforms from 2010, the proportion of children adopted from care increased to as much as 8 per cent of all children in care, and the numbers of children adopted from care have been high compared to the previous 25 years. However, underlying these statistics, the number of placement orders granted (where children are placed in pre-adoptive placements pending the granting of an Adoption Order) has fallen markedly since 2013/14 and this has now started to result in lower numbers and proportions of children being adopted in England.

The fall in placement orders and adoptions has been attributed to two high-profile appeal court judgments in 2013 – *Re B* and *Re B-S*[2] – where birth parents challenged prior court judgments which had granted decisions in favour of adoption. Neither appeal was successful. However, the judgments voiced criticisms of the reasoning given for adoption by social workers in their court reports. Between them, the judgments highlighted that adoption should be viewed as a last resort and that social workers should weigh the positives and negatives of each plausible placement option, rather than ruling out all placement options other than adoption until adoption appeared as the only option left. The National Adoption Leadership Board (2014) in England was sufficiently concerned about the impact the reputation of these cases had had on falling numbers of placement orders that it issued clarification about what the judgments did and did not say. This clarification emphasised, above all, that the legal test for adoption remained the same as before the judgments.

Controversies over the promotion and use of adoption

Adoption's stability and the outcomes children generally achieve within it make it an attractive placement option (Triseliotis, 2002b). Once adoption has been chosen as the preferred placement route for a child, moves to reduce delays in the adoption process make sense given the research suggesting that the younger a child is placed the more likely their placement will last and the better developmental recovery will be if there is developmental delay (Van IJzendoorn and Juffer, 2006; Biehal et al., 2010).

However, adoption's permanence – one of its benefits viewed from one viewpoint – may also be problematic viewed from another, given that it terminates all birth parental rights. The UK stands distinct from other European countries in its use of adoption without birth parental consent. Research into differing approaches to adoption across European Union (EU) countries has found, despite previous claims, that there are in fact legal mechanisms in a number of EU countries to facilitate adoption without parental consent (Fenton-Glynn, 2016). However, the UK differs from these other EU countries in the frequency with which non-consensual adoption is used in practice (Fenton-Glynn, 2016).

The vast majority of children coming into care are from families living in poverty (Bebbington and Miles, 1989; Bywaters et al., 2016). Poverty is only one issue facing such families – domestic violence, parental substance misuse and mental health difficulties are often combined in the most complex of families (Brandon et al., 2009). However, poverty is linked to and exacerbates each of these difficulties. It has long been questioned whether more generous and effective family support systems might lead to fewer children needing to be permanently looked after outside of parental care in the first place (Jordan, 1981; Selman, 2004) or whether care in extended family networks might be better identified and supported where parental care is not feasible (Wang et al., 2012).

Such concerns have increased over recent years with the successive drives to increase the numbers adopted in England and Wales, with concerns that this is likely to limit the support given to birth families to make appropriate changes which would allow for reunification to happen (Dale, 2013; Shaw et al., 2014; Ward and Smeeton, 2017). The use of adoption targets to increase adoption under the New Labour governments was the cause of some alarm and continues to be so. When the policy document *An Action Plan for Adoption* (DfE, 2011a) introduced performance indicators for local authorities via the Adoption Scorecard these related only to the speed with which an authority placed children for adoption and assessed prospective adopters. It subsequently transpired that local authorities were being publicly ranked by *the numbers of* children they had placed for adoption (Transparency Project, 2015). Further concerns were raised by the discovery that some local authorities appeared to have targets for the numbers or proportions of children in care it should place for adoption (Transparency Project, 2016). While it is not clear how these targets were used, it raises the possibility that they might have inappropriately skewed decision-making in favour of adoption.

In recognition of concerns such as these, the British Association of Social Workers (BASW) conducted an inquiry into the role of the social work in adoption (Featherstone et al., 2018). As part of this inquiry, Bilson's (2016) analysis of adoption trends in England highlights that the numbers of children leaving care by adoption varies from 3 to 30 per cent according to local authority area. The top third of authorities using adoption the most also saw the greatest rise in numbers of children coming into care, while those using adoption the least showed a reduction in numbers in care. He therefore concludes that current adoption policy has not achieved its stated goal of reducing the numbers of children in care and 'at worst appears to be part of a mass and growing removal of children from parental care based on an ever wider definition of what constitutes abuse and neglect' (Bilson, 2016, p. 7). John Simmonds (2017) of CoramBAAF responded by questioning suspicious attitudes towards adoption. He argues that there is a rigorous legal process in place for deciding whether adoptions are necessary, which provides appropriate safeguards for parents while promoting the interests of children needing long-term care, many of whom have been subject to abuse.

Practice Pointer 7.3

Read Andy Bilson's summary analysis of adoption data and the concerns he raises about the use of adoption and John Simmonds' response statement in defence of current practice and policy (both available on Community Care's website):

www.communitycare.co.uk/2017/02/09/the-governments-adoption-drive-isnt-doing-what-it-set-out-to-do/

www.communitycare.co.uk/2017/03/07/people-suspicious-adoption/

Which points do you agree and disagree with in each article?

Assessing and matching prospective adopters

There is currently a two-stage process for the assessment of prospective adopters. The first consists of an adoption agency gaining background information on an applicant's family situation and undertaking medical, criminal history and person reference checks. If successful, the applicant moves to the second stage which involves attending preparation groups to learn more about adoption alongside other prospective adopters, and an in-depth assessment via completion of the

Prospective Adopter's Report (PAR) – also known as the 'Form F' – which is presented to an adoption panel who decide whether or not an applicant should be approved as an adopter. Overall, the process should take six months (First4adoption, 2017).

The completion of the PAR includes consideration of an applicant's personal and family background and circumstances, comprising a chronology of an applicant's family history and their family tree; current relationship and history of the relationship (where a couple application); previous adult relationships; educational background; adult occupations; adult health history; any criminal record issues; who else is in the current household; and the family home and how it will be set up for a new child. There will also be a discussion on the applicant's sense of their own identity and their views on identity matters relevant to the upbringing of a child: guidance specifically names issues of class, ethnicity, gender, sexuality, culture, language and spirituality. Applicants will also be asked about their motivations to adopt, their expectations about the child or children they may adopt and their understanding of the likely needs of adoptive children, including their attitudes to openness around the adoption and birth family contact. Finally, applicants are asked about their formal and informal support networks and local community relationships, activities and resources (CoramBAAF, 2016).

In the past adoption agencies had their own exclusion criteria for applicants which could comprise different upper age limits for applicants, restrictions on both individuals in a couple working full-time and different restrictions on the health of applicants (Lowe et al., 1999). The process has now been simplified and the only automatic restrictions are on those aged under 21, non-UK residents and those with particular criminal records (convictions against children and serious sexual offences against an adult). Other criminal convictions and health issues are considered as part of the application process in terms of ability to provide appropriate care throughout a child's upbringing, but are not an automatic bar.

Research previously suggested the need for the provision of support to those turned down as adopters (Parker, 1999) and policy has taken this on board in terms of rights of explanation and appeal, if not support beyond this. Adoption agencies must now provide applicants with a full written explanation of why they have been deemed unsuitable to adopt and they can choose to appeal the decision, either to the agency itself or to an independent reviewing panel, within 40 working days of notification of the decision (DfE, 2011b). Those who are approved as adopters will go on to be matched with a child or children awaiting adoption. If prospective adopters have not been matched after three months then their details are forwarded to the Adoption Register.

The arguments in favour of matching children waiting to be adopted, based on their needs, with prospective adopters, based on their characteristics and parenting qualities, are both rights-based (matching for identity issues, particularly ethnicity) and ends-based (better outcomes for children) (Quinton, 2012). There is, however, currently limited information on how these matching decisions are made and their impact. An Adoption Research Initiative (ARI 2011a) study did investigate the matching decisions made for 149 children and found they had an impact on the success of placements. The researchers did not directly assess the quality of matching *per se* but analysed the extent to which compromises had been made in respect of children's stated needs and adopters' stated preferences for what kind of children they wished to care for. When greater compromises were made in matching, placements tended to be less successful: in two-thirds of disrupted or unstable placements, the match was categorised as 'poor', defined as involving serious compromises. However, one of the difficulties in matching children with prospective adopters is the context that there is considerably more demand for adoptive children with some characteristics rather than others. Young, single, white children are still more likely to be adopted than those who are defined by their social worker as being disabled, as BME or who required adoption alongside siblings (Sinclair et al., 2007).

Quinton (2012, p. 58) reports the general parenting qualities of effective adopters found in a 2004 Evan B. Donaldson Institute review of adoption are:

- Commitment as parents.

- A flexible and relaxed approach to parenting.

- Realistic expectations about the experience of adoption.

- And an ability to work effectively with the adoption agency in support of the child.

Quinton notes that an awareness of such a general list of qualities may aid assessors in being able to identify prospective adopters who evidently do or do not possess them, but whether an adopter is able to put them into practice when they have a particular child placed with them will still be unclear until that actually happens. He concludes that there is a need for further research to underpin a more scientific understanding of matching in adoption.

A contrasting approach has been to note the importance of 'chemistry' between children and their potential adopters. Such thinking is behind adoption agencies offering activity days where prospective adopters meet with children who are awaiting adoption – usually children who have been waiting longer for an adoptive match to be found. The sessions are organised on the basis that a face-to-face meeting can better bring across a child's qualities to those looking to adopt than a word-based description and there are some powerful anecdotal examples of where this has worked very well (Cousins, 2009; Moorhead, 2014).

Practice Pointer 7.4

'If adopters have the correct qualities they should be able to parent any child.'

'Matching adopters' particular characteristics, qualities and wishes for a child with a child's characteristics and needs is crucial to adoption succeeding.'

What are the arguments for and against each of these statements?

Supporting adopters

Preparation for prospective adopters

Alongside individual assessment of prospective adopters, most adoption agencies run 'preparation groups' for those interested in becoming adopters, which are normally mandatory. Both the individual assessment and preparation groups serve a dual purpose of giving information to prospective adopters about adoption of children from care while also gaining insights into their suitability as adopters. Typically the preparation group sessions will be led by family placement social workers with extensive experience of adoption and will cover issues including adopted children's needs, parenting styles, working with challenging behaviour, working with support services and managing birth family contact. Typically, experienced adopters are invited along to some sessions to talk about their own experiences of adoption.

Post-adoption support

However good the assessment process for prospective adopters may be it is hard to know how a particular child will settle once placed in their care, and how adopters will be able to respond to the expressed needs a particular child shows (Triseliotis, 1973; Quinton, 2012). This puts the focus on post-adoption support.

As part of Selwyn and colleagues' (2014) study of adoption disruption, interviews were also conducted with adoptive parents where parenting difficulties had emerged. Most difficulties initially manifested before adolescence but escalated after, and in hindsight several adoptive parents recognised there would have been value in earlier help when the difficulties first emerged. The most common difficulties were adolescent-to-parent violence and going missing or running away from home which applied to over half of children in the identified families. Adopted children making apparently false allegations of abuse about adults in the household and serious child offending behaviour were also issues for a substantial minority of adoptive families. The majority of families had received some post-adoption support from their local authority. Social work support combined with therapeutic input, and the input of particular individual educational professionals, was valued by parents. However, some school responses, barriers to support via eligibility criteria and a lack of available specialised input to address problems were the source of difficulties. A similar picture was found in a separate UK study, where, though a small majority of parents were satisfied with support services, a third of adoptive parents had had to wait over a year for specialist input (Monck and Rushton, 2009).

The UK government has introduced changes to better support adopters in England and Wales via the Children and Families Act 2014. Statutory adoption leave from work has been enhanced so it matches that of birth parental leave, adoption agencies are required to inform adopters of their rights to post-adoption support and local authorities must provide adopters with personal budgets (allowing adoptive parents to determine the type of support they receive directly) if adopters request this. The Adoption Support Fund was established in 2015 providing £19 million of investment for England-wide support (DfE, 2014e; 2015c) and offering funding for specific therapeutic inputs and specialised assessments for adoptive children and families. Adopted children and young adults up to the age of 21 are eligible, as are those up to the age of 25 where they have a Special Educational Needs Statement or Education, Health and Care Plan. From 2016 the fund was enlarged to include children in special guardianship arrangements who were previously looked after, but at the same time all new claims were also limited to a 'fair access limit' of £5,000 per child in one year. For the year 2017/18 the £5,000 limit still applies but a separate £2,500 funding for specialised assessment may be sought, in addition to match funding which local authorities may provide (Adoption Support Fund, 2017).

The use of parenting programmes tailored towards adoptive parents has been recently trialled and evaluated in the UK. Both evaluations revealed the programmes were well received by parents, but they had limited impact on children's behaviour. Rushton and colleagues (2010) used an experimental design to compare the impact of: (1) a CBT parenting programme; (2) a tailored home-delivered parenting programme for adopters devised by Rushton and colleagues which was influenced by behavioural and attachment approaches; and (3) support services as normal. Those attending either of the two parenting programmes showed greater satisfaction with their parenting than those who did not. However, despite this, there were no statistically significant improvements in difficulties for any of the children in the study.

The AdOpt parenting programme is a group programme for adoptive parents of 3 to 8 year olds piloted by the National Implementation Service. The evaluation (Harold et al., 2017) found that adoptive parents were very positive about the programme in terms of peer support and its perceived impact on their parenting and children's behaviour. Again, however, there was limited impact on child behaviour. Positively, children's overall problems and conduct problems reduced, but not their emotional problems, hyperactive and impulsive problems or peer problems, and there was no improvement in pro-social behaviours.

Similar to the comments on foster carer training these mixed findings should not be interpreted as suggesting that parenting programmes for adopters are without value. An improvement in an adoptive parent's view of their own parenting is likely to be important in helping them cope positively with problematic behaviours their child may display. However, the findings do suggest that an improvement in adopters' view of their own parenting does not easily translate through to better outcomes for children. This may be because the children's difficulties are deep-seated and not easy to affect and/or because further follow-up support is needed for adopters to be able to fully put into practice skills learnt on a parenting programme. Either way, the need for adoptive parents to be able to access further specialist support for their child, should this be felt necessary, is emphasised.

Adopted children's views

A strong message coming from children who were old enough to remember their adoption is that while they were informed of the adoption itself, their views and preferences for what type of family they wanted were not discussed with them (Owen, 1999; Morgan, 2006a). The children interviewed in the study by Thomas and colleagues (1999) recalled having very specific preferences about the characteristics and qualities of the parents and families they wanted, and wished they had been consulted on how they were presented to potential adopters. This suggests, as the social studies of childhood has claimed, that adults tend to underestimate the age at which children can make choices and wish to be consulted about their preferences (James, 2013).

For children who are aware of the plan for adoption, the length of time between the plan being made and an adoption match being found is a source of frustration, worry and distress which can reinforce feelings of rejection (Thomas and Beckford et al., 1999; Morgan, 2006a). There is some evidence that children who have been adopted are glad this happened and that they prefer the security that adoption provides to the less legally and emotionally secure option of long-term foster care (Triseliotis, 2013). This point is reinforced by the finding in another study that children viewed their adoptive parents as their primary supports (Thomas et al., 1999). While children's experiences of contact with both birth parents and siblings are varied, whatever the nature of these relationships, a common theme from children's accounts is the need for them to have space within their adoptive families to be able to discuss their, often complex, feelings and wishes about their birth families (Thomas et al., 1999; McSherry et al., 2013).

Practice Pointer 7.5

Adopters' openness to discussing their children's birth family roots and their feelings around their birth family and adoption have been found to be highly important. What can social workers do to prepare adopters around the importance of having such discussions?

Adoption by LGBT parents

Since the Adoption and Children Act 2002 and the Adoption of Children (Scotland) Act 2007, same-sex applicants, as well as unmarried couples, have been able to apply jointly in England, Scotland and Wales. Previously they could apply to be adopters but only as notionally 'single' applicants – this restriction still applies in Northern Ireland at the time of writing. An early study of LGBT adoption was conducted by Mellish and colleagues (2013) which explored family relationships in 130 adoptive families where children had been placed for at least 12 months. Roughly a third of the families were parented by gay male couples, a third lesbian couples and a third heterosexual couples. The research found that the three types of families had different pathways to becoming adopters – gay fathers in particular and lesbian mothers to some extent were less likely to have tried to have biological children, and gay fathers were more likely to have adopted older children who had spent longer in care. This suggests the need to take account of differences in motivation to adopt during the assessment process and, particularly, preparation groups involving LGBT applicants – much as a previous study of single adopters found the need to ensure that their particular needs and circumstances were included in this stage of the process (Owen, 1999). All the families in the Mellish and colleagues study were found to be functioning well in terms of parental and child well-being and family life, with few significant differences between them. Nine per cent of lesbian and gay parents did report their children had been subject to some form of homophobic bullying, but were confident in their ability to handle this and satisfied with the responses from schools and other parents when homophobic comments had been made and challenged.

The adoption of BME children

The adoption of BME children by white adopters has been an issue of substantial debate. The Children and Families Act 2014 controversially amended existing legislation so that adoption agencies no longer have a duty to give 'due consideration' to a child's religious persuasion, racial origin and cultural and linguistic background when placing a child for adoption in England. The duty to do so in other parts of the UK remains. The change in England followed calls from several prominent politicians and political advisers from the mid-1990s who claimed that social workers were blocking so-called 'transracial adoptions' due to ideologically dogmatic views that BME children should only be placed with BME families (Kirton, 2000; Barn and Kirton, 2012). The Narey Report on adoption, claimed that 'for some years now prospective adopters with everything else in their favour ... have been thwarted simply because of their race' (Narey, 2011, p. 12) and quoted the then Secretary of State for Education, Michael Gove, stating that:

> Edicts which say children have to be adopted by families with the same ethnic background and prevent other families because they don't fit left-wing prescriptions are denying children the love they need. (Gove, cited in ibid., p. 13)

Though these statements could apply to any 'transracial adoption', the political discourse has almost exclusively focused on the adoption of BME children by white adopters and the politics of ethnicity is implicit within this debate (Barn and Kirton, 2012). Notably, Sir Martin Narey (2011) claimed that he could not envisage a situation whereby if there were ever an 'over-supply of white children we would turn otherwise well qualified black adopters away' (n.p.). However, it has recently emerged that an Asian couple were discouraged by a Conservative local authority from applying to be adopters, on the basis that the children in the area waiting to be adopted were white (Rawlinson, 2017). The case is currently subject to legal appeal and it remains to be seen what the impact of the case will be.

There is evidence that some social work practice can be overly rigid when seeking adoptive placements for *some* groups of BME children. The most recent government-commissioned studies on adoption found lower adoption rates for Asian and black children which could, in part, be connected to attempts to ethnically match children, greater delays in decision-making around permanence and greater pessimism on the part of social workers about finding a match for these children, allied with a failure to proactively promote the children's need for an adoptive placement (Selwyn et al., 2010; ARI, 2011a).

However, evidence of the implied systemic dogmatism in social work practice is harder to find. Barn and Kirton's (2012) analysis suggests that while there could be localised pockets of rigid decision-making, these were isolated. This is given some support by the finding in the study of Farmer and colleagues (2011, cited by Thomas, 2013, p. 45) that though there were delays in finding BME children adopters through attempts to match to ethnicity, 29 per cent of adopted BME children were in fact 'transracially' placed after all. Barn and Kirton (2012) also found no clear evidence that white adopters were turned down solely on the basis of their ethnicity. One adoption agency manager, for example, explained that in her experience most white applicants looking to adopt black children wanted to adopt younger children for whom there is already the greatest demand, rather than older, harder to place, black children.

A look at the surface figures on ethnicity for 2016 in England does suggest disparities between the proportions of children in care categorised by ethnicity and the proportions adopted, although these disparities do not apply to all BME groups (see Table 7.2).

White and 'mixed' ethnicity children are approximately equally likely to be adopted from care, while Asian and, particularly, black children are less likely. The surface figures also hide some underlying issues. Firstly, within the category of 'Asian' it is principally Bangladeshi and Pakistani children, rather than Indian children, who are less likely to be adopted; and with the category of 'black' it is particularly black African children who are less likely to be adopted – and such disparities may be partly related to traditional religious and cultural objections to stranger adoption within Islamic and black African culture (Barn and Kirton, 2012).

Table 7.2 The proportions of children adopted from care by ethnic background in England, 2016 (DfE, 2017a)

Ethnicity	%age in care	%age adopted from care
White	75	83
'Mixed'	9	11
Asian	4	2
Black	7	2

Additionally, other demographic factors can be influential in different placement pathways for groups of children – for example, in the study of adoption pathways by Selwyn and colleagues (2010) black African children were significantly less likely to be adopted, but were also on average two and a half years older than white and mixed ethnicity children on entry into care.

The findings from the main government-commissioned study on placement pathways for BME children (Selwyn et al., 2010) also had nuanced detail. The study confirmed that age, and not ethnicity, was the single largest determinant of whether a child is adopted: the younger a child when the decision for adoption is made, the more likely they are to be adopted. The researchers did find social workers struggled around some aspects of BME children's identity; when trying to decide how to match children of mixed ethnicity, social workers tended to view them as 'black' even though many of these children had been brought up in the primary care of white birth mothers. However, this did not have a significant adverse impact on these children's chances of adoption – mixed ethnicity children were *not* statistically significantly less likely to be adopted than white children. Asian and black children were significantly less likely to be adopted but there were complex reasons behind this, and the researchers caution that the small numbers of Asian and black children in their study make generalisations difficult.

The evidence of child outcomes from the UK and the USA suggests that BME children placed with long-term white carers or adopters are no more likely to have placement breakdowns or poorer developmental outcomes than children who are ethnically matched (Thoburn et al., 2000; Quinton, 2012). However, qualitative accounts from *some* BME adults who were 'transracially' placed, particularly those who were placed in largely white communities, do suggest there can be ongoing issues of identity questioning and a sense of otherness from their communities and families (Parker, 1999; Howe and Feast, 2000; Thoburn et al., 2000; Carroll, 2015). Though such experiences are far from universal among those who have been 'transracially' placed, they do highlight the need for consideration of how adopters will respond to a child's identity needs throughout their childhood when that child is of a different ethnicity.

The recruitment of more BME adopters would be one way of increasing the number of BME adoptions (Triseliotis et al., 1997). There is some evidence that targeted recruitment campaigns for BME adopters can be effective and thereby support the greater use of same ethnicity placements for BME adoptees (Wainwright and Ridley, 2012). However, it is also evident that social workers need to proactively consider compromises in matching for BME children where an exact ethnic match is not readily available. This may include consideration of a child staying with a current foster carer with whom they are settled though not ethnically matched (Selwyn et al., 2010; Thomas, 2013). Ethnicity is undoubtedly important but social workers should be open to the fact that a child's ethnicity is only one part of their personal and social identity and that ethnic identities themselves have become increasingly complex and diverse in the twenty-first century. At the same time, whether a child's positive identity formation and sense of self will be supported in an adoptive placement should remain a core consideration for social workers. Notably, the removal of the legal *duty* for adoption agencies in England to give due consideration to a child's religion, ethnicity, linguistic background and culture does not prohibit social workers from giving these things attention. The principles of holistic assessment suggest that, for any child, consideration of how well prospective adopters may meet their identity needs should remain an essential, rather than optional, task in adoption placement.

Practice Pointer 7.6

What are your views on 'transracial adoption'? Identify what assumptions underlie your views.

Disabled children and adoption

In comparison to the adoption of BME children, the adoption of children with a disability has received relatively little attention. The most detailed analysis of this issue explored whether there was a 'reverse ladder of permanence' for disabled children with them less likely to be either adopted or returned home (Baker, 2007). There was partial evidence of this. Disabled children were overall less likely to return home and more likely to remain in foster care. Though they were not less likely to be adopted overall, there were greater delays in finding adoptive matches and a greater number of foster carer adoptions for them. The research also found those children with a learning disability were indeed less likely to be adopted.

These findings were enhanced by the subsequent large-scale study of permanence in England by Sinclair and colleagues (2007) which found three differing categorisations of children who were disabled. Firstly, those children looked after *due to* their disability and who mainly had serious organic impairments constituted 4 per cent of the looked after child population. Secondly, those judged to have a disability by local authorities' differing definitions were 8 per cent of the looked after population. And, thirdly, those judged by social workers to be looked after children *with a* disability were 18 per cent of the looked after population. The first category of disabled children were not less likely to be adopted, but the other two groups were. The likely explanation for this was that, similar to the Baker (2007) analysis, severe organic impairments were not a barrier to adoption, but other kinds of disability, where the impact of the disability on the child's future learning and care needs were unclear, were.

There is also a suggestion that there might be considerable variation in practice between different agencies – a survey of adoption agencies found the proportion of children placed for adoption who had special health needs or disabilities varied from 0 to 29 per cent between agencies (ARI, 2011b). Though the researchers noted the differences could be related to differing definitions of disability it is also suggestive of different policies and practice commitment in respect of placing disabled children for adoption. Recommendations for improving practice have included adoption agencies putting more resources into recruiting a greater pool of adopters willing to adopt children with a disability (ARI, 2011b), particularly those willing to adopt children with disabilities related to learning and behaviour (Baker, 2007); greater effort put into the matching of children with a disability with adopters (Cousins, 2009); and giving greater consideration and support to foster carer adoption for children with a disability (Baker, 2007).

Birth parents' experiences of adoption

Alongside the needs of adoptive children and adoptive parents, there has been recognition since the 1990s of the third side of the 'adoption triangle' – birth parents. Data from birth parents whose children have been adopted suggest that they endured feelings of loss that affected their future life courses and often their mental health (Howe et al., 1992; Smeeton and Boxall, 2011; Clapton and Clifton, 2016). Clapton and Clifton separately conducted studies on birth fathers' experiences 30 years apart. While the two samples of men had seen their children adopted when the character of adoption differed, and were of contrasting socio-economic backgrounds, there were common feelings of grief and powerlessness. The men in Clifton's study, whose children were adopted due to concerns about parental care, differed in harbouring a sense of shame that impacted on their self-image as fathers. The fathers in the latter study also harboured an ongoing sense of injustice and mistrust of social workers and formal agencies, which was mirrored in the study by Smeeton and Boxall (2011) of three sets of birth parents whose children had been adopted without their consent.

The recognition experiences such as these has led, slowly and somewhat patchily, to the development of adoption support services for birth parents. It is now the case, under s.3 of the Adoption and Children Act 2002 and *National Minimum Standards* for adoption (DfE, 2014a), that birth parents in England and Wales must be provided with an independent support worker from the time adoption is chosen as the plan for their child. Neil and colleagues' (2010) study of support to birth parents found that they were more likely to take up support services if they self-referred than if referred by children's services. Birth parents had high levels of psychological distress but this did reduce somewhat for those who continued to access support services. The researchers suggest that thought needs to be given to the best referral routes for birth parents to facilitate their engagement, and that support services need to proactively engage birth parents, including via outreach work, offering routes into a range of flexible support.

Key messages for practice

- Adoption has been the preferred permanence placement choice for young children for successive governments since the 1990s, partly due to its stability and the outcomes children tend to achieve within it. Due to the fact it severs all birth parental rights, often without birth parental consent, it is also a controversial option, the use of which some argue could be reduced if better support were given to birth parents or kinship carers.

- Good preparation of adopters for the reality of adopting and effective post-adoption support are both important. A number of adopted children will exhibit some challenging behavioural issues, particularly in adolescence, and many adopters will need non-judgemental support from social workers to help them and their children navigate these difficulties.

- Certain groups of children are currently less likely to be adopted: BME children from some ethnic backgrounds, children with some kinds of disability and children in sibling groups. The need for proactive matching efforts, efforts to recruit prospective adopters looking to care for such children, consideration of foster carer adoption and some flexibility in matching consideration are suggested by this.

- The needs of birth parents whose children have been adopted have, traditionally, been poorly considered. Birth parents in England and Wales must now be provided with an independent support worker from the time adoption is chosen as the plan for their child. Take-up of such services is currently mixed and thought needs to be given to providing support in a way that is likely to match the circumstances of the birth parents to whom it is offered.

Suggested reading

Baker, C. (2007) 'Disabled children's experience of permanency in the looked after system', *British Journal of Social Work*, 37 (7): 1173–1188 – A paper shedding light on a neglected area of practice and policy.

Lord, J. and Lucking, M. (2016) *The Adoption Process in England: A Guide for Children's Social Workers*. London: CoramBAAF – A focused guide providing greater detail on the process of adoption.

Online resources

CoramBAAF is a national UK charity with expertise on adoption (as well as fostering). Some of its resources are available at: https://corambaaf.org.uk

Thomas, C. (2013) *Adoption for Looked After Children: Messages from Research*. London: BAAF. The summary of the most recent series of government-commissioned studies on adoption in England and available at: www.adoptionresearchinitiative.org.uk/docs/ARi%20overview_WEB.pdf

Notes

1   Abortion was legalised in England, Scotland and Wales but not Northern Ireland where it continues to be allowed only in very restrictive circumstances.
2   *Re B (A Child)* [2013] UKSC 33 and *Re B-S (Children)* [2013] EWCA Civ 813.

CHAPTER 8

RESIDENTIAL CARE

> ## Chapter Overview
>
> This chapter considers the fluctuating use of residential care provision in the UK before detailing the different, and varied, types of residential provision which are used to provide care to looked after children. The current relative lack of focus within, and use of, the residential sector is described with consideration given to the question of what the future direction of the sector might be. The discussion goes on to consider effective practice in residential care, drawing on the concept of the 'life space' and the use of social pedagogy, before exploring young people's views of residential care and what support residential care workers need to deliver good quality care. The chapter concludes by considering the issues of ethnicity, gender and the provision of care for young people with a disability in residential settings.

Residential child care in context

Since 2012 around 10 per cent of the looked after population in England have been in residential care provision (DfE, 2017a, 2017c). This follows a period of sharp decline in the use of the sector since the 1970s. However, before the late 1970s there had been fluctuations in the use of residential placements. In the immediate post-war period there was an initial move away from the use of residential child care following the Curtis Report (1946) in England and the Clyde Report (1946) in Scotland. Both were critical of the quality of care they found provided by large-size institutional care, particularly the emotional care offered to children. They argued that fostering was preferable and where residential care continued it should be in smaller-sized units. The reports coincided with Bowlby's (1951) early development of attachment theory which suggested that it was preferable for a child to be cared for within their known family networks environment, or where this was not possible, in another family-based setting.

Following a decline in the use of residential care, the 1960s and early 1970s saw a significant renewal and expansion of the residential sector – not for very young children, but for most others, such that at its peak in the mid-1970s the residential sector had around 40,000 children in it, or around 40 per cent of all children in care (Narey, 2016), a greater number than were in foster care (Hutchinson, 2005). From the late 1970s the use of residential child care reduced significantly. The initial decline in the use of residential care could be related to falling numbers in care overall and the relatively greater cost of residential care compared to fostering during a period of economic downturn (Sen et al., 2008). From the mid-1980s a more dramatic reduction in the use of sector followed a series of inquiries into child abuse within residential child care provision (ibid.).

Today those in residential care are mainly aged 12 and over. In some cases children under 12 with a disability and/or marked health needs and children with serious emotional or behavioural problems may be placed in residential care, but this is still rare (Sinclair et al., 2007). Three-quarters of young people in residential care in England are aged between 14 and 17 and residential care will be the first placement for around a third of those aged 10 to 15 coming into care (Narey, 2016). Young people in residential care are more likely to have marked emotional and behavioural problems, mental health issues, offending behaviour and educational support needs than children in the care system overall (Berridge et al., 2012).

Types of residential child care

Though we talk of 'residential child care', it is, of all the care placement options, the most diverse. The main types of residential provision are:

● *Children's homes* – A residential home where young people live in group care but go to schools in the community. There has been changing terminology and types of care provided in this type of care. The terminology of 'children's homes' went out of fashion for a time, to be replaced by 'children's units' or 'residential units'. The terminology of 'children's homes' now seems to be back in favour but some local authorities currently refer to 'children's houses'. The size of children's homes has reduced over time. The move away from large dormitory-style residential child care units started with the Curtis and Clyde reports. However, large homes of up to 20–30 children were the norm until the twenty-first century. Since then there has been a trend towards ever smaller units with some children's homes now only providing care to a few young people at any one time – typically these are young people with particularly marked emotional and behavioural needs or other high-level care needs.

● *Residential schools* – A residential home where the young people live in group care and also attend education on-site. Residential schools have been of two main types: firstly, facilities for young people with emotional behavioural problems and/or engaged in offending behaviour, typically who have had poor engagement with mainstream education; secondly, specialist provision for children with severe disabilities, some of whom will be looked after children (Connelly and Milligan, 2012). Compared to modern-day children's homes, residential schools are larger but organised in smaller group clusters. There is some evidence that residential schools appear to achieve relatively good outcomes (Triseliotis et al., 1995a).

- *Children's residential care facilities and hospitals* – These include places where young people are resident due to illness and physical needs as well as residential facilities providing psychological and psychiatric care.

- *Hostels* – This accommodation is generally provided to young people who are due to age out of care as part of the process of leaving care and whose previous placement ended before they were 18.

- *Family centres and mother and baby units* – Looked after children who are young mothers may have a care placement in such units which, alongside care and support for mother and child, may include an assessment element to determine if the young mother is able to provide long-term care for her child.

- *The Secure Estate/Youth Detention Accommodation* – Collectively known as 'the secure estate', in England this comprises three types of locked accommodation for young people: secure children's homes, secure training centres (STCs) and young offenders institutions (YOIs).

  - Secure children's homes (also known as 'secure care') are provided by local authority or voluntary sector providers for young people whose behaviour poses a significant risk to themselves or others.
  - STCs and YOIs both provide accommodation for young people charged or convicted of repeat or serious offending. These facilities are under the structural management of the Youth Justice Board but the service providers are a mixture of private sector companies and the prison service. STCs provide structured education and care, principally for 15 to 17 year olds, while YOIs are juvenile prisons for those aged between 15 and 20. Though there were STCs and YOIs for both genders in England and Wales until 2013, due to low demand the remaining YOIs for women were closed. Therefore all young women under 18 who are placed in the secure estate are now either accommodated in secure care or STCs (Elwood, 2013).

Any young person remanded to the secure estate after being charged with a serious offence becomes a looked after child for the duration of time they are remanded. However, if convicted and given a custodial sentence only those young people subject to Care Orders at the time of the offence remain 'looked after' while those who were subject to voluntary s.20 accommodation and those not looked after at the time of the offence do not (DfE, 2014b). This is the same in Northern Ireland and Wales, but in Scotland most young offenders under 16, or under 18 if subject to a Supervision Requirement, will be managed through the Children's Hearing System and those placed in the secure estate via a Children's Hearing will become looked after.

There were overall 9,090 young people in residential settings in England on 31 March 2017; this comprised 13 per cent of the overall numbers of children in care on that date (see Table 8.1).

Table 8.1 Numbers and proportions of young people in different types of residential care in England, 31 March 2017

Type of residential care	Number of young people and proportion of total numbers in residential care this represents
Children's homes and hostels subject to children's homes regulations	6,070, 67%
Semi-independent accommodation not subject to children's home regulations[1]	1,640, 18%
Residential care homes and hospitals providing medical and nursing care	670, 7%
Secure estate	420, 5%
Family centres and mother and baby units	160, 2%
Residential schools	130, 1%

[1] Semi-independent accommodation not subject to the Children's Homes Regulations comprises residential accommodation where some supervisory or advice staff are employed but staff may not live on the premises. Placements in this category are distinguished from those in independent living where no formal support structure is provided as part of the accommodation.

From this summary it can be seen that the residential sector is diverse with functions ranging from assessment, respite and short-term care to therapeutic treatment, the meeting of complex care and health needs and longer-term care. While foster care also has a diverse variety of functions, the context of delivery (a family in their own home) is very similar from one type of fostering to the next. Residential child care, by contrast, is delivered in contexts that are, sometimes subtly, but often markedly, physically, structurally and culturally different. This means that making general comments about the sector as a whole is difficult, and it is worth nothing that most literature on the sector tends to be focused on children's homes as the most common type of residential child care.

Practice Pointer 8.1

Look at the different types of residential care establishments listed above. What similarities and differences do you think each of them is likely to have in terms of: (1) ethos; (2) aims of their work with young people; and (3) the needs of the young people in them?

The legacy of inquiries into abuse in residential child care

The most high-profile inquiries into abuse in the residential sector occurred between 1990 and 2000. There have been others before and after, but these arguably had the greatest impact on the sector (Sen et al., 2008). It is indisputable that the different inquiries catalogued a range of physical, sexual and emotional child abuse occurring in some residential child care establishments. However, it has also been pointed out that child abuse occurs in all settings and therefore argued that the focus on abuse in residential child care has been unbalanced (Gallagher, 2000). Smith (2009) challenges the resulting image of the residential sector as rife with, and more likely to lead to, child abuse. The question of whether child abuse was, or indeed is, more likely in residential child care than in other care settings is ultimately an impossible one to answer conclusively. There are challenges in distinguishing between reported and unreported, substantiated and unsubstantiated, child abuse. And the UK does not routinely collect data on abuse prevalence within the care system (Biehal, 2014). Having said that, we do have more evidence of abuse occurring in residential child care than other care placements, and, as already noted, young people in residential child care have also been found to be at greater risk of child sexual exploitation (CSE) than other young people in care (Sen, 2017).

Concerns about care in the residential sector led to reviews in England and Scotland in the early 1990s (Utting, 1991; Skinner, 1992) and it was also given substantial focus in reviews of safeguards for children in the late 1990s in Scotland and England (Kent, 1997; Utting, 1997), as well as a review of progress in implementing safeguarding developments (Stuart and Baines, 2004). The evidence from inquiries into abuse in institutional care does point, importantly, towards certain organisational factors which make the 'corruption of care' more likely. These factors include cases where establishments are inward-looking; where there is a failure of management; and where lines of accountability are lacking between front-line staff and management and between the organisation as a whole and external agencies (Wardhaugh and Wilding, 1993). The key safeguards which have been identified in terms of preventing future abuse in residential care are effective external inspection against clear standards; more rigorous recruitment practices for staff and better support and training for those in post; and ensuring that young people have a clear voice about the care they are receiving (Sen et al., 2008).

What place does the residential child care sector have in the twenty-first century?

Residential child care currently occupies an ambiguous space within the UK child welfare system in the twenty-first century. Alongside some mixed evidence of its effectiveness, the significantly higher cost of residential care compared to other placements raises questions about what future role it should have as a placement choice (Sinclair et al., 2007). Other than the introduction of national minimum standards for children's homes (DOH, 2002a) the three New Labour governments from 1997 to 2010 gave relatively little specific policy attention to the sector despite the significant focus on improving outcomes for children in care overall via the *Quality Protects* (DOH ,1998b) agenda and several additional initiatives around looked after children's educational attainment and the adoption of looked after children from care.

The lack of focus has also been reflected by a lack of recent large-scale research on the sector. In the early 1990s several large-scale government-funded studies of residential child care were commissioned (DOH, 1998a); however, following this, there have been few. The last Labour government did commission a pilot evaluation of the introduction of social pedagogy in English children's homes (Berridge et al., 2011) as well as a linked subsequent study of life an arising study of life in residential child care (Berridge et al., 2012) (both studies reported after the Labour government had left power in 2010), but this represents a small investment in research on the sector compared to the large number of significant studies commissioned on fostering (Sinclair, 2005) and adoption (Thomas, 2012) around the same time.

Care Matters: Time for a Change (DCSF, 2007) signalled the then Labour government's belief that further improvement in the care provided to looked after children was needed. The residential sector's place within such improvement was unclear. The policy paper referred to placing children in residential homes with 'high standards' but also described the need to increase the scope of foster placements such that it could meet the needs of those with high and complex needs. Taken together, this seemed to indicate the further marginalisation of residential care as a placement choice. The lack of governmental attention to the sector was reinforced under the Liberal Democrat–Conservative coalition government when their early policy statement *Improving Outcomes for Children and Young People and Families* (DfE, 2010) made no mention of residential child care. However, David Cameron's second government did subsequently commission a wide-ranging national review of residential child care in England (Narey, 2016) (hereafter called 'the Narey Review'). It remains to be seen whether this represents the start of increasing governmental support for the sector.

The lack of mainstream policy and research focus on residential care is reflected in contemporary practice. Sinclair and colleagues (2007) found that only one of the 13 local authorities in their study actively promoted residential child care as a placement choice. In others social workers and team leaders were reported to accept residential care as the best placement for some children only reluctantly. Some local authorities have moved to close all their residential child care provision (Narey, 2016); however, past experience suggests such authorities merely then end up using out-of-area residential placements for children (DOH, 1998a), with the downside that these are further away from young people's home communities. Government statistics show that nearly 60 per cent of residential children's home and hostel placements are now out-of-authority (DfE, 2017a). There has also been increasing privatisation of the sector. Twenty years ago 90 per cent of children's homes were run by local authorities (House of Commons Health Committee, 1998 cited in Hill, 2000, p. 12). Now two-thirds of residential child care places come from private, profit-making, providers (Narey, 2016). This includes some residential child care establishments which are run by large multinational companies, such as G4S and Serco, alongside others run by smaller private providers.

This context creates two tensions. The first is that the sector which cares for young people with the highest level of need has been given the least attention and focus out of all the placement choices in recent years. The second is that while there has been a long-standing call to view residential care as a positive placement choice for children (e.g. Wagner, 1990; Utting, 1991), in practice it has increasingly been viewed as a residual option when all other family-based options have failed. Underlying these tensions is the lack of a clear theoretical base and rationale for the sector in the twenty-first century (Berridge and Brodie, 1998; Sinclair, 2006). Its most common functions involve explicitly short-term care: assessment, respite and as a bridging placement before family-based care, independent living or leaving care. This short-term focus is reflected in the fact that over three-quarters of residential placements in English children's homes last less than a year (Narey, 2016). By the same token, nearly a fifth of placements do though last a year or more (ibid.).

Boddy (2013) also draws attention to the difference between the point in time numbers for children in residential care and the numbers coming into it during a year (see Chapter 1 on this distinction), suggesting that there is greater usage of the residential sector than there may seem to be at first glance. For example, on 31 March 2017 there were 9,090 children in residential care. But, during the year preceding this date the residential sector had provided 17,380 placements to young people at some point during the year (DfE, 2017c). These 17,380 placements are not all necessarily different young people – a young person who leaves residential care, returns home and then returns to residential care would be included twice, for example. However, putting the data together suggests there is a mixture of stays in modern residential provision: on the one hand there is considerable turnover in the population in most residential units but, on the other, a minority of young people will stay in a given residential unit longer-term. Drawing on examples from other Western European countries, which tend to use residential care for young people much more than in the UK, and with better outcomes, Boddy (2013) repeats the call for residential care to be seen as a first-choice placement option for those with high-level and complex needs, as well as a longer-term placement for some young people in care.

Practice Pointer 8.2

In their day-to-day practice how can (1) residential care workers and (2) field social workers challenge the perception of residential care as a residual 'last choice' placement option for young people?

Effective practice in residential work

In field social work there are discrete and largely boundaried locations in which the job role occurs (the office, home visit and placement visit) and given processes and procedures to complete (assessments, interventions, formal meetings, referrals, reports) which provide a certain definition to the work. In residential work most roles and tasks take place within the residential space. While there has been an increasing tendency for residential workers to do outreach work (for example, to birth parental homes) and to attend significant outside meetings for a young person such as Looked After Child Reviews and Children's Hearings in Scotland, the focus of residential care work remains within the residential space where the working tasks are more fluid and less concretely defined than in field social work. This lack of definition can lead those workers new to the residential environment – myself included as a student social worker on placement in a residential school – to initially question what their role and function as a worker is within the setting.

The concept of the 'lifespace' helps provide a framework for conceptualising residential practice. The framework recognises that the residential home is a physical and emotional environment shared by staff and young people, which is consequently both a workplace and home environment (Connelly and Milligan, 2012). The emphasis is on how engagement in daily living tasks in this environment offers opportunities for developing relationships and supporting children's development (Ward, 2007). An approach which has different roots but is consistent with the lifespace framework is that of social pedagogy – a European model of practice, used widely in Denmark, France and Germany, as well as a number of other European countries. It is focused on the idea of using daily activities to support children's social education – their upbringing in the broadest sense (Cameron and Moss, 2011). Several prominent writers on residential child care in the UK have argued for its adoption in residential practice (Smith, 2009; Cameron and Moss, 2011; Connelly and Milligan, 2012).

Social pedagogy firstly emphasises the importance of building a relationship between the pedagogue and young person, with the goal of effecting change and supporting the development of the young person (Storø, 2013). Emphasis is given to engaging in shared activities that support intellectual, emotional and practical skill development (the 'head, heart, and hands'). The concept of 'common third' is prominent in this work. The pedagogue and young person find a new activity – usually a practical skill or physical activity – to which they are both new and which they learn together. This positions them as equals in respect of the new activity, and emphasises the relational, as well as the technical, aspects of the learning journey (Berridge et al., 2011). Social pedagogy stresses the importance of the pedagogue's reflexivity and of the pedagogue working in collaboration with others, including other young people and colleagues in the group setting, as well as individuals outside it, such as family members (Connelly and Milligan, 2012). It has been argued that social pedagogy supports better interprofessional working in residential care through encouraging the development of a shared language around young people's needs and wishes and a more nuanced understanding of issues of risk in the residential environment (McPheat and Vrouwenfelder, 2017).

The Narey Review (2016) noted the successful use of social pedagogy in other European countries but questioned whether the better outcomes for young people in those countries could be attributed to social pedagogy given wider systemic differences. It also voiced the common question as to whether social pedagogy was not in fact merely good residential practice, rather than a distinct model of working. These are both reasonable cautionary points which remind us of the need to be realistic about what social pedagogy is, and what its introduction might achieve in the UK. However, they are also not arguments against the use of social pedagogy *per se*. One of the promises of introducing social pedagogy in the UK is that it offers residential child care work a unified theoretical and practice orientation (Hannon et al., 2010) which it has lacked in recent decades (Sinclair, 2006).

The use of social pedagogy was piloted and evaluated in three residential care sites in England, with a fourth used as a comparator (Berridge et al., 2011) and there have also been other, smaller, evaluations of its use in Scotland (Crimmens and Milligan, 2012). The Scottish studies were positive, finding that residential workers felt more confident and reflective and that they were undertaking more activities with young people after the introduction of social pedagogy (Crimmens and Milligan, 2012). The English pilot (Berridge et al., 2011) consisted of several social pedagogues from Germany coming to work in English children's homes alongside existing staff. The pedagogues were experienced in other areas of work but a third had no prior experience of residential child care. The pedagogues were generally well received both by other staff and by young people and introduced some new ways of working in the homes, but there was also a lack of clarity as to how the pedagogues' roles differed from that of other residential workers. The ability of social pedagogic practice to influence cultures of practice in the homes in the three sites was uneven, and overall limited. Neither short-term nor long-term outcomes in terms of young people's well-being in the three pilot sites were any better (or any worse) than the comparator site, though true comparisons were difficult to make due to a number of differences between the sites. Despite the inconclusive findings on outcomes, the researchers did find there was sufficient merit in what they saw to recommend there should be further exploration of social pedagogy in children's homes in England. Currently, some local authorities in England as well as some individual residential care providers in Scotland are implementing social pedagogy in their children's homes, while *The Fostering Network* is also involved in a training programme for foster carers in social pedagogy.

Practice Pointer 8.3
_____

What potential benefits can you identify in the adoption of social pedagogy within residential child care practice in the UK?

Young people's views of residential care

There is some evidence that young people in residential care may prefer it to foster care, although for some this view may be influenced by their arrival in residential care after a fostering placement breakdown (Sinclair and Gibbs, 1998; Hadley Centre/Coram Voice, 2015). The centrality of trusting relationships and belonging – and sometimes the absence of them – comes over as a key theme in young people's experience of residential care (Morgan, 2009b; Hadley Centre/Coram Voice, 2015). In one of the few more recent large-scale studies of children's homes, young people identified that they appreciated staff with good listening skills who were sensitive, reliable and who had a sense of humour. Despite the large turnover of young people in the units studies, a number of the young people interviewed also expressed a wish for relationships that resembled family-like ones (Berridge et al., 2012).

Drawing on theoretical literature about changing conceptualisations of what family is and empirical studies of residential child care, Kendrick (2013) highlights how some young people describe their experiences of residential care in family-like terms, including notions of staff being there for them, familiarity, relatedness and closeness to both staff and some other young people. Peer relationships in residential care have been under-researched but the data there are suggest that while young people do forge close and supportive relationships with each other, there can also be a considerable degree of wariness, if not fear, of other young people (Barter et al., 2004; Morgan, 2009b; Berridge et al., 2012). In a study by Sinclair and Gibbs (1998) nearly half of all young people said they had been bullied in residential care while over a fifth of female residents stated that another young person had tried to 'take sexual advantage of them'. Barter and colleagues' (2004) study of peer violence in residential homes identified examples of physical assault, destruction of belongings, verbal abuse and unwanted sexual behaviours. Staff awareness of the possibility of bullying and peer violence and proactive steps to address this are clearly important in supporting young people's ease within the residential setting as well as a positive culture within a unit overall.

A number of young people in residential care report badly missing their birth families (Berridge and Brodie, 1998; Sinclair and Gibbs, 1998; Berridge et al., 2012). Prior research has suggested that residential establishments were successful at promoting contact with birth families (Bilson and Barker, 1995; Berridge and Brodie, 1998). A possible explanation of this is that family contact also suits the needs of residential homes – for example, weekend home leave for young people may suit the staffing patterns common in children's homes. Over a third of young people in residential care are now placed over 20 miles from their home *and* in out-of-authority provision (Narey, 2016). Sinclair and Gibbs (1998) found that children's homes further away from young people's home communities, with on-site education, tended to allow the staff to manage the environment more positively, but they also noted that this meant the units had to adopt different strategies to support young people to keep in touch with their families. There is general agreement that young people should be placed as close to home as possible unless this is inconsistent with their needs (Morgan, 2006b). However, due to the relatively small number of children's homes that now exist and the fact that some authorities have no residential provision at all, a placement of some distance is now likely for a large minority of young people in residential care. As a result, social workers and residential workers must think through ways in which young people's needs and wishes for contact with family and friends networks may be facilitated in these circumstances.

Young people in residential care and offending

According to official statistics around 8 per cent of looked after children in care commit an offence each year which is around double the recorded rate for other children (Schofield et al., 2014). Though this higher rate of offending is worrying, it is worth acknowledging that this statistic also suggests that the vast majority of looked after children will not come into contact with the criminal justice system.

There has though been concern about the rates of offending by young people in residential care and a related but separate concern about their criminalisation; some have expressed concerns that young people in residential care may be charged with offences for behaviour which would not be treated as criminal if the young person were living at home or living in a substitute family setting. It is common for young people, particularly males, to commit a criminal offence at some point in their youth. For example, the Youth Lifestyles Survey of 1998/9 found that 57 per cent of males and 37 per cent of females aged 12–30 admitted to committing at least one offence in their lives (Campbell and Harrington, 2000). Subsequent to their offending, most of these young people would not have had significant involvement with the adult criminal justice system. Therefore, whether a young person commits an offence is not the key issue. Rather the seriousness of the offence, whether it develops into repeat offending and whether and how the offending is picked up and responded to by the child welfare and youth justice systems are more significant.

The practice of residential child care facilities in responding to misdemeanours by young people in the residential space has come into the spotlight in this regard, with questions raised about whether residential establishments are unduly and unnecessarily criminalising young people's minor offending or behavioural problems (Schofield et al., 2014; Shaw, 2014; Howard League, 2016). Issues have also been identified regarding a lack of support and advocacy for young people in care going through the youth justice system: when young people in residential care are charged with an offence it is possible that no one, including their social worker, attends the court hearings with them or advises them through the process; or, if someone does attend, it is someone with whom the young person does not have an established relationship (Schofield et al., 2014; Shaw, 2014).

By contrast, the Narey Review (2016) strongly refuted the assertion that residential child care facilities were systematically criminalising young people in care without good reason. The review did report an estimate that young people in residential care were up to six times as likely as other young people to be involved in criminal justice proceedings, but argued this was principally due to offending committed outside the residential units, some of which pre-dated entry into care. Where police were called by residential staff, the review asserted that this was likely to be due to serious criminal activity by young people in the residential unit rather than trivial behaviour (Narey, 2016). The Howard League (2016) has taken a very different view. They argued that government statistics provide a partial picture of looked after young people's offending, as they only record offences by young people who are looked after for 12 months or more. Based on their own research they claim that young people in residential child care aged 16–17 are 'at least' 15 times more likely to be involved in the criminal justice system, and have stated a belief that young people are indeed being unduly criminalised within residential care.

Practice Pointer 8.4

What practical steps can (1) residential workers and (2) field social workers take to reduce the criminalisation of young people in residential child care?

That individual-, family- and community-level vulnerabilities and disadvantages underpin the offending of young people in care is broadly accepted (Schofield et al., 2014; Shaw, 2014; Prison Reform Trust, 2016). However, 'child welfare' and 'youth justice' responses tend to be very differently focused – the first based around the notion of children as 'victims' who are in need of help and support; the second based on the notion of children as 'threats' whose behaviour needs sanctioning and modifying. These long-standing framings have been challenged at particular points within the history of child welfare. For example, the Kilbrandon Committee, which established the Children's Hearing system in Scotland, explicitly formulated the system on the 'needs not deeds' premise that children who have welfare issues and children who offend both have underlying unmet needs which require addressing (Hill et al., 2006). This perspective, however, tends to rub against wider public concerns about crime and youth offending and political rhetoric reflecting these concerns which verbalises the need to be 'tough on' crime.

The importance of addressing the emotional, behavioural and mental health needs that are likely to underpin much of the offending behaviour of young people in residential care is highlighted (Prison Reform Trust, 2016). This may involve specialist therapeutic input of the sort discussed in Chapter 3, but it will also likely involve finding a stable placement where a young person is offered the chance to build trusting relationships with the care staff around them. Where there is offending behaviour the use of restorative justice as an alternative to disposals through the youth court system, or the shortening of the rehabilitation period for offences such that they do not show on young people's future criminal records checks when applying for training and jobs, has been recommended (Prison Reform Trust, 2016). Such greater use of diversion and early rehabilitation for young people in residential care will require close liaison between staff in residential care units, field social workers, the police and officials connected to the youth justice system.

Supporting the residential workforce

The low status of residential care work has been an enduring issue, with the work tending to be viewed as a 'lesser' role than field social work, and residential staff less well qualified and remunerated (Skinner, 1992; Berridge et al., 2012). The recruitment of appropriate residential care staff has also been a recurrent concern since the 1990s. The Warner (1992) inquiry noted the haphazard methods which had generally been used when recruiting residential staff. It recommended that selection processes be tightened up, including the routine use of criminal records checks and the involvement of young people in assessment and selection processes. A study of overall progress towards implementing safer recruitment processes in Scotland found limited progress had been made (Kay et al., 2007).

By contrast, one Scottish local authority studied by McPheat (2007) had implemented a rigorous recruitment process for all front-line residential child care staff posts. This comprised of an interview and a three-day residential assessment centre where there were a variety of individual and group exercises including a psychometric test and a residential unit visit. While young people might happen to see applicants on their visit to the unit they were not, however, part of the selection process. Residential managers generally viewed the process positively in terms of the skills and child-centredness of staff successfully coming through the process. Staff disciplinary concerns in residential units in the local authority also reduced after the process was introduced. However, the selection process was noted to be heavily resource-intensive, and there were some concerns that suitable candidates may have been deterred from progressing with an application due to its intense nature.

Targets for improving the level of qualifications among the residential workforce have been in place for some time, with slow progress made towards them (Sen et al., 2008). There are, however, mixed views as to whether this will improve practice. The Scottish government has announced plans for all staff in Scottish residential homes to be graduates from 2018. The Narey Review (2016) cast doubt on whether this will improve the quality of the residential workforce and urged the UK government not to follow suit in England. There is a mixed evidence base regarding the relationship between residential workers' qualification levels and better outcomes for young people. Some previous studies have found little relationship between them (DOH, 1998a), while another study did find positive associations between different qualification levels of staff in England, Denmark and Germany and outcomes for young people – with English staff the least well qualified (Cameron and Boddy, 2008). Recently a pilot of a new specially tailored training programme for residential care staff ('RESuLT') has been positively evaluated in terms of its content, and staff and young people's views of it (Berridge et al., 2016). The researchers also acknowledged, however, the methodological difficulties in clearly demonstrating that any form of training has 'led to' improvements in outcomes for young people. As in the case of training delivered to foster carers and adoptive parents, this mixed evidence base should not be read as suggesting that training is unimportant for residential staff providing good-quality care. However, it again focuses attention on the fact that one-off good-quality training, while important, is not a panacea for staff members' ability to meet all the complex needs which young people have while in residential care.

Ethnicity and gender in residential care

Though the data we have are imperfect they suggest there is some disproportionality in the use of residential child care according to ethnic background. The reasons for this are not well understood. Research from 20 years ago suggested that young people of African-Caribbean heritage might be over-represented within the residential sector, while those of South Asian heritage might be under-represented (DOH, 1998a). This finding was supported by the more recent study by Owen and Statham (2009) which found that African-Caribbean young people were twice as likely as Bangladeshi young people to be placed in residential care, despite being on average younger on entry into care.

Berridge and Brodie (1998) noted the lack of explicit attention to BME issues in the residential child care homes they studied and spoke of the 'identity stripping' of young people from minority cultures, including that staff sometimes did not have details of young people's ethnicity or religion. They identified that the residential homes lacked strategies for meeting the needs of BME young people. Kendrick (2008) suggested that there appeared to have been a positive change from the 1990s, when research found overtly racist attitudes on the part of both young people and sometimes staff, to the early 2000s when Barter and colleagues (2004) found zero-tolerance policies towards racism in children's homes, low levels of racist behaviour from young people and young people's own willingness to challenge other young people displaying racist attitudes. Culturally competent practice requires that residential workers have the capacity to engage with an individual young person's own sense of what their culture is and the ways in which it is important to them.

The lack of explicit focus given to issues of gender in residential care is also notable given the gendered aspects of caregiving in this environment (Green, 2005). Smith and colleagues (2013) note that around two-thirds of residential workers are women and approximately the same proportion of residents are young men. In mixed residential establishments, the environment may nonetheless be a male-dominated one with young women expected to fit into an environment set up primarily to meet the needs of young men (O'Neill, 2008). Gender differences in the reasons that bring young women and young men into care, and in the ways they are likely to seek help and respond to services, need to be acknowledged. Young women in care are considerably more likely to be have been subject to sexual abuse and CSE and to have entered care due to family relationship break-down (O'Neill, 2008; Sen, 2017). Young men are more likely to have emotional and behavioural difficulties, conduct and hyperkinetic disorders, educational support needs and be involved in serious offending (Smith et al., 2013).

Young people with a disability in residential child care provision

Young people with a disability are more likely to be placed in residential care than non-disabled young people (Sinclair et al., 2007) and this has been argued to be part of a 'reverse ladder of permanency' for them (Baker, 2007). We also know relatively little about this group of young people, the lack of basic information on them reflecting a more general lack of focus on the needs, interests and wishes of children with a disability (McConkey et al., 2004; Stalker, 2008). We do know that, like other looked after children, they are more likely to have experience of child abuse and neglect and come from difficult home situations; they are also likely to have multiple and profound disabilities (McConkey et al., 2004). A number of young people with a disability placed in residential special schools are not looked after children, meaning that though they have high levels of need and vulnerability and are placed away from home, their care will not be subject to the same legal requirements and oversight as children who are looked after. This is something which is questionable given that we know children with a disability are more likely to be subject to abuse and neglect (Stalker and McArthur, 2012). Stalker (2008) makes a number of recommendations for good practice in this area. These include assessing whether or not the use of family-based care is a more appropriate for young people with a disability; viewing residential care as a placement of choice for those young people who do need it; gaining young people's views of their care, including the use of independent advocates; and supporting families to keep in contact with young people in residential establishments as much as possible.

Key messages for practice

- The decline in the use of residential placements has stopped and different types of residential provision have provided just over 10 per cent of young people with placements in England in recent years. Residential provision is now principally used for young people who are 12 and older. Young people with a disability are more likely than other young people to have a placement in residential care.

- The residential sector continues to be largely regarded as a residual option when other options have failed or are untenable. A lower priority has been given to the sector in recent policy and research and residential child care workers tend to be less well paid and trained than field social workers.

- Relatively poor outcomes for those in and leaving residential care and its considerably greater expense than other placement options have led to questions about whether residential provision should be further reduced. At the same time, the ongoing role for some residential provision is suggested by the fact that local authorities that have closed all of their residential provision still then place some young people in out-of-authority residential placements. This practice partly explains why a large minority of young people in residential care are now placed a long distance from their home communities, creating challenges in keeping young people in touch with family and friends.

- In the UK modern residential provision has tended to lack a coherent practice and theoretical orientation. There are some strong advocates for the use of social pedagogy in UK residential child care – a model developed in some European countries where there is greater use of residential provision, and outcomes for young people in, and leaving, residential care are better.

Suggested reading

Kendrick, A. (2008) *Residential Child Care: Prospects and Challenges*. London: Jessica Kingsley – A wide-ranging set of chapters on core areas of practice and policy relating to residential care.

Shaw, J. (2014) *Residential Children's Homes and the Youth Justice System*. London: Palgrave – Provides a thorough treatment of issues related to offending in residential care.

Smith, M. (2009) *Rethinking Residential Child Care*. Bristol: Policy – Partial but passionate overview of the state of the residential sector in the UK in the twenty-first century.

Online resources

The Fostering Network sought to introduced social pedagogy into fostering services. The material from the project and its evaluation are of relevance to those interested in social pedagogy more generally and can be accessed at: www.thefosteringnetwork.org.uk/policy-practice/head-heart-hands/what-social-pedagogy

Jackson, L. (2015) '"The last place was like a prison": care leavers' stories of children's homes', *The Guardian*, 2 June, www.theguardian.com/social-care-network/2015/jun/02/childrens-homes-care-leavers-neil-morrissey-lemn-sissay – This article outlines the good and not so good experiences of a few well-known celebrities who spent time in residential care facilities.

CHAPTER 9

EDUCATION AND HEALTH

Chapter Overview

This chapter focuses on the education of looked after children up until the age of 16, and their mental and physical health. Post-16 education and training are considered in Chapter 10. This chapter examines the key roles, in addition to a social worker's, in promoting looked after children's education and health. It then considers the evidence in terms of looked after children's comparative educational attainment, mental ill health and physical health. Explanations for why looked after children fare comparatively poorly are explored in terms of pre-care and in-care experiences. The chapter concludes by summarising the evidence on effective support for looked after children in these three areas.

Key roles in looked after children's education and health

Alongside a social worker's own responsibility for overseeing a looked after child's education and health needs, other professionals have key roles and responsibilities in these areas. In education, the *Every Child Matters* (DfES, 2003) programme created the role of the *designated teacher* and the provision of personalised programmes of support for every looked after child through Personal Education Plans (PEPs). The Children and Young Persons Act 2008 made the role of the designated teacher mandatory in all state schools. The role is to be fulfilled by a qualified teacher in every school where there is a looked after child. The designated teacher has responsibility for promoting the educational attainment of looked after children in their school and advocating for their interests in the school; secondary legislation has made clear this requirement applies to the new state-funded, but organisationally independent, academies and free schools (DfE, 2014d).

Following the successful pilot of the *Virtual School Head* (VSH) role in 11 authorities (Berridge et al., 2009), the Children and Families Act 2014 amended the Children Act 1989 so that all local authorities in England are now required to appoint a VSH. The role of the VSH is authority-wide and principally strategic but it also has operational responsibilities for identifying suitable school placements for children in care and negotiating with schools where they are at risk of exclusion (Berridge et al., 2009). The VSH is expected to be a former senior teacher or educationalist.

Secondary legislation specifies that where a PEP has not already been completed for a looked after child in preparation for their entry into care, it is the child's social worker's responsibility to initiate its completion within ten working days of the care placement starting, supported by the VSH. The designated teacher should then lead on how the PEP is used in the child's school to support and monitor their progress (DfE, 2014d). A written report summarising the PEP should be fed into the child's first Looked After Child Review, which should take place within 20 working days of their placement, and formally reviewed at subsequent Looked After Child Reviews, with additional review of the PEP undertaken on an ongoing basis such that it is a live document (ibid.).

In England, the schools which looked after children, and children who have previously been looked after, attend are given a government Pupil Premium Grant (PPG) of £1,900 per pupil per year in order to raise 'the attainment of disadvantaged pupils of all abilities to reach their potential' (DfE, 2017d, n.p.). Though this grant is paid per looked after, or previously looked after, pupil, the policy allows that the grant may be used for provision which also has educational benefit for other pupils at the school in question (ibid.).

In terms of health, in England each Clinical Commissioning Group (CCG)[1] in the NHS should have a *designated doctor* and *designated nurse* for looked after children (DfE/DOH, 2015). These roles are strategic rather than operational, and designed to ensure that commissioners of health services are aware of the strategic areas of unmet health needs for looked after children and meet their responsibilities to them (DfE/DOH, 2015). Previous statutory guidance (DOH, 2002b) specified that the designated doctor should be a senior paediatrician while the designated nurse should be a senior nurse or health visitor. Evidence from 2007, however, suggested not all health areas had appointed these positions – three-quarters of NHS regional areas had a designated doctor and 93 per cent a designated nurse (DCSF and DOH, 2009).

Separate to the strategic roles of the designated doctor and designated nurse, each looked after child should have a *named GP* at the practice with which they are registered, responsible for the co-ordination of services under the GP contract (DfE and DOH, 2015). There should also be a *named health professional* for looked after children at the GP practice who may be a named nurse or a named doctor. The named health professional should be the principal health contact for children's social care; be responsible for co-ordinating the information contained in the child's health assessment and ensure such assessments are completed on time and of good quality; co-ordinate the provision of health services for an individual child; and act as a liaison point for the child and their carer where they have difficulties accessing health services (ibid.).

Under the Care Planning, Placement and Case Review (England) Regulations (2010) (DfE, 2010) local authorities are responsible for ensuring an assessment takes place of the physical, emotional and mental health needs of every looked after child on entry into care. The initial assessment needs to be carried out by a registered medical practitioner who should produce a written health plan which should be available for the first statutory Looked After Child Review. The regulations specify that the assessment should include an assessment of the child's current physical, emotional and mental health; the child's and their family's health history; the effect of this history on the child's development; arrangements for the child's health care and monitoring including dental, vision and hearing checks and treatment plans; advice on promoting the child's health and effective personal care; and the role of any other person, such as a foster carer, residential worker, school nurse, social worker or teacher, in promoting the child's health.

The review of the child's health plan must happen at least once every six months for children under five, and annually for looked after children above this age. Health review assessments can be undertaken by a registered medical practitioner, registered nurse or registered midwife. Where a child is placed 'out of area' the responsible CCG should liaise with the CCG where the child is placed in order to 'reach agreement without delay as to which CCG's service will carry out the health assessment' (DfE/DOH, 2015, p. 18).

Practice Pointer 9.1

Write down the key roles and responsibilities for looked after children's health and education. Which professional has primary responsibility for which tasks?

The evidence on educational attainment, mental and physical health

Educational attainment

From the late 1990s, local authorities were required to produce figures on the educational attainment of looked after children and compare them with those of other children. This provided evidence of the 'attainment gap' between the educational attainment of children from the general population and the educational attainment of looked after children – a gap which has narrowed slightly since the early 2000s but is still substantial (see Table 9.1).

Practice Pointer 9.2

Look at Table 9.1. What stands out to you about the educational performance and attainment of looked after children compared to other groups of children?

Table 9.1 Comparative educational data for children in care in England, 2012–2016

	2012	2013	2014	2015	2016
%age of children achieving 5+ GCSEs at A*–C grades including English and Maths++					
Looked after children+	15	15.5	12.2	13.9	13.6
Non-looked after children	58.8	58.6	52.9	53.2	53.1
Children in need	15.2	16.1	15.1	14.9	14.9
Adopted from care				22.6	25.3
SGO from care				20.9	25.3
CAO from care				19.7	28.7
%age of children with identified Special Educational Needs (SEN)					
Looked after children+					57.3
All children					14.4
Children in need					46.7
%age of 'Persistent Absentees' across state primaries, secondaries and special schools					
Looked after children+		10.1	8.9	9	9.1
Non-looked after children		13.6	10.7	11	10.5
Children in need				28.2	28.3
%age of children with at least one fixed period of exclusion					
Looked after children+	11.3	10.2	10.2	10.4	
Non-looked after children	2.1	1.9	1.9	1.9	
Children in need	7.5	6.6	6.5	7.2	
%age of children permanently excluded					
Looked after children+	0.15	0.13	0.12	0.14	
Non-looked after children	0.07	0.06	0.06	0.07	
Children in need	0.31	0.18	0.17	0.2	

Source: DfE (2017d)

+ Looked after children are defined here as those continuously looked after for 12 months or more.

++ The methodology for calculating this changed in 2014, meaning comparison with previous years is limited.

As can be seen in Table 9.1 looked after young people perform poorly at Key Stage 4 (GCSE level) compared to young people in the general population, with an attainment gap – the difference in proportions of the two groups who passed five GCSEs with A*–C grades – of 39.5 per cent. Evidence from Australia (Fernandez,

2012) and other European countries (Weyts, 2004) suggests this is not just a UK phenomenon. Over the last two years, the government has also collected the results of those children who left care via adoption, a Special Guardianship Order (SGO) or Child Arrangement Order (CAO). This early data suggest that these former looked after children educationally outperform those children who are in care, but their results are still some way behind the educational attainment of children in the general population.

The number of looked after young people gaining five A*–C passes at GCSE has risen from 8 per cent in 2002 (SEU, 2003) to its current level of close to 14 per cent. Though the proportion of looked after young people achieving this target has actually fallen since 2014, this has followed modifications to the GCSE exam system which have seen the proportion of all children getting five A*–C grades falling. Wider data on educational attainment further indicate that while there has been improvement in looked after young people's educational attainment in the 2000s there is still a substantial attainment gap – for example, in 2007, 64 per cent of looked after young people passed one GCSE, grade A*–G, compared to only 49 per cent in 2000. However, this still compared poorly with the general population of young people, nearly all of whom (99 per cent) achieved this standard (Berridge and Saunders, 2009; O'Sullivan et al., 2013). Similarly, while the proportion of looked after children who are excluded and permanently excluded has fallen since the 1990s, when looked after children were ten times as likely to be excluded from school as others (SEU, 1998), the proportion is still notably higher than for other children (see Table 9.1).

A more balanced picture of looked after children's education attainment may arguably be provided by comparing it with that of young people living in 'similar' circumstances at home. Recent data from both government statistics and research studies (McClung and Gayle, 2010; Sebba et al., 2015) suggest that when this comparison is made, young people in care for over a year in fact do similarly well to, if not better than, young people living at home under social work supervision. The proportion of *Young People in Need* (YPN)[2] gaining five A*–C grades at GCSE was comparable to the proportion of looked after young people in 2016, and looked after children actually performed slightly better than *Children in Need* (CIN) at Key Stage 2 at the end of primary school in 2016 (DfE, 2017d). Government statistics in England also show there are fewer looked after children who are persistent absentees or permanently excluded than CIN (ibid.).

Sebba and colleagues (2015) compared the educational performance of young people in England in the general child population with YPN, looked after young people in care for more than a year, and looked after young people who had been in care for less than a year at the end of Key Stage 4 (GCSE level). They found young people in the general population fared the best, followed by young people who had been in care for more than a year, then YPN and finally young people who had been in care for less than a year. There was some complexity to the findings in that, despite the overall findings, young people who had entered care before the age of five and stayed in care long-term (an average of 11 years) fared relatively poorly. Nonetheless, like the DfE statistics and a study of education attainment in Scotland conducted by McClung and Gayle (2010), the findings suggest that young people in care for sustained periods of time are equalling or bettering the educational performance of young people living in parental care with social work support. This may suggest that greater focus on the educational attainment of CIN, as well as children in care, is now needed (Welbourne and Leeson, 2012), particularly as there is some evidence that children living in parental care with social work support may receive less educational support despite displaying higher levels of need (McSherry et al., 2013).

Mental health

Mental health disorder classifications are agreed and set out in the internationally referenced *Diagnostic and Statistical Manual of Mental Disorders* (DSM) produced by the American Psychiatric Association and the *International Classification of Diseases – Classification of Mental and Behavioural Disorders* (ICD) produced by the World Health Organization (WHO). The two classification manuals contain some differences but are viewed as complementary publications (APA, 2013) which are each regularly reviewed and updated. The latest versions are DSM-5, released in 2013 (APA, 2013), and ICD-10, which was released in 1992 (WHO, 1992), but subject to updates, with ICD-11 due out in 2018 (WHO, 2017).

The latest definition of a mental health disorder in DSM-5 is:

> a syndrome characterized by clinically significant disturbance in an individual's cognition, emotion regulation, or behavior that reflects a dysfunction in the psychological, biological, or developmental processes underlying mental functioning. Mental disorders are usually associated with significant distress or disability in social, occupational, or other important activities. An expectable or culturally approved response to a common stressor or loss, such as death of a loved one, is not a mental disorder. Socially deviant behavior (e.g., political, religious or sexual) and conflicts that are primarily between the individual and society are not mental disorders unless the deviance or conflict results from a dysfunction in the individual, as described above. (APA, 2013, p. 20)

This definition leaves open the possibility, therefore, that a looked after child may experience mental distress that is not severe enough to meet the level of a 'clinically significant disturbance' required for diagnosis of a disorder.

The main classifications of mental health disorder applied to children are:

- Conduct Disorders – for example, repetitive patterns of anti-social behaviour including aggression, defiance and offending behaviour.

- Developmental Disorders – for example, autism, language disorders, learning disorders.

- Eating Disorders – for example, anorexia, bulimia.

- Emotional Disorders – for example, anxiety, depression, phobias.

- Habit Disorders – for example, soiling, sleeping problems.

- Hyperkinetic Disorders – for example, ADHD, other disorders related to problems of inattention, hyperactivity and impulsivity.

- Psychotic Disorders – for example, bipolar disorder, psychosis, schizophrenia (Walker, 2003, p. 24).

The variety of disorders covered in this list is notable, from those which are primarily defined by behaviours towards others (for example, conduct disorders) to those which relate to biological functions (for example, soiling), to primarily inwardly orientated (for example, emotional disorders) and those which are primarily organic neurodevelopmental disorders (for example, autism, ADHD). A distinction is sometimes made between 'internalising disorders' – for example, emotional disorders and eating disorders where problems are individually internalised by a child – and 'externalising orders' – conduct disorders and hyperkinetic disorders – where problems are manifested outwardly in behaviour towards others. There are some patterns within this distinction – boys are more likely to experience externalising disorders, and girls internalising disorders (Green et al., 2005) – which can be important to recognise when seeking to find an appropriate placement match for a child. For example, it is widely known that children with emotional and behavioural difficulties have a greater chance of placement breakdown (Sinclair et al., 2007) and therefore carers with the correct skill set to manage such needs will be required to reduce the likelihood of a breakdown occurring. However, the label of 'emotional and behavioural difficulties' can mask important underlying differences. In a study of teenagers in foster care, Farmer and colleagues (2004) found that placement instability was connected to a young person displaying emotional and behavioural problems that could be classed as 'externalising'. Young people with 'internalising' problems in fact had more stable placements than average, but the researchers also raised concerns about whether the needs of the latter group of young people, mainly teenage girls, slipped under the radar because of the internalising nature of their difficulties.

Practice Pointer 9.3

Take one of the mental health disorders listed above. What do you think might be the key challenges and key supports for a looked after child identified as experiencing this disorder?

Questions about the mental health paradigm

The knowledge base of mental health is a contested one. The social model of disability argues that the treatment of disability, including mental illness, is influenced by a medical model which identifies and responds to health impairment as a deficit, abnormality or limitation located within the individual person (Oliver et al., 2012). Expert knowledge of the impairment rests within the hands of the medical professional and the focus is on finding individual medical remedies to best mitigate the perceived deficit (Goodley, 2014). The social model originated within the disability movement itself and distinguishes between disability and impairment (Oliver et al., 2012). Disability is defined as the social, economic and cultural barriers which excludes those with an impairment from living the same lives as those without an impairment (Goodley, 2014). Arising from this it argues for social, economic, legal and cultural change to address disablism, foregrounding the inclusion and participation of those with impairments as experts in their own lives. A social model is consistent with the recognition of the links between social factors such as poverty, poor housing, stress and discrimination and physical and mental ill health (Venkatapuram, 2011), and a key implication of it is that 'in working with disabled people the social work task should no longer be one of adjusting individuals to personal disasters but rather helping them to locate the personal, social, economic and community resources to enable them to live life to the full' (Oliver et al., 2012, p. 26). The social model itself has, however, been criticised for failing to adequately recognise the lived reality of pain and distress which can be caused by impairment (Goodley, 2014).

There are also criticisms of the construction and classification of mental disorders. At one end of the spectrum are those who question the validity of all psychiatric classifications (Rogers and Pilgrim, 2015). That the classifications in the DSM and ICD are subject to societal influence, rather than value free, is supported by the way categories have changed over time to reflect changing social norms. For example, homosexuality was categorised as a mental disorder in the DSM until 1973 and in the ICD until 1992. The number of mental health classifications has increased markedly – the forerunner of the APA recognised 59 psychiatric disorders in 1917; by the time DSM-IV was published in 1994, this had grown to 347 (Pilgrim, 2017). This growth had led some to question whether psychiatric diagnosis may be pathologising everyday emotional and psychological responses to stress and adversity as mental health disorders (Stein et al., 2010). However, perspectives questioning the classification of all mental disorder have themselves been criticised for overlooking the lived reality of distress which can be caused by mental ill health (Rogers and Pilgrim, 2015). A middle position has been to argue for the value of mental health disorder classifications in identifying, treating and researching mental health problems, while simultaneously acknowledging their use and application require professional judgement (Stein et al., 2010). Ethical consideration of the purpose and use of mental disorder diagnoses is essential. The ever growing number of mental health disorders classifications may blur the boundaries between mental health disorders and common psychological and emotional responses to adversity (ibid.). Such blurring can potentially expose people to inappropriate medical treatment as well as using up scarce mental health resources unnecessarily (Goodley, 2014).

Practice Pointer 9.4

The credibility of the dominant mental health paradigm is a long-standing point of debate with implications for practice with looked after children. What are your views on this debate and on what do you base them?

Mental ill health prevalence

There has been an increase in the number of mental health disorders diagnosed in all children in developed countries, with longitudinal assessment suggesting that over half of young people will meet the criteria for at least one psychiatric disorder by the age of 21 (Maughan and Collishaw, 2015). The rates of mental disorder in the looked after child population are, however, far greater, a finding which has been consistent across studies over the last 60 years (Sempik, 2010). Conduct disorders, emotional disorders and hyperkinetic disorders are particularly common among looked after children (DOH, 2002b; Meltzer et al., 2003) as illustrated in Table 9.2, derived from national surveys of the mental health of children in England in the general child population (Meltzer et al., 2000) and the looked after child population (Meltzer et al., 2003). Although not included in Table 9.2 it is worth noting that comparable results were found in a survey of looked after children in Scotland (Meltzer et al., 2004).

Table 9.2 shows that younger looked after children were found to have over five times the rate of mental disorder compared to that of children of their age in the general population, while looked after young people had four and half times the rate of their peers. In both the younger and older age groups of looked after children, nearly half were found to have a mental disorder, and levels of conduct disorder were particularly high for both age groups compared to their peers. In addition, nearly half (43 per cent) of the looked after children in the survey who were not clinically assessed as having a mental disorder had emotional, behavioural or hyperactivity problems in their carers' opinions (Meltzer et al., 2003). Sempik's (2010) review of the UK evidence similarly concluded that, in addition to 45 per cent of children who had a diagnosed mental disorder, 70–80 per cent of looked after children have recognisable problems.

In a follow-up study to those of Meltzer and colleagues, Ford and colleagues (2007) compared the mental health of children in the care system in England, Scotland and Wales with both children living in the community in the poorest households socio-economically and children in the general population. Children in

Table 9.2 Comparison of rates of mental health disorders in the general child population and the looked after child population

	%age of general population of children with the following	%age of looked after children with the following
	5–10 year olds	
Emotional disorders	3	11
Conduct disorders	5	36
Hyperkinetic disorders	2	11
Any childhood mental disorder	**8**	**42**
	11–15 year olds	
Emotional disorders	6	12
Conduct disorders	6	40
Hyperkinetic disorders	1	7
Any childhood mental disorder	**11**	**49**

Source: Meltzer et al. (2003)

the poorest households were more likely than children in the general population to have psychiatric difficulties, but looked after children had greater psychiatric difficulties than both other groups at a statistically significant level. The authors also reported that looked after children were found to be particularly likely to have psychiatric disorders associated with environmental factors such as post-traumatic stress disorder (PTSD) and conduct disorder. The absence of a psychiatric disorder does not, however, mean a child is in good mental health, therefore the study also looked at indicators of psychological adjustment as a measure of well-being. Again, looked after children fared comparatively poorly on this measure, with less than a tenth assessed as having 'good psychological adjustment' compared to one in two children in the general child population. The study further found that children experiencing psychiatric difficulties, with the exception of depression, were more likely to be struggling at school, suggesting that difficulties in one area could reinforce or compound others.

Practice Pointer 9.5

Data suggest that looked after children now do as well, if not better, than children living at home with their parents with social work support in terms of educational attainment. However, they fare significantly worse than children living at home in poverty in terms of mental ill health. What can you identify about looked after children's circumstances which might explain this difference?

Disinhibited Social Engagement Disorder (DSED) and Reactive Attachment Disorder (RAD)

Attention is given to these disorders here as they have been found to be much more prevalent in the looked after and adopted children populations than for other children (Millward et al., 2006). There also has been considerable debate, and sometimes controversy, over the use of the classifications, therefore practitioners should have an awareness of them.

Importantly, attachment and engagement disorders are different classifications to the categories of attachment security and insecurity set out in Chapter 2 – they developed in an attempt to explain the behaviour of children whose behavioural traits did not correspond to any of these standard classifications (Zeanah and Gleason, 2011). Attachment and engagement disorders are believed to develop in children who have experienced severe abuse or neglect in early childhood (Millward et al., 2006) and are defined as disorders which begin before the age of 5 but persist over time (Rutter et al., 2009). Children with both types of disorder show marked difficulties in achieving key developmental milestones, most notably around emotional, behavioural and social development (Zeanah and Gleason, 2011).

Children's indiscriminate friendliness and physical tactility towards adult and peer strangers, alongside the absence of checking back with primary carers or trusted adults during times of stress or upset, is the key indicator of DSED (Rutter et al., 2009). RAD is characterised by a child's rejection of intimacy at the same time as demanding close attention from carers, displays of hypervigilance, where a child is constantly watchful and very easily aroused by small changes in their environment, and a lack of emotional self-regulation whereby a child is prone to emotional and behavioural outbursts that do not have an obvious trigger (Millward et al., 2006; Zeanah and Smyke, 2015).

To complicate matters, DSED was previously classified as a type of attachment disorder ('Disinhibited Reactive Attachment Disorder') but was reclassified in DSM-5. The reclassification was based on systemic observations that despite indiscriminate attachment to strangers, these children could still display secure attachment to their primary carers, making the classification as an 'attachment disorder' problematic (Zeanah and Smyke, 2015). By contrast, RAD is associated with difficulties a child has in forming a secure attachment to their primary carers, hence the ongoing description of this as an attachment disorder (Zeanah and Gleason, 2011). This difference is also held to be significant in the way the two disorders develop over childhood; current evidence suggests that while children diagnosed with RAD improve considerably in response to warm, consistent caregiving, children with DSED will continue to manifest some difficulties into later childhood and adulthood (Rutter et al., 2009).

Opinions on how widespread the disorders are in children diverge wildly, ranging from 'rare' to over 1 million children, including half of all adopted children in the USA alone (Barth et al., 2005). Some social work researchers working within an attachment theory paradigm have questioned whether the behavioural traits described by DSED and RAD are in fact significantly different from those described by insecure disorganised attachment (Shemmings and Shemmings, 2011). Within the field of child psychiatry there is, however, substantial support for the reliability and validity of the classifications of both DSED and RAD (Zeanah and Smyke, 2015), though the need for greater research into the disorders' core features and causes is also acknowledged (Zeanah and Gleason, 2011).

Despite the very measured statements by prominent child psychiatric research-ers, there is some evidence that the label of 'attachment disorder' has become more widely sensationalised and misunderstood. Assertions that children with an attachment disorder are prone to lying, stealing and have an inability to show empathy have led to non-evidenced-based claims of an association between RAD and later psychopathic traits (Barth et al., 2005). It also appears that there has been word-of-mouth advice among some carers and adopters in the USA suggest-ing prospective carers should avoid offering placements to children diagnosed with RAD (Quinton, 2012, p. 104). Professionals working with looked after chil-dren should therefore be aware of the classifications of DSED and RAD, but also recognise their potential misuse and the developing, and sometimes contested, nature of these diagnostic constructs. As in other areas of mental health diagnosis, the critical question of whether applying a diagnostic label will help or hinder a child to get the support they require should be asked.

Physical health

Though the evidence suggests that looked after children fare worse in respect of physical health than peers in the general population, there is a more positive pic-ture here than in respect of mental health, with research indicating most looked after children are in good general physical health (Scott, Ward and Hill, 2007). Meltzer and colleagues (2003) found the most commonly reported physical com-plaints in the looked after child population were eye and/or sight problems (16 per cent), speech or language problems (14 per cent), bed wetting (13 per cent), difficulty with co-ordination (10 per cent) and asthma (10 per cent). Other than asthma, eczema and allergies, physical health difficulties were more prevalent in looked after children than in the general population. The study also found that children in foster care were more likely to be rated by their carers as being in good health (69 per cent), compared to young people in residential care (41 per cent) or independent living (31 per cent).

Less positively, one relatively recent study of obesity in foster care children found that children were more obese than their peers, and their Body Mass Index increased after entry into care (Hadfield and Preece, 2008). Young people in care are also up to four times more likely to use drugs, alcohol and smoke and do these things problematically at a younger age than other young people (Meltzer et al., 2003). While government data for the years 2014–2016 show a small proportion of all looked after children in England (4 per cent) were specifically classed as having a 'substance misuse problem' by their local authorities (see Table 9.3), this figure increases to 9–10 per cent for 16 and 17 year olds (DfE, 2017a).

In summary, while looked after children's educational attainment, mental health and physical health are worse than those of children in the general population there are substantial differences. When compared to children in similarly difficult circumstances living at home, children in care for a substantial period of time do at least as well, if not better, educationally. Looked after children's physical health is worse than peers, with some noted issues, but has been found to be reasonably good overall. By contrast, looked after children are far more likely to have a diagnosed mental health disorder than other children, and to experience greater mental ill health more broadly.

Explanations of the poorer educational attainment and health of looked after children

For all three areas covered in this chapter there are essentially two broad explanations – children's pre-care experiences and their in-care experiences.

Pre-care experiences

Firstly, attachment theory argues that separation from primary caregivers – even where that caregiving has been in some ways inadequate – is likely to be experienced by a child as traumatic and can have an impact on a child's later development (Bowlby, 1997). Additionally, many children entering the care system will also have had other difficult pre-care experiences, including experience of poverty and poor housing, and there is evidence that living in persistent poverty in the early years has an impact on cognitive development (Dickerson and Popli, 2016).

Thirdly, most children entering care will have experienced some form of maltreatment. Maltreatment in early life can affect a child's brain development and hormonal and nervous systems (Glaser, 2000), and maltreatment at any stage of childhood can have an adverse impact on both later mental and physical health, as well as cognitive development (Jones, 2010). A recently completed study by the University of York found that, in a large sample of looked after children, mental health difficulties were primarily attributable to pre-care rather than in-care experiences (Medical Press, 2017).

The question of whether children who have adverse childhood experiences will go on to manifest other difficulties or resilience later in life is a complex one to which we do not have the full answer. The ecological-transactional model emphasises that there is a complex interplay between a substantial number of factors that makes predicting futures difficult. Factors related to the individual child (biology, psychology, developmental history at the time of the adverse experience, choices the child makes), their environment (social contexts, the broader experiences of the child) and the adverse experiences themselves (their nature, timing and duration) are all influential (Cicchetti, 2010). Among the complexity there is a positive message that later difficulties are not inevitable following adverse childhood experiences, but also a realism that they are substantially more likely.

We know that many children enter the care system with some educational delay, mental health difficulties or physical health issues. To take one indicator of this, Table 9.1 shows that well over half of looked after children have Special Educational Needs (SEN) compared with only 14.4 per cent of all children taken together. A child's health and behavioural issues on entry to the care system are also likely to mean that they will, at least initially, struggle to make as much progress in their placement and educational settings as children without these issues. In particular, behavioural problems also make a child more vulnerable to the possibility of exclusion from school and placement breakdown (SEU, 2003; Welbourne and Leeson, 2012) which can further negatively affect their progress. This can generate a negative cycle whereby a child with greater needs experiences a greater likelihood of placement and school placement breakdowns, generating further difficulties in turn. This example illustrates how 'pre-care experiences' may be related to 'in-care experiences' to which we now turn in more detail.

In-care experiences

It has been argued that the care system has failed to adequately prioritise aspects of children's care. Low commitment to looked after children's educational attainment on the part of carers and social workers and multiple care and school placements undermining stability for children have been noted as issues (SEU, 2003; Jackson, 2010). Studies from the 1990s reported that there were very high rates of non-attendance at school by young people in residential care (Berridge and Brodie, 1998; Sinclair and Gibbs, 1998). A lack of private study space, poor access to educational materials and a lack of staff support for study were also noted in studies of the care system around this time (Rees, 2001; Francis, 2007). It was also argued that schools were reluctant to offer looked after children placements in an environment where there was strong pressure to perform in national school league tables (Bourne, 2005; Jackson, 2010). In Harker and colleagues' (2004) study of looked after young people's education young people highlighted social workers as the greatest *barrier* to their educational achievement. This was related to the perceived lack of focus which social workers gave to young people's education when their care placements changed.

Since the mid-2000s considerably greater priority has been given to looked after children's education, addressing some of these systemic gaps. Sebba and colleagues (2015) found that young people in care were overwhelmingly positive about the effect that coming into care had had on their education. Young people commented on more settled and nurturing care environments and greater access to resources to support their education. Sebba and colleagues also found there had been improvements in the prioritisation of education in residential care, with nearly a fifth (18.5 per cent) of looked after young people in residential settings taking GCSEs. However, it is still the case that the attainment gap between looked after children and their peers widens as young people progress through their educational careers, suggesting a cumulative effect whereby early educational differences are compounded rather than reversed (Welbourne and Leeson, 2012; Sebba et al., 2015). The government target, set in 2011, that 20 per cent of looked after children should achieve five A*–C GCSEs (Welbourne and Leeson, 2012) also remains some way off being met and Jackson (2010) has highlighted the large variation in the performance of local authorities in respect of the educational attainment of looked after children in their care – such a large variation may suggest that some local authorities give a lower priority to the education of their care populations than others.

Practice Pointer 9.6

Choose a local authority area in England and explore the looked after young people Key Stage 4 (GCSE or equivalent) results data for this area. An explanation of how to find these data is provided in the online resources section at the end of this chapter.

How does the local authority perform compared to other local authorities in the same geographical region and the national average? What practice issues do you think might be behind any differences?

In terms of mental health, there is evidence that multiple placement moves in care negatively affect children's mental health (Stanley et al., 2005) and that the mental health needs of looked after and adopted children are insufficiently addressed (Selwyn et al., 2006; Ford et al., 2007). A recent Children's Commissioner's report (2016) has emphasised the systemic gaps in specialist mental health services for all children. Over a quarter of children referred were not provided with a service while nearly two-thirds of the 3,000 children referred with a life-threatening mental health condition were not allocated to service provision or were put on a waiting list. Given the far greater prevalence of mental health disorders among the looked after child population, they will be disproportionately affected by such systemic service gaps.

In respect of physical health, there is some older evidence that health assessment in residential care used to be haphazard and medical services were only used in response to illness rather than preventatively (Utting, 1991). Subsequent evidence indicated that children in care were still missing out on routine vaccinations and medical assessments (Scott et al., 2007), and that limited attention was given to health promotion (Ridley and McCluskey, 2003). One study found young women in care were twice as likely as those living at home to have missed having the Meningococcal C immunisation, while data from

Table 9.3 Children looked after in England continuously for 12 months or more, health indicators 2014–2016

Year	%age with immunisations up to date	%age with teeth checked by a dentist in last year	%age who have had annual/ bi-annual health assessment	%age identified as having a substance misuse problem
2014	87	84	88	4
2015	88	86	90	4
2016	87	84	90	4

2007 suggested only 80 per cent of looked after children, in care for a year or more, were fully up to date with health immunisations (C. Hill, 2009). The most recent data does, however, suggest some improvement in this area. Close to 90 per cent of looked after children have been fully immunised over recent years in England (DfE, 2017a; see Table 9.3) and there is also evidence that the longer children are in care the better their physical health becomes (Meltzer et al., 2003).

Summary

Both pre-care and in-care experiences are important in explaining the poorer educational attainment and mental and physical health of looked after children. Children are likely to enter care with some educational delay, physical health issues and mental health problems, or underlying issues which make the development of mental health problems later on more likely. Once in care there have been, and still remain, some systemic failures in responding fully to looked after children's needs. There remain divergences of opinion as to whether pre-care factors, in-care factors or the interplay between better explain the comparatively poorer outcomes for looked after children.

Support

Education

Carers and significant adults who support and encourage a looked after child's learning and have high, but grounded, expectations of their educational achievement are a key ingredient in their educational success (Jackson and Martin, 1998; Harker et al., 2004; Bentley, 2013; Sebba et al., 2015). Children whose carers have low levels of educational qualifications themselves may need to be provided with additional support for academic work (Jackson, 2010). Peer group influences are also important – having friends who achieve educationally is a supportive factor

(Jackson and Martin, 1998), although the extent to which a young person's friendships can, and perhaps should, be strongly influenced by carers and professionals is open to question.

Good literacy is a key foundation for children's later educational success (Jackson and Martin, 1998), promoting self-esteem, a desire to learn more and providing a child with the platform from which they can explore learning by themselves. Given that many children in care will have had disrupted school experiences and will be behind educationally the importance of targeted support is emphasised. Two schemes which seek to provide such extra support are paired reading, whereby foster carers are supported to read with children in their care for a minimum of three times a week for at least 20 minutes (Osborne et al., 2013), and the Letterbox Club (Griffiths, 2013), whereby reading and mathematics learning materials are attractively packaged and periodically sent directly to a looked after chid, in order to promote their interest and enthusiasm in the learning – the scheme is open to all UK local authorities. The early evaluation of both schemes found notable increases in children's reading skills as well as broadly very positive feedback from children and carers.

Stability and continuity in care and school relationships are important for children's educational attainment – looked after children whose care careers are more stable attain better results (Biehal et al., 2010) while looked after children who have multiple placement moves and changes of school, particularly in the year of their GCSE exams or the year preceding them, do not achieve their potential at GCSE level (O'Sullivan et al., 2013). Young people in care have also been critical of social workers' failure to prioritise their education in placement moves (Harker et al., 2004). We know, however, that some placement moves will be inevitable. Not all placement breakdowns can be prevented and placement moves (as opposed to placement breakdowns) are also likely to occur for many children who are in care for substantial periods of time; due to the structure of fostering placements many children will have planned moves from short-term to medium-term placements before finding a permanent placement (Sinclair et al., 2007). While it can strongly be argued that foster placements should be more flexible and open-ended, we also know there is a huge shortage of them, making this goal very hard to achieve currently. Therefore, the focus should be on minimising any unnecessary placement moves while ensuring that children's schooling is prioritised in any school and placement moves which do occur. Information about a child's educational needs should be transferred to their new school as soon as possible and the child provided with the greatest available support to settle in their new school.

Positive experiences within school are central – young people in care have identified teachers to be the most important people in terms of their educational support (Harker et al., 2004). Gilligan (2000) identified how a child enjoying school can help them develop more broadly by positively impacting on other areas of their emotional, health and social development. Sinclair and colleagues (2005a) provided some empirical support to this – those children who had educational psychologist involvement were more likely to have a stable placement, suggesting that a child receiving tailored educational support, and presumably doing better in school as a result of it, supported the success of their care placement. Gilligan (2000) has also illustrated the value of out-of-school activities for children who have faced adversity. There is evidence that such activities tend to have a small, but positive, impact on children's educational attainment (Gilligan, 2007). Their greater impact is seen in children's wider development: in addition to the specific skills a child develops they can help a child build resilience through giving them a forum where they gain respect and a sense of contribution; through the development of a close relationship with an adult mentor; and through the building of peer networks (Gilligan, 2000; 2007).

Health promotion

Venkatapuram (2011) argues for a capabilities approach to health, whereby people's right to good health is recognised and the supports they need to achieve this are provided to them. In a similar vein, the importance of health promotion with looked after children around good self-care, how to access health services, mental health, physical fitness, healthy eating, sexual health, pregnancy and relationships has been emphasised (SCIE, 2004; Ford et al., 2007; Scott et al., 2007).

Mental well-being

Mental health diagnosis may, unintentionally, lead to increasing stigmatisation of a looked after child. A mental health label can negatively affect the way a child is considered in school, current and potential future care placements and job and training applications, even though it should not. Given that half of all children will meet the criterion for a psychiatric disorder at some point in their youth (Maughan and Collishaw, 2015) and most will overcome these difficulties (Buchanan, 2005) there is an argument that looked after children with less severe mental health difficulties will best be supported through the provision of a settled, nurturing, care placement and a stable educational experience, rather than via formal child psychiatric services (Dozier et al., 2001; Ford et al., 2007).

Looked after children have voiced that they want to be given preferences about available mental health services and whom they can speak to about their problems (Meltzer et al., 2003; Buchanan, 2005), with some voicing active opposition to accessing mental health services which they feel they have not been consulted about attending (Stanley, 2007). There is some evidence that looked after children prefer help and support to be provided through professionals and carers they already know well and trust (Hill, 1999), including support around mental health issues (Piggot et al., 2004; Buchanan, 2005). This suggests there would be merit in providing additional child mental health training to professionals such as carers, health professionals, social workers and teachers who ordinarily work with looked after children such that those with established trusting relationships with a child may be able to give mental health support knowledgeably outside of the provision of specialist mental health services.

Box 9.1 Considerations when there is a prospective mental health diagnosis for a child in care

- What is the meaning of the diagnosis and on what basis is it being made?

- How has, or will, the diagnosis be explained to the child and their carers?

- How will the diagnosis be recorded, who else will know, and what implications will this have for the child now and in the future?

- What are the implications of the diagnosis for the current care of the child?

- What additional support will the diagnosis give rise to for the child and their carers? What expected improvements are envisaged through its provision?

- What are the child's views, and what are the carers' views, about the diagnosis and the proposed additional support?

Equally, formal diagnosis of a psychiatric disorder can facilitate access to a scarce specialist input which is required. Such input may prevent placement breakdown where a placement is under pressure due to these difficulties (Ford et al., 2007), thereby stopping a vicious circle developing. Many of the interventions described in Chapter 3 are examples of specialist support which may be more easily facilitated with a mental health diagnosis. That there appears to be an association between many childhood mental health disorders and educational difficulties suggests that earlier provision of specialist mental health input for some looked after children is required to prevent a downward spiral where one difficulty compounds another (ibid.).

There is also a strong association between childhood mental ill health and adult psychopathology (Rutter and Stevenson, 2010). While it is a strong association rather than a causal link, it suggests the need for appropriate help to be given to children at the time difficulties emerge in order to minimise the chances that mental health difficulties persist, emerge or re-emerge in later life. There is, however, currently a dire shortage of child mental health services based on epidemiological study of the needs of children for such services (Rutter and Stevenson, 2010; Children's Commissioner, 2016). The survey conducted by Meltzer and colleagues (2003) found that less than half of looked after children with a mental health disorder were in touch with child mental health specialists. The extent to which this was because of children refusing, rather than being refused, a service is unclear from the research report. However, it is reasonable to expect that appropriate specialist support should always be offered alongside a formal mental health diagnosis for a looked after child.

In terms of DSED and RAD, attachment theory-informed interventions, play therapy and CBT have been suggested as therapeutic supports (Pearce, 2009). In terms of caregiving, the suggested responses are similar to the general qualities of providing good care more broadly: consistency, persistent warmth and sensitivity while providing clear boundaries (Pearce, 2009). The advice also suggests that caregivers establish a very clear structure for the child, holding appropriate developmental expectations according to developmental stage rather than age, and providing a level of emotional connectedness that the child is able to tolerate and manage (Pearce, 2009). In terms of RAD specifically, children are noted to tend to communicate behaviours and feelings through acting out in unacceptable ways. Therefore, verbalising the child's presenting emotional state back to them is suggested in order to encourage the child to recognise their own emotional and behavioural states, as well as supporting the child to see that their feelings and thoughts have been recognised and understood (Pearce, 2009).

Physical health

Modelling healthy lifestyle choices within the care environment – for example, by providing healthy food options and opportunities for exercise which carers also partake in – is important, as is consistent and open discussion around sexual relationships and substance misuse. The latter may be particularly important for young people who have missed substantial periods of schooling when aspects of personal, social and health education will have been covered (Cairns, 2004; Nelson, 2015). Ensuring that children in care, particularly young people in residential care, have constant access to all conventional health services and information (for example, GP, dentist, school nurse, sexual and personal health information) is also important (Scott et al., 2007). Access to additionally targeted or specialised health care information and support around particular issues such as sexual health and substance misuse will also be needed by some young people. The provision of health services on a more flexible and 'open door access' basis, centred around the needs and likely engagement patterns of young people in care, should be a key consideration for service providers (Scott et al., 2007).

Cairns (2004) emphasises the importance of finding a supportive GP. He describes this as a GP willing to fight for resources to meet the identified health needs a child has, as well as one who is sensitive to their circumstances and presentation at health appointments. Some of the foster children in Cairns' care, particularly those who had been abused, found intimate medical examinations very difficult. On top of this, though statutory guidance requires looked after children over five to have an annual medical, children in his care could find the review an intrusive reminder of their care status. Finally, he notes that some children in care may minimise, exaggerate or appear to invent symptoms as they struggle to express their health and emotional experiences clearly (ibid.).

While total abstention from smoking, alcohol and drug use is the safest health promotion message, it is also one that may be unrealistic for many young people both in care and outside it. Research indicates that the majority of young people who do try drugs will not go on to experience significant harm (DOH, 2002b). Cairns (2004) notes that while young people in their care were prohibited from smoking inside the foster home, they were allowed to do so outside it. He also notes that he and his wife tended to 'take a relatively relaxed position on cannabis' (p. 47), stressing to young people its illegality and the adverse health consequence of using it, but seeing its use as different to 'harder' drugs. Other carers and professionals may take a different position on the rules and boundaries which should apply in this respect – indeed, social attitudes towards smoking have hardened over the last 15 years. However, the importance of open discussion with young people in care around smoking, drug and alcohol use which balances positive health promotion, young people's agency and the avoidance of overly simplistic 'just say no' messages is emphasised.

Where young people have developed serious substance misuse problems, they will need tailored intervention and support. Of those looked after young people with an identified substance misuse problem in England, just over half receive a tailored intervention for their substance use, and around a third were offered an intervention but refused it (DfE, 2017a). There is no national data on the effectiveness of these interventions, but a research trial to investigate them issues is currently under way (Alderson et al., 2017).

Key messages for practice

- The key roles and responsibilities for looked after children's education and health over and above that of the child social worker are the Virtual School Head (VSH), the designated teacher, the designated doctor, the designated nurse, the named GP for looked after children and the named health professional for looked after children.

- Looked after children's educational attainment, mental health and physical well-being are worse than those of children in the general population. However, when compared to children in similarly difficult circumstances living at home, children in care for a year or more do at least as well, if not better, educationally. And, looked after children's physical health is generally good, and mostly improves over time in care. However, looked after children are far more likely than other children to have a diagnosed mental health disorder and, over and above this, to experience mental ill health.

- The explanations of the poorer educational attainment and health well-being of children in care relate to pre-care, in-care experiences and the interplay between them. There are ongoing debates about which is more significant.

- Whatever the causes, the markedly higher levels of mental health needs in looked after children make this a priority area to address in practice. Given that specialist mental health provision is currently far too scarce to meet identified levels of need, practitioners will need to be proactive and persistent in accessing appropriate supports for those children they work with.

Suggested reading

Gilligan, R. (2000) 'Adversity, resilience and young people: The protective value of positive school and spare time experiences', *Children and Society, 14*: pp. 37–47 – An important article on education and extra-curricular activities.

Jackson, S. (ed.) (2013) *Pathways through Education for Young People in Care: Ideas from Research and Practice.* London: BAAF – An excellent resource on policy, practice and research around looked after children's education.

Scott, J., Ward, H. and Hill, M. (2007) 'The health of looked after children in residential child care', in A. Kendrick (ed.) *Residential Child Care: Prospects and Challenges.* London: Jessica Kingsley – Informative chapter focused on residential child care, but which also provides an overview of key physical health issues in respect of looked after children more broadly.

Walker, S. (2003) *Social Work and Child and Adolescent Mental Health.* Lyme Regis: RHP – An incisive and accessible introduction for social workers working with children with mental health issues.

Online resources

The Children's Society has produced a report on promoting children's health and well-being in the UK. Links to the report can be found at: www.childrenssociety.org.uk/what-we-do/research/well-being/publications/promoting-positive-well-being-children

Explore the government statistics on the education of looked after children for yourself: www.gov.uk/government/collections/statistics-looked-after-children – Look under the section titled 'Outcomes for looked-after children'.

Website of the Letterbox Club: www.letterboxclub.org.uk

Notes

1   Following NHS reorganisation in England, since 2013 Clinical Commission Groups (CCGs) have replaced Primary Care Trusts (PCTs) as the commissioners of most health services in England.

2   A 'Child in Need' or 'Young Person in Need' is one who receives social work supervision and support in England and Wales, while living in the community, generally in the full-time care of a birth parent or parents.

CHAPTER 10

LEAVING CARE

Chapter Overview

This chapter focuses on young people leaving care when they 'age out' of care when they reach, or approach, adulthood. Due to their circumstances young people leaving care are likely to have greater needs than young people in the general population and yet they have tended to leave care at an earlier age – between 16 and 18 – while the national average age for leaving home is approximately 25 years old. This chapter considers the historically poor levels of support given to care leavers and the policy and legislative changes which have been introduced to try to address imbalances between the practice support given to care leavers and that given to young people leaving parental care from their birth families. It looks at the mixed impact of these changes by exploring a classification developed by Mike Stein of three types of pathway for care leavers on leaving care. Elements of effective throughcare and post-care support are then discussed, with consideration of the evidence base for effective support around housing, education and young parenthood. While care leavers' experience is varied, with some experiencing smooth transitions, experiences of unemployment, poverty, homelessness and involvement in the criminal justice system are common for a sizeable number in the years after care. Getting the right support to those care leavers facing the greatest challenges remains an ongoing practice challenge.

The developing legislative context for leaving care

In the initial post-war period, the Children Act 1948 set out powers and duties which local authorities had in respect of those young people leaving care. However, following the reorganisation of social services in the 1970s research identified that many of those in care were leaving care at 16 with minimal support (Stein, 2012). The Children Act 1989 started to address this by providing a duty under s.24 to 'advise, assist and befriend young people' leaving care between the ages of 16 and 21. However, rather than giving local authorities specific duties to support care leavers it instead largely gave them discretionary powers. As a result, while some local authorities established specialist leaving care services there was a great variety in the type, quality and effectiveness of leaving care support between different local authority areas (Stein, 2012). The Children (Leaving Care) Act 2000 sought to remedy this imbalance by delaying the age at which young people left care and improving local authorities' assessment, planning and support for transitions from care. The 2000 Act gives local authorities specific duties to:

- Assess and meet the needs of young people leaving care. This includes the mandatory use of a Pathway Plan for every young person in care from the age of 16, which details their future route to independence.

- Assist care leavers until the age of 21, or until 25 if they are in approved education or training programmes, by keeping in touch with them, providing general and financial assistance and supporting them to access suitable accommodation.

The Children and Young Persons Act 2008 further augmented local authority duties by legislating that young people in care must receive a statutory review before leaving care so that they do not leave before they are ready, providing a statutory entitlement to a Personal Adviser and requiring local authorities to provide a bursary for those young people going on to higher education (Stein, 2012). The *Staying Put* policy (explored in greater detail below) was introduced in the Children and Families Act 2014 and places a duty on local authorities to support eligible young people to stay in their foster placement between the ages of 18 and 21 where the young person wishes to do so and their foster carer agrees to this. Finally, the recently enacted Children and Social Work Act 2017 (s.2) requires each local authority in England to publish a 'local offer for care leavers' containing information about services which the local authority provides for care leavers under the Children Act 1989, and other services which the local authority offers that may assist care leavers. Section 3 of the 2017 Act requires local authorities to provide Personal Advisers (who may or may not be qualified social workers) to care leavers up until they reach the age of 25, thereby extending this provision beyond the age of 21 whether or not a young person is in further education or training.

Care leavers' eligibility for entitlement

The Children Act 1989, as updated by subsequent leaving care legislation, provides categories of eligibility for care leavers to receive support. The detailed rules of eligibility are complex but there are four categories of young people about which practitioners should be aware.

1. *Eligible Young People* are those who are still in care at 16 or 17 and have been in care for at least 13 weeks since their 14th birthday. Before the age of 18 they are entitled to a Personal Adviser, a needs assessment and a Pathway Plan.

2. *Relevant Young People* are those aged 16 or 17 who have been in care for at least 13 weeks since their 14th birthday and at some point after 16, but who are no longer in care (for example, they have returned home to parental care at age 16 or 17). They are entitled to a Personal Adviser, a needs assessment, a

Pathway Plan and accommodation and maintenance. A young person, however, ceases to be a *Relevant Young Person* if they have returned to parental care for six months or more, and consequently they will not be entitled to leaving care support on reaching 18. However, if the return home then breaks down before the young person reaches 18, they will once again become a *Relevant Young Person,* with eligibility for support after reaching 18.

3. *Former Relevant Young People* are care leavers aged 18 to 21, or aged up to 25 if in further education or training, who were either *Eligible Young People* or *Relevant Young People.* They are entitled to a Personal Adviser and their Pathway Plan must remain under regular view. The local authority must keep in touch with them, provide general assistance, support with employment, education or training and suitable accommodation and help with living costs. As noted above, following the Children and Social Work Act 2017, *Former Relevant Young People* are entitled to a Personal Adviser and a Pathway Plan up until the age of 25 if they want this, regardless of whether they are in further education or training.

4. *Qualifying Young People* include those who were in care after the age of 16 but who are not *Eligible Young People* or *Relevant Young People* because they do not fulfil the 13-week in care criterion set out above; those young people who have successfully returned home from care for six months or more after reaching 16; and those young people who are in Special Guardianship Order (SGO) arrangements at the age of 16, having been a looked after child directly before the SGO was granted. *Qualifying Young People* are entitled to advice and assistance from their local authority, including some financial assistance and help in securing vacation accommodation where they are in further education. This support lasts until they are 21, or 25 if in further education or training.

Practice Pointer 10.1

Young people's entitlements to leaving care support are important for their future yet complex and difficult to grasp. How can practitioners help young people to understand and enforce their entitlements to support in preparation for leaving care and post-leaving care?

Pathways for young people leaving care

The headline outcomes for care leavers are typically poor. They include high(er) rates of early mortality, offending behaviour and imprisonment, mental health difficulties, homelessness, teenage parenthood and struggles with unemployment, poverty and social isolation (Biehal et al., 1995; Wade and Dixon, 2006; Munro et al., 2012; Scottish Government, 2013). Evidence suggests that outcomes are better for those leaving foster care than residential care (Stein, 2008) but again the issue of comparability arises given that the young people with greater difficulties tend to be in residential provision. These depressing findings do rather mask the fact that outcomes for care leavers are quite varied and some care leavers cope well on leaving care. While international evidence suggests there are poor outcomes for those leaving care in other developed countries, there is also some evidence of more positive outcomes for those leaving small-group residential care in Switzerland and German residential provision where the social pedagogic model is used (Stein, 2008). This illustrates that poor outcomes for those leaving care, and leaving residential care, are far from inevitable. Recognising the variability in outcomes, Stein (2012) outlines a typology of three categories of young people leaving care based on their pathways before and after care, as set out below.

Care Leavers Moving On – This group of care leavers successfully transition from care and will be in education, training or employment which they want to be in. They are likely to have had greater placement stability during their time in care and to have left care gradually. They are more likely to have come to terms with the nature of birth family relationships, and had at least one supportive adult relationship in their lives, be that someone from their care setting, birth family, friendship network or an intimate partner and their family network.

Survivors – This group of care leavers will have experienced considerable instability in the care system and left care earlier than those *Moving On*. While experiencing some of the same difficulties as *Strugglers* in terms of unemployment, homelessness and periods of isolation they are also likely to have some experience of work, if casual and poorly paid, and to be able to overcome some of the key challenges they face with effective, persistent, specialist leaving care support.

Strugglers – This group of care leavers are likely to have had the most difficult pre-care experiences, undergone many placement moves and disruption in care and to have had marked emotional and behavioural difficulties and struggles at school. They are the most likely to have left care at the youngest age and experience the poorest outcomes. *Strugglers* are likely to have poor personal networks of support and to have alienated or refused professional support. While leaving care services are unlikely to be able to fully address the entire range of needs and issues this group of young people encounter, these care leavers can benefit from specialist support which continues to try and work with them despite the difficulties in engagement there are, at times, likely to be.

Practice Pointer 10.2

Mike Stein's classification of those *Moving On*, *Surviving* and *Struggling* strongly suggests that unstable placement histories in care negatively influence the immediate life trajectory of care leavers once they leave care. What can practitioners working with young people approaching adulthood, who have had unstable placement histories, do to better prepare them for life after care?

Leaving care support

Support before leaving care

Support for young people in preparation for leaving care is often termed 'through-care'. Some local authorities have specific throughcare teams with a remit to work with those looked after children who are approaching adulthood, while in others support will be carried out within mainstream child and family social work teams. Young people will leave care between 16 and 18, depending on their circumstances. Where young people are in stable foster, kinship and residential placements this will likely be 18. While there have been moves to try to ensure that as many young people leave care at 18 rather than before, this is dependent on their wishes, which in turn are likely to be influenced by their views and experiences of the care placements available to them. Those young people who are not in stable foster, kinship or residential placements will be offered 'semi-independent' or 'supported lodging' living accommodation. In these kinds of accommodation, support staff are available to help with practical issues and wider advice but they are not necessarily available 24 hours a day, and the accommodation is not subject to the same statutory regulations as apply to children's homes and other residential accommodation.

There is, unsurprisingly, evidence of a connection between services effectively preparing young people prior to leaving care and their ability to cope successfully on leaving care (Dixon and Stein, 2005). Data in a Scottish context, collected in 2000, highlighted that while most authorities offered throughcare programmes, only a minority of young people had been through one and almost three-quarters left care at either 15 or 16. Nearly half of all young people leaving care in the study also reported feeling they had little choice in the matter (Dixon and Stein, 2005). Since 2000, legislative duties on local authorities in Scotland to assess the needs of young people leaving care have been introduced through the Regulation of Care (Scotland) Act 2001 and associated guidance, and it would be expected that leaving care support has improved.

There has been some evidence that specialist leaving care services over-zealously trying to prepare young people for leaving care can inadvertently undermine their established networks of support by encouraging them to move into independent living support as they approach adulthood (Schofield and Ward, 2008; Sinclair et al., 2007). Indeed, the potential importance of foster care as a support for young people beyond the age of 18 has been highlighted (Schofield, 2009), as has the importance of reliable formal and informal supports to which young people can return as and when they require after formally leaving care (Dixon and Stein, 2005; Sinclair et al., 2007).

As noted, it is a statutory requirement in England that every young person must have a Pathway Plan. Under the Children (Leaving Care) Act 2000 this can happen at any point after a young person's 15th birthday but must happen within three months of their 16th birthday. It should be reviewed every three to six months and sooner than that if the young person requests it, or if there is a pressing issue in the young person's life which suggests the plan needs to be reconsidered. The content should be based around a young person's future hopes and goals until they are 25 and the supports they are likely to need to achieve these goals. More specifically, the Pathway Plan should include:

- The personal supports which a young person will have.
- Their accommodation during this time.
- An education and training plan and a plan for employment.
- The family and social relationships a young person has.
- Practical skills support.
- Financial support and issues.
- Health needs and supports.
- Contingency plans if the initial plans do not work out (Wheal, 2005).

More detailed preparation work with a young person is likely to include issues such as:

- Relationships – friendships, personal relationships, sexual health and relationships, family and professional support.
- Accessing support if in difficulty.
- Accessing and safely maintaining identity and other formal documentation, such as exam certificates, which may be needed in the future.
- Accessing health services in the community and what a young person might do to maintain and promote their personal physical and mental well-being.
- The young person's entitlement to financial, housing and professional support on leaving care and what they need to do to access these.
- Making training/university/job applications and learning interview skills.
- Tenancy maintenance – the practicalities of paying rent, managing bills, physically maintaining a flat, respecting tenancy rules.

Post-care support

Wade and Munro (2008) summarise that current evidence suggests leaving care services in the UK can make a considerable positive difference to care leavers by supporting them to find housing and helping them settle in new accommodation. Leaving care services can also be effective in supporting young people to build new networks and social relationships. However, they appear to be less effective at supporting care leavers in accessing training, further and higher education and suitable employment opportunities; at meeting young people's mental health and emotional needs; and at supporting young people to negotiate relationships with their birth families.

The Children and Family Act 2014 has introduced the *Staying Put* policy. This requires local authorities in England to facilitate, monitor and support staying put arrangements for previously fostered young people between the ages of 18 and 21, where this arrangement is wanted by the young person and their former foster carer and where the local authority considers that it is consistent with the young person's welfare.[1]

Staying Put can be viewed as a recognition of the association between unstable care experiences, insecure housing and poor outcomes for care leavers (Dixon and Stein, 2005; Wade and Dixon, 2006) and an acknowledgement of evidence that placements open to young people beyond 18 can be a significant source of support (Sinclair et al., 2005a, 2007). Young people have themselves also voiced the desire for placements to remain open as a source of both formal and informal support (Care Inquiry, 2013). A government-funded evaluation of the pilot of *Staying Put* was generally very positive (Munro et al., 2012). Most foster carers were willing to leave open the placement for the young person they had cared for beyond 18 and in the vast majority of cases it was the young person who determined whether or not to remain in the placement beyond 18. Transitions for those who did 'stay put' were more settled – young people were twice as likely to remain in full-time education and slightly more likely to be in full-time training or employment (ibid.), although this may in part reflect the different characteristics of those care leavers who chose to 'stay put' in the first place.

Since the *Staying Put* programme was made a legislative duty and rolled out nationally, the government has stated that over half of those young people eligible have chosen to take part (Hansard, 2016). It is not clear from this statement how many care leavers were eligible given that 'staying put' requires not only the young person but their former foster carer (or another foster carer) to agree to it, as well as the relevant local authority to approve that it is in the young person's best interests for the arrangement to be made. However, the 2016 government statistics do suggest that there has been a significant uptake of the *Staying Put* offer, with 30 per cent of 19-year-old care leavers and 16 per cent of 20-year-old care leavers still living with their former foster carers (DfE, 2017a).

Some more critical observations of the policy and its implementation have also been made. The first is that, though the government did provide some extra funding to local authorities to meet their new duties under *Staying Put*, it has not been sufficient to meet all of the extra cost (Stevenson, 2015). The second concern is that *Staying Put* has drastically cut some foster carers' incomes (Stevenson, 2017). Though former foster carers are paid an allowance for participating in *Staying Put* arrangements, the allowances are sometimes as little as a third of that which the carer would have received for fostering. This can have significant implications for foster carers' income, particularly when fostering is their main or sole occupation.

There are also suggestions that this aspect of the policy can make those young people 'staying put' feel uncomfortable as a result (Driscoll, 2013). Thirdly, *Staying Put* arrangements are only currently open to those in foster care and not residential care in England. Given that a considerable proportion of older young people in care are in residential provision, and those in residential care tend to have greater levels of needs, this is a considerable gap. The government is currently trialling versions of *Staying Put* for residential care in England (*Staying Close*), though there is at the time of writing no statutory requirement for local authorities to offer it.

Finally, evidence from a study of asylum seeking care leavers suggests it is likely that those young people who do stay in their previous foster placements beyond 18 are those who already had better relationships with their carers, were more engaged in education or training and were generally coping better (Wade et al., 2012). In Stein's typology, those 'staying put' are also those most likely to *Move on* as care leavers. *Survivors* and *Strugglers* – those care leavers with greater levels of need and greater instability and whom need the help the most – are then less likely to benefit. There remains, therefore, an ongoing need to provide flexible housing support and other assistance to those care leavers who do not benefit from *Staying Put*.

Housing and homelessness

Two large-scale studies of leaving care in Scotland (Dixon and Stein, 2005) and England (Dixon et al., 2006; Wade and Dixon, 2006) found that about a third of care leavers were homeless at some point in the two years after leaving care. Though short periods of homelessness did not always lead to longer-term housing insecurity, Wade and Dixon (2006) did identify that housing was a gateway issue such that having secure housing and employment was associated with positive mental well-being as well as a range of other positive outcomes, while the absence of secure housing and employment was associated with poor outcomes for young people. However, the direction of causality is unclear as young people with greater levels of need and more difficult behaviours in the first place are less likely to maintain secure accommodation and employment.

Stein (2012) identifies that certain groups of care leavers will be particularly vulnerable to homelessness: those leaving care at 16 and 17, particularly through placement breakdown; young people with emotional and behavioural difficulties, mental health problems and substance misuse problems; and young offenders leaving secure care. Biehal and colleagues (1995) noted that there was a gendered aspect to housing security for care leavers: young women were twice as likely to sustain a tenancy as young men, due to possessing better practical and social skills. As noted above, housing support, as well as social support, are two areas in which research has found leaving care services have made a clear positive impact on care leavers' welfare (Wade and Munro, 2008). But as Stein's (2012) typology suggests those groups of care leavers with greater difficulties and therefore most in need of care leaving support (*Survivors* and *Strugglers*) are the most likely to either reject or alienate professional and personal support. Therefore consideration needs to be given to providing flexible help for these groups of young people in such a way that it is available for them even after they might have rejected previous offers of help, or engaged in behaviours which have undermined previous efforts to help.

Practice Pointer 10.3

Housing is a 'gateway' issue in that acquisition and maintenance of a secure tenancy is linked to several other positive outcomes for care leavers. Which other professionals will social workers or Personal Advisers need to liaise with in order to support care leavers in securing and maintaining a stable tenancy?

Education, training and unemployment

Few care leavers go on to higher education. In the early 2000s it was estimated that only 1 per cent of care leavers went to university (SEU, 2003). While the latest figures show that 8 per cent of care leavers in 2016 were in higher education (DfE, 2017a) this compares to around half of all young people in the general population (Sebba et al., 2015). Jackson (2010) is critical of what she views as social workers' failure to duly prioritise looked after young people's education post-16. Financial hardship can lead care leavers to drop out of educational opportunities post-16 (Wade and Dixon, 2006), alongside the challenges of managing the challenges of having less social support, greater social demands, and the changes associated with transitioning to leaving care teams and living independently (Driscoll, 2013). Jackson and Ajayi (2007) and Jackson and Cameron (2012) found that tailored support and careers advice, financial funding and encouragement from carers could increase the chances of care leavers entering higher education. It is also important to recognise that those care leavers going into higher education are more likely to take non-linear, and lengthier, paths into it (Jackson and Cameron, 2012).

At the same time, the range of alternatives for training and employment other than higher education need to be acknowledged. Data from the 1990s and 2000s suggested that between half and three-quarters of looked after young people left school with no qualifications and the majority of them did not go on to further education, work or training on leaving school (Francis, 2007). Research suggests that looked after young people attending courses that are suited to where they are at educationally at that point in time is important (Wade et al., 2012). Government statistics from 2016 suggested that a huge 40 per cent of care leavers were not in education, employment or training in 2016 – a proportion which has increased slightly over recent years (DfE, 2017a). One report has identified that while the few care leavers going into higher education are provided with a local authority bursary of at least £2,000, as standard, those following apprenticeship routes or looking for financial support to buy things like smart clothing for interviews face a much harder task in getting such support (CSJ, 2015a).

Practice Pointer 10.4

Sally is an 18-year-old care leaver. You have supported her in making several job applications in the local area. She now has two job interviews next week. One for a position of a server in a fast-food restaurant (which she says she really wants), the other for a position as a receptionist within a local authority library (which she says she doesn't want). Sally is very nervous about both interviews. What would you do to support her?

Young parenthood

Government statistics for 31 March 2017 (DfE, 2017c) indicate that of the young women in care aged 12 and over in England, only a small proportion (2 per cent or 270 young women) were mothers. Both the number and proportion of young mothers in care have also been in decline over the last five years (DfE, 2017a; 2017c). However, a higher proportion of care leavers aged 19–21 – 7 per cent, or 1,780 care leavers in 2016 (DfE, 2017a) – are recorded as being outside of education, employment or training due to pregnancy or parenthood.

This figure is, however, very unlikely to accurately reflect all care leavers who are young parents. Other data have suggested considerably higher rates of young parenthood among care leavers. In the late 1990s it was estimated that young women in care were two and a half times more likely to become pregnant as teenagers than other young people (SCIE, 2004), with looked after young people also more likely to become sexually active at a younger age and have poorer access to sexual health information (ibid.). More recently, a think tank press release claimed that 22 per cent of female care leavers become teenage mothers every year (CSJ, 2015b). Although the source of the data on which this claim is made is not clear from the press release, it is broadly consistent with previous research findings that the proportion of care leavers who become pregnant or young parents within a few years of leaving care is high. One study found that a quarter of care leavers had become, or were due to become, young parents within a year of leaving care (Dixon et al., 2006), while a more dated study found a third of care leavers, and nearly half of young women leaving care, had become parents within two years of leaving care, with over half of the pregnancies unplanned (Biehal et al., 1995).

Parenthood is generally celebrated and it should be acknowledged that young parenthood can be a very positive choice for some care leavers and their children (Dixon et al., 2006). At the same time, research does suggest that those care leavers who are not in secure housing, education, employment or training, or who become involved in substance misuse or offending behaviour, are more likely to become young parents (Biehal et al., 1995; Dixon et al., 2006). There are associations between teenage/young parenthood and greater health complications for expectant mothers (Scott et al., 2007), greater parental experience of educational and health difficulties, social isolation and poverty (Biehal et al., 1995; SCIE, 2004) and poorer outcomes for children (Scott et al., 2007). There are also suggestions that care leavers are themselves considerably more likely than other parents to have their own children placed in state care (Selwyn et al., 2006; CSJ, 2015b).

The provision of targeted sexual health advice and information to young people in care has been suggested as a necessary strategy to reduce teenage parenthood among care leavers (SCIE, 2004). The narratives of care leavers who have become parents suggests that the rewards of parenthood are combined with fears of being seen to be an inadequate parent and having history repeat itself such that their own children are placed in care (Maxwell et al., 2011; Sen, 2016). This suggests the need for professionals to be sensitive to overcoming the potential ambivalence there may be among young care leaving parents when parenting support is offered. Research evidence suggests that young parents do value such input when it is clear it involves providing genuine support rather than just the monitoring of their parenting; Stein (2012) indicates that care leavers have indicated the support they welcome for parenthood includes help finding suitable accommodation; financial support to purchase child clothing and equipment; birthing information and support around pre-natal classes; support to develop parenting skills; efforts to involve young fathers; and linking parents with other peer and professional support networks.

Key messages for practice

- Though there have been considerable advances in support given to care leavers in the UK, it is still likely that care leavers will have a more unsupported transition to early adulthood than many other young people who are living with their birth parents.

- Those care leavers who have experienced greater stability in care and a gradual transition to independence are most likely to have the best outcomes. This transition is likely to be linked to appropriate preparation before leaving care, as well as support to leave care when the young person feels they are ready. The acquisition of stable housing and securing a path into training, education or desired employment are associated with achieving broader well-being.

- A number of other care leavers will have experienced greater instability in the care system and earlier and more abrupt departures from care. It is these young people who are likely to both require support the most and be the most difficult to engage in leaving care work. However, persistent and empathic support from leaving care services can make a very positive difference to them. Indeed, care leavers' pathways in the immediate years after leaving care tend to be very influential on a young person's later adult life course.

Suggested reading

Stein, M. (2012) *Young People Leaving Care: Supporting Pathways to Adulthood*. London: Jessica Kingsley – Comprehensive text written by a researcher whose work has done much to raise the profile of care leavers' needs and perspectives.

Wheal, A. (2005) *The Leaving Care Handbook: Helping and Supporting Care Leavers*. Lyme Regis: RHP – Edited collection providing detailed, practical advice on preparing and supporting care leavers.

Online resources

Two well-known charities that provide support, advocacy and information for care leavers are:

The Care Leavers' Association: www.careleavers.com

Rees, Care Leavers Foundation: www.reesfoundation.org

Note

1   Though operating slightly differently, the equivalent of *Staying Put* policies operate in Northern Ireland as the *Going the Extra Mile Scheme*, in Scotland as *Staying Put Scotland*, and in Wales as *When I am Ready: Planning Transitions to Adulthood*.

CONCLUSION

Looked after children share in common the fact that they are not living with their birth parents and are formally cared for by the state. They are a 'vulnerable' group of young people both because of this fact and because many will have had challenging backgrounds prior to entering care which may include difficult family relationships and experiences of being parented; managing disabilities; experience of fleeing persecution abroad; experience of poverty and poor-quality housing; and experience of neglect or abuse. Social work practice with looked after children will have either a positive or a negative impact on their lives, and some practice decisions can have profound implications for looked after children's future life courses.

A number of looked after children fare very well. A number experience difficulties but manage to overcome these with time. And a number struggle. Those who do better tend to have more stable placements and relationships in care; those who do less well experience far more fragmented placement experiences and relationships. These differences within care tend to be exacerbated on leaving care, and the early years of adulthood tend to be highly influential in shaping most young people's future life courses; though some care leavers will succeed in 'turning their lives around' after experiencing great challenges in early adulthood, it becomes increasingly difficult for any adult to do so as the life course progresses. It also needs to be recognised that looked after children and care leavers are a diverse group of people with their own particular histories, characteristics and individuality who will also exercise their own agency as to how they set about trying to achieve their life aspirations. Social workers and carers need to balance realism about the challenges which looked after children face in care, and on leaving care, with respect for their ability to make their own choices, and optimism and belief about what they can achieve with the correct support.

REFERENCES

ARI (Adoption Research Initiative) (2011a) 'Summary 4: Family finding and matching A survey of adoption agency practice in England and Wales'. Available at: www.adoption-researchinitiative.org.uk/summaries/ARi_summary_4.pdf.

ARI (Adoption Research Initiative) (2011b) 'Summary 5: An investigation of family finding and matching in adoption'. Available at: www.adoptionresearchinitiative.org.uk/summaries/ARi_summary_5.pdf.

Adoption Support Fund (2017) Adoption Support Fund Q&A. Available at: www.adoption-supportfund.co.uk/FAQs.

Ainsworth, M.D.S., Bell, S. and Stayton, D. (1971) 'Individual differences in strange-situation behaviour of one-year-olds', in H. Schaffer (ed.), *The Origins of Human Social Relations.* New York: Academic Press.

Alderson, H., McGovern, R., Brown, R., Howel, D., Becker, F., Carr, L., Copello, A., Fouweather, T., Kaner, E., McArdle, P., McColl, E., Shucksmith, J., Steele, A., Vale, L. and Lingam, R. (2017) 'Supporting Looked After Children and Care Leavers In Decreasing Drugs, and Alcohol (SOLID): Protocol for a pilot feasibility randomised controlled trial of interventions to decrease risky substance use (drugs and alcohol) and improve mental health of looked after children and care leavers aged 12–20 years', *Pilot and Feasibility Studies, 3* (1): 25.

Aldgate, J. and Bradley, M. (1999) *Supporting Families Through Short-Term Fostering.* London: The Stationery Office.

Aldgate, J. and MacIntosh, M. (2006) *Looking After the Family: A Study of Children Looked After in Kinship Care in Scotland.* Edinburgh: SWIA. Available at: www.gov.scot/Publications/2006/06/07132800/14.

APA (American Psychiatric Association) (1994) *Diagnostic and Statistical Manual of Mental Disorders,* 4th Edition. Washington, DC: APA.

APA (American Psychiatric Association) (2013) *Diagnostic and Statistical Manual of Mental Disorders,* 5th Edition. Washington, DC: APA.

Ariès, P. (1982) 'The discovery of childhood', in C. Jenks (ed.), *The Sociology of Childhood Essential Readings.* London: Batsford.

Ashley, C. and Nixon, P. (eds) (2007) *Family Group Conferences: Where Next? Policies and Practices for the Future.* London: Family Rights Group.

Austerberry, H., Stanley, N., Larkins, C., Ridley, J., Farrelly, N., Manthorpe, J. and Hussein, S. (2013) 'Foster carers and family contact: Foster carers' views of social work support', *Adoption and Fostering, 37* (2): 116–129.

BAAF (2006) *Attachment Disorders, their Assessment and Intervention/Treatment. BAAF Position Statement 4.* London: BAAF.

BASW (British Association of Social Workers) (2016) 'Adoptions – a social work enquiry'. Available at: www.basw.co.uk/adoption-enquiry/.

Baker, C. (2007) 'Disabled children's experience of permanency in the looked after system', *British Journal of Social Work, 37* (7): 1173–1188.

Bakermans-Kranenburg, M.J., Van IJzendoorn, M.H. and Juffer, F. (2003) 'Less is more: Meta-analyses of sensitivity and attachment interventions in early childhood', *Psychological Bulletin, 129* (2): 95–215.

Bakermans-Kranenburg, M.J., Van IJzendoorn, M.H. and Juffer, F. (2005) 'Disorganized infant attachment and preventative interventions: A review and meta-analysis', *Infant Mental Health Journal, 26* (3): 191–216.

Ballantyne, N., Duncalf, Z. and Daly, E. (2010) 'Corporate parenting in the network society', *Journal of Technology in Human Services, 28* (1–2): 95–107.

Bandura, A. (1977) *Social Learning Theory.* New York: General Learning Press.

Barn, R. and Kirton, D. (2012) 'Transracial adoption in Britain: Politics, ideology and reality', *Adoption and Fostering, 36* (3–4): 25–37.

Barter, C., Renold, E., Berridge, D. and Cawson, P. (2004) *Peer Violence in Children's Residential Care.* Hampshire: Palgrave.

Barth, R.P., Crea, T.M., John, K., Thoburn, J. and Quinton, D. (2005) 'Beyond attachment theory and therapy: Towards sensitive and evidence-based interventions with foster and adoptive families in distress', *Child and Family Social Work, 10* (4): 257–268.

Barth, R.P. and Lee, B.R. (2014) 'Common elements and common factors approaches to evidence-informed children's services: Stacking the building blocks of effective practice', in A. Shlonksy and R. Benenishty (eds), *From Evidence to Outcomes in Child Welfare: An International Reader.* Oxford: Oxford University Press.

Baumrind, D. (1967) 'Child care practices anteceding three patterns of preschool behavior', *Genetic Psychology Monographs, 75* (1): 43–88.

Baynes, P. (2008) 'Untold stories: A discussion of life story work', *Adoption and Fostering, 32* (2): 43–49.

Bebbington, A. and Miles, J. (1989) 'The background of children who enter local authority care', *British Journal of Social Work, 19* (1): 349–368.

Beck, A.T. (1991) *Cognitive Therapy and the Emotional Disorders.* New York: Penguin.

Beckett, H. (2011) *Not A World Away: The Sexual Exploitation of Children and Young People in Northern Ireland.* Belfast: Barnado's.

Beek, M. and Schofield, G. (2004) *Providing a Secure Base in Long-Term Foster Care.* London: BAAF.

Bell, M. (2011) *Promoting Children's Rights in Social Work and Social Care: A Guide to Participatory Practice.* London: Jessica Kingsley.

Bentley, C.I. (2013) 'Great expectations: Supporting "unrealistic" aspirations for children in care', in S. Jackson (ed.), *Pathways Through Education for Young People in Care: Ideas from Research and Practice.* London: BAAF.

Berridge, D. (1997) *Foster Care a Research Review.* London: The Stationery Office.

Berridge, D. (2007) 'Theory and explanation in child welfare: Education and looked-after children', *Child and Family Social Work, 12* (1): 1–10.

Berridge, D., Biehal, N. and Henry, L. (2012) *Living in Children's Residential Homes. DfE Research Report 201.* London: Department for Education.

Berridge, D., Biehal, N., Lutman, E., Henry, L. and Palomares, M. (2011) *Raising the Bar? Evaluation of the Social Pedagogy Pilot in Residential Children's Homes.* London: Department for Education.

Berridge, D. and Brodie, I. (1998) *Children's Homes Revisited.* London: Jessica Kingsley.

Berridge, D. and Cleaver, H. (1987) *Foster Home Breakdown.* Oxford: Blackwell.

Berridge, D., Henry, L., Jackson, S. and Turney, D. (2009) *Looked After and Learning: Evaluation of the Virtual School Head Pilot.* London: DCSF.

Berridge, D., Holmes, L., Wood, M., Mollidor, C., Knibbs, S. and Bierman, R. (2016) *RESuLT training, Evaluation Report*. London: DfE.

Berridge, D. and Saunders, H. (2009) 'The education of fostered and adopted children', in G. Schofield and J. Simmonds (eds), *The Child Placement Handbook, Research, Policy and Practice*. London: BAAF.

Biehal, N. (2006) *Reuniting Looked After Children with Their Families. A Review*. London: National Children's Bureau.

Biehal, N. (2007) 'Reuniting children with their families: Reconsidering the evidence on timing, contact and outcomes', *British Journal of Social Work, 37* (5): 807–824.

Biehal, N. (2014) 'Maltreatment in foster care: A review of the evidence', *Child Abuse Review, 23* (1): 48–60.

Biehal, N., Clayden, J., Stein, M. and Wade, J. (1995) *Moving On: Young People and Leaving Care Schemes*. London: HMSO.

Biehal, N., Dixon, J., Parry, E., Sinclair, I., Green, J., Roberts, C., Kay, C., Rothwell, J., Kapadia, D. and Roby, A. (2012) *The Care Placements Evaluation (CaPE) Evaluation of Multidimensional Treatment Foster Care for Adolescents (MTFC-A)*, Research Report, RR 194. London: DfE.

Biehal, N., Ellison, S., Baker, C. and Sinclair, I. (2010) *Belonging and Permanence: Outcomes in Long-term Foster Care and Adoption*. London: BAAF.

Biehal, N., Ellison, S. and Sinclair, I. (2011) 'Intensive fostering: An independent evaluation of MTFC in an English setting', *Children and Youth Services Review, 33*: 2043–2049.

Bilson, A. (2016) *Written Submission to BASW's Adoption Enquiry*, Unpublished report. London: British Association of Social Workers.

Bilson, A. and Barker, R. (1995) 'Parental contact with children fostered and in residential care after the Children Act 1989', *The British Journal of Social Work, 25* (3): 367–381.

Boddy, J. (2013) *Understanding Permanence for Looked after Children: A Review of Research for the Care Inquiry*. The Care Inquiry, Online.

Bond, C., Woods, K., Humphrey, N., Symes, W. and Green, L. (2013) 'Practitioner review: The effectiveness of solution focused brief therapy with children and families: A systematic and critical evaluation of the literature from 1990–2010', *Journal of Child Psychology and Psychiatry, 54* (7): 707–723.

Borland, M., Hill, M., Laybourn, A. and Stafford, A. (2001) *Improving Consultation with Children and Young People in Relevant Aspects of Policy-Making and Legislation in Scotland*. Edinburgh: The Stationery Office.

Borland, M., Pearson, C., Hill, M., Tisdall, K. and Bloomfield, I. (1998) *Education and Care Away from Home*. Edinburgh: The Scottish Council for Research in Education.

Borthwick, S. and Donnelly, S. (2013) *Concurrent Planning – Achieving Early Permanence for Babies and Young Children*. London: BAAF.

Bourne, J. (2005) 'Education for children and young people in care', in A. Wheal (ed.), *The RHP Companion to Foster Care*. Lyme Regis: RHP Publishing.

Bowlby, J. (1951) *Maternal Care and Mental Health*. Geneva: World Health Organization.

Bowlby, J. (1997) [1969] *Attachment and Loss, Volume I: Attachment*. New York: Basic Books.

Bowyer, S., Wilkinson, J. and Gadsby Waters, J. (2015) *Impact of the Family Justice Reforms on Front-line Practice Phase Two: Special Guardianship Orders*. London: Department for Education.

Boyle, C. (2017) '"What is the impact of birth family contact on children in adoption and long-term foster care?" A systematic review', *Child and Family Social Work, 22* (1): 22–33.

Brandon, M., Bailey, S., Belderson, P., Gardner, R., Sidebotham, P., Dodsworth, J., Warren, C. and Black, J. (2009) *Understanding Serious Case Reviews and their Impact: A Biennial Analysis of Serious Case Reviews 2005–7*. Research Report DCSF-RR129. London: Department for Children Schools and Families.

Brandon, M. and Thoburn, J. (2008) 'Safeguarding children in the UK: A longitudinal study of services to children suffering or likely to suffer significant harm', *Child and Family Social Work*, 13 (4): 365–377.

Bratton, S.C., Ray, D., Rhine, T. and Jones, L. (2005) 'The efficacy of play therapy with children: A meta-analytic review of treatment outcomes', *Professional Psychology: Research and Practice*, 36 (4): 376–290.

Broad, B. (2008) *Aspirations: The Views of Foster Children and their Carers*. London: The Adolescent and Children's Trust.

Brodzinsky, D.M. (2006) 'Family structural openness and communication openness as predictors in the adjustment of adopted children', *Adoption Quarterly*, 9 (4): 1–18.

Bronfenbrenner, U. (1979) *The Ecology of Human Development*. Cambridge, MA: Harvard University Press.

Brown, K. (2015) *Vulnerability and Young People, Care and Social Control in Policy and Practice*. Bristol: Policy Press.

Brown, L. and Sen, R. (2014) 'Improving outcomes for looked after children: A critical analysis of kinship care', *Practice: Social Work in Action*, 26 (3): 161–180.

Brown, R. and Ward, H. (2013) *Decision Making within a Child's Timeframe*. Loughborough: Childhood Wellbeing Research Centre. Available at: www.gov.uk/government/uploads/system/uploads/attachment_data/file/200471/Decision-making_within_a_child_s_timeframe.pdf.

Buchanan, A. (2005) 'The mental health of children who are fostered', in A. Wheal (ed.), *The RHP Companion to Foster Care*, Lyme Regis: RHP Publishing.

Bullock, R., Courtney, M.E., Parker, R., Sinclair, I. and Thoburn, J. (2006) 'Can the corporate state parent?', *Children and Youth Services Review*, 28 (11): 1344–1358.

Byrne, J.G., O'connor, T.G., Marvin, R.S., and Whelan, W.F. (2005) 'Practitioner review: The contribution of attachment theory to child custody assessment', *Journal of Child Psychology and Psychiatry*, 46 (2): 115–127.

Bywaters, P., Brady, G., Sparks, T. and Bos, E. (2016) 'Inequalities in child welfare intervention rates: The intersection of deprivation and identity', *Child and Family Social Work*, 21 (4): 452–463.

The Care Inquiry (2013) *Making Not Breaking: Building Relationships for Our Most Vulnerable Children. Findings and Recommendations of the Care Inquiry*. Care Inquiry, Online.

Cairns, B. (2004) *Fostering Attachments: Long-term Outcomes in Family Group Care*. London: BAAF.

Cameron, C. and Boddy, J. (2008) 'Staff, training and recruitment: Outcomes for young people in residential care in three countries', in A. Kendrick (ed.), *Residential Child Care, Prospects and Challenges*. London: Jessica Kingsley.

Cameron, C. and Moss, P. (eds) (2011) *Social Pedagogy and Working with Children and Young People: Where Care and Education Meet*. London: Jessica Kingsley.

Campbell, S. and Harrington, V. (2000) *Youth Crime: Findings from the 1998/99 Youth Lifestyles Survey, Research Findings No. 126*. London: Home Office. Available at: http://webarchive.nationalarchives.gov.uk/20110218143155/http://rds.homeoffice.gov.uk/rds/pdfs/r126.pdf.

Carroll, R. (2015) 'For years the stories of adoptive children were not heard. That's finally changing', *The Guardian*, 28 November.

Chamberlain, P. (2003) 'The Oregon multidimensional treatment foster care model: Features, outcomes, and progress in dissemination', *Cognitive and Behavioral Practice, 10* (4): 303–312.

Children's Commissioner for England (2016) *Lightning Review: Access to Child and Adolescent Mental Health Services, May 2016.* London: Children's Commissioner.

Child Law Advice (2017) 'Special Guardianship'. Available at: http://childlawadvice.org.uk/information-pages/special-guardianship/.

Churchill, H. (2013) 'Retrenchment and restructuring: Family support and children's services reform under the coalition', *Journal of Children's Services, 8* (3): 209–222.

Cicchetti, D. (2010) 'Resilience under conditions of extreme stress: A multilevel perspective', *World Psychiatry, 9* (3): 145–154.

Clapton, G. and Clifton, J. (2016) 'The birth fathers of adopted children: Differences and continuities over a 30-year period', *Adoption and Fostering, 40* (2): 153–166.

Cleaver, H. (2000) *Fostering Family Contact.* London: HMSO.

Colton, M.J. (1988) *Dimensions of Substitute Child Care: A Comparative Study of Foster and Residential Care Practice.* Aldershot: Gower.

Connelly, G. and Milligan, I. (2012) *Residential Child Care.* Edinburgh: Dunedin.

CoramBAAF (2016) *Prospective Adopter's Report: Guidance Note and Additional Resources.* London: CoramBAAF. Available at: http://corambaaf.org.uk/webfm_send/4592.

Corsaro, W.A. (2004) *The Sociology of Childhood,* 2nd Edition. Thousand Oaks: Pine Forge Press.

Coulshed, V. and Orme, J. (2012) *Social Work Practice,* 5th Edition. Palgrave: Basingstoke.

Cousins, J. (2009) 'Placing disabled children with permanent new families', in G. Schofield and J. Simmonds (eds), *Child Placement Handbook.* London: BAAF.

Coy, M. (2009) '"Moved around like bags of rubbish nobody wants": How multiple placement moves can make young women vulnerable to sexual exploitation', *Child Abuse Review, 18* (4): 254–266.

Coyle, S. (2008) *Lawyer for the Child: The Road Ahead? Role of the Lawyer for the Child, Child Law Conference 2008.* Auckland: LexisNexis.

Crittenden, P.M., Claussen, A.H. and Kozlowska, K. (2007) 'Choosing a valid assessment of attachment for clinical use: A comparative study', *Australian and New Zealand Journal of Family Therapy, 28* (2): 78–87.

CSJ (Centre for Social Justice) (2015a) *Finding their Feet, Equipping Care Leavers to Reach Their Potential.* London: CSJ. Available at: www.centreforsocialjustice.org.uk/core/wpcontent/uploads/2016/08/Finding.pdf.

CSJ (Centre for Social Justice) (2015b) 'Press release: Nearly a quarter of girls in care become teenage mothers, reveals CSJ'. Available at: www.centreforsocialjustice.org.uk/core/wp-content/uploads/2016/08/CSJ-press-release-care-16.01.15.pdf.

CYPSP (2017) *Children and Young Peoples Strategic Partnership.* Available at: www.cypsp.org/children-and-young-peoples-strategic-partnership/.

Dale, P. (2013) 'Restrictions on natural parent contact with infants during care proceedings where forced adoption may be the outcome: Some cautions about recent research and developing practice', *Families, Relationships and Societies, 2* (2): 175–191.

Daniel, B., Wassell, S. and Gilligan, R. (2010) *Child Development for Child Care and Protection Workers,* 2nd Edition. London: Jessica Kingsley.

DCSF (Department for Children, Schools and Families) (2007) *Care Matters: Time for Change,* White Paper. London: DCSF.

DCSF (Department for Children, Schools and Families) (2010a) *Care Planning, Placement and Case Review (England), Regulations 2010.* London: DCSF.

DCSF (Department for Children, Schools and Families) (2010b) *Statutory Guidance on How to Safeguard and Promote the Welfare of Disabled Children Using Short Breaks.* London: DCSF.

DCSF (Department for Children, Schools and Families) and DOH (Department of Health) (2009) *Statutory Guidance on Promoting the Health and Well-being of Looked After Children.* London: DCSF and DOH.

Delgado, S.V. (2008) 'Psychodynamic psychotherapy for children and adolescents: An old friend revisited', *Psychiatry (Edgmont),* 5 (5): 67–72.

de Shazer, S. (1994) *Words Were Originally Magic.* New York: Norton.

DfE (Department for Education) (2010) *Improving Outcomes for Children and Young People and Families: A National Prospectus.* London: DfE.

DfE (Department for Education) (2011a) *An Action Plan for Adoption: Tackling Delay.* London: DfE.

DfE (Department for Education) (2011b) *Adoption Guidance, Adoption and Children Act 2002, First revision, February 2011.* London: DfE.

DfE (Department for Education) (2011c) *The Fostering Services (England) Regulations 2011.* London: DfE.

DfE (Department for Education) (2013a) '£16 million boost to attract more adopters'. Available at: www.gov.uk/government/news/16-million-boost-to-attract-more-adopters.

DfE (Department for Education) (2013b) *Assessment and Approval of Foster Carers: Amendments to the Children Act 1989 Guidance and Regulations Volume 4: Fostering Services.* London: DfE.

DfE (Department for Education) (2014a) *Adoption: National Minimum Standards.* London: DfE.

DfE (Department for Education) (2014b) *The Children Act 1989 Guidance and Regulations, Volume 2: Care Planning, Placement and Case Review Care Planning, Placement and Case Review [supplement], Looked after Children and Youth Justice.* London: DfE.

DfE (Department for Education) (2014c) *Draft Statutory Guidance on Adoption in England.* London: DfE.

DfE (Department for Education) (2014d) *Promoting the Education of Looked after Children Statutory Guidance for Local Authorities.* London: DfE. Available at: www.legislation.gov.uk/uksi/2015/495/pdfs/uksi_20150495_en.pdf.

DfE (Department for Education) (2014e) 'Policy Paper: Improving the adoption system and services for looked after children'. Available at: www.gov.uk/government/publications/2010-to-2015-government-policy-looked-after-children-and-adoption/2010-to-2015-government-policy-looked-after-children-and-adoption.

DfE (Department for Education) (2015a) *The Care Planning and Fostering (Miscellaneous Amendments) (England) Regulations 2015.* London: DfE.

DfE (Department for Education) (2015b) *The Children Act 1989 Guidance and Regulations, Volume 2: Care Planning, Placement and Case Review Care Planning, Placement and Case Review.* London: DfE.

DfE (Department for Education) (2015c) 'National Roll-out of the Adoption Support Fund'. Available at: www.gov.uk/government/uploads/system/uploads/attachment_data/file/416050/Letter_to_DCSs-Adoption_Support_Fund.pdf.

DfE (Department for Education) (2016) *Special Guardianship (Amendments) Regulations 2016.* London: DfE.

DfE (Department for Education) (2017a) *Children Looked After in England Including Adoption: 2015 to 2016 National tables: SFR41/2016.* London: DfE. Available at:

www.gov.uk/government/statistics/children-looked-after-in-england-including-adoption-2015-to-2016.

DfE (Department for Education) (2017b) *Children Looked After in England Including Adoption 2016 to 2017*. London: DfE: Local authority tables: SFR50/2017. Available at: www.gov.uk/government/statistics/children-looked-after-in-england-including-adoption-2016-to-2017.

DfE (Department for Education) (2017c) *Children Looked After in England Including Adoption 2016 to 2017, National tables: SFR50/2017*. London: DfE. Available at: www.gov.uk/government/statistics/children-looked-after-in-england-including-adoption-2016-to-2017.

DfE (Department for Education) (2017d) 'Guidance, Pupil premium 2016 to 2017: Conditions of grant'. Available at: www.gov.uk/government/publications/pupil-premium-conditions-of-grant-2016-to-2017/pupil-premium-2016-to-2017-conditions-of-grant.

DfE (Department for Education) (2017e) *Outcomes for Children Looked After by LAs: 31 March 2016. National tables: SFR12/2017*. London: DfE. Available at: www.gov.uk/government/collections/statistics-looked-after-children.

DfES (Department for Education and Skills) (2003) *Every Child Matters*. London: DfES.

DfES (Department for Education and Skills) (2005) *The Special Guardianship Regulations 2005*. London: DfES.

DfE (Department for Education) and DOH (Department of Health) (2015) *Promoting the Health and Well-Being of Looked-After Children: Statutory Guidance for Local Authorities, Clinical Commissioning Groups in NHS England*. London: DfE and DOH.

Dickerson, A. and Popli, G.K. (2016) 'Persistent poverty and children's cognitive development: Evidence from the UK Millennium Cohort Study', *Journal of the Royal Statistical Society: Series A (Statistics in Society)*, *179* (2): 535–558.

Dixon, J. and Stein, M. (2005) *Leaving Care: Throughcare and Aftercare in Scotland*. London: Jessica Kingsley.

Dixon, J., Wade, J., Byford, S., Weatherly, H. and Lee, J. (2006) *Young People Leaving Care: A Study of Costs and Outcomes*. London: DfES.

DOH (Department of Health) (1995) *Looking After Children: Good parenting, Good Outcomes*. London: HMSO.

DOH (Department of Health) (1998a) *Caring for Children Away from Home: Messages from Research*. Chichester: John Wiley & Sons.

DOH (Department of Health) (1998b) *Quality Protects*. London: DOH.

DOH (Department of Health) (2000a) *Assessing Children in Need and Their Families: Practice Guidance*. London: The Stationery Office.

DOH (Department of Health) (2000b) *Adoption a New Approach,* White Paper, Cm 5017. London: The Stationery Office.

DOH (Department of Health) (2002a) *National Minimum Standards for Children's Homes*. London: The Stationery Office.

DOH (Department of Health) (2002b) *Promoting the Health of Looked After Children*. London: DOH.

Doolan, P., Nixon, P. and Lawrence, P. (2004) *Growing up in the Care of Relatives or Friends: Delivering Best Practice in Family and Friends Care*. London: Family Rights Group.

Dozier, M. (2003) 'Attachment-based treatment for vulnerable children', *Attachment and Human Development*, *5* (3): 253–257.

Dozier, M., Stoval, K.C., Albus, K.E. and Bates, B. (2001) 'Attachment for infants in foster care: The role of caregiver state of mind', *Child Development*, *72* (5): 1467–1477.

Driscoll, J. (2013) 'Supporting care leavers to fulfil their educational aspirations: Resilience, relationships and resistance to help', *Children and Society*, *27* (2): 139–149.

Elwood, C. (2013) *HM Inspectorate of Prisons Youth Justice Board, Children and Young People in Custody 2012–13*. London: The Stationery Office.

Fahlberg, V. (2012) *A Child's Journey Through Placement*. London: BAAF.

Family Law Week (2013) '*R (on the application of X) v London Borough of Tower Hamlets [2013] EWHC 480 (Admin)*. Available at: www.familylawweek.co.uk/site.aspx?i=ed112455.

Farmer, E. (2009) 'Reunification with birth families', in G. Schofield and J. Simmonds (eds), *The Child Placement Handbook: Research, Policy and Practice*. London: BAAF.

Farmer, E. (2014) 'Improving reunification practice: Pathways home, progress and outcomes for children returning from care to their parents', *British Journal of Social Work, 44* (2): 348–366.

Farmer, E. and Moyers, S. (2008) *Kinship Care: Fostering Effective Family and Friends Placements*. London: Jessica Kingsley.

Farmer, E., Moyers, S. and Lipscome, S. (2004) *Fostering Adolescents*. London: Jessica Kingsley.

Farmer, E. and Parker, R.A. (1991) *Trials and Tribulations: Returning Children from Local Authority Care to their Families*. London: The Stationery Office.

Farmer, E. and Wijedasa, D. (2013) 'The reunification of looked after children with their parents: What contributes to return stability?', *British Journal of Social Work, 43* (8): 1611–1629.

Featherstone, B., Gupta, A. and Mills, S. (2018) *The Role of the Social Worker in Adoption – Ethics And Human Rights: An Enquiry*. London: BASW.

Featherstone, B., White, S. and Morris, K. (2014) *Re-Imaging Child Protection: Towards Humane Social Work with Families*. Bristol: Policy Press.

Fenton-Glynn, C. (2016) *Adoption with Consent, Update 2016 Policy Department for Citizens' Rights and Constitutional Affairs*. Brussels: European Parliament.

Fernandez, E. (2012) *Accomplishing Permanency: Reunification Pathways and Outcomes for Foster Children*. New York: Springer.

First4adoption (2017) The adoption process. Available at: www.first4adoption.org.uk/the-adoption-process/.

Fisher, P. and Chamberlain, P. (2000) 'Multi-dimensional treatment foster care: A program for intensive parenting, family support and skill building', *Journal of Emotional and Behavioural Disorders, 8* (3): 155–164.

Fonagy, P., Steele, M., Higgitt, H. and Target, M. (1994) 'The theory and practice of resilience', *Journal of Child Psychology and Psychiatry, 35* (2): 231–257.

Fonagy, P., Target, M., Cottrell, D., Phillips, J. and Kurtz, Z. (2002) *What Works for Whom? A Critical Review of Treatments for Children and Adolescents*. New York: The Guildford Press.

Ford, T., Vostanis, P., Meltzer, H., Goodman, R. and Ord, T.F. (2007) 'Psychiatric disorder among British children looked after by local authorities: Comparison with children living in private households', *British Journal of Psychiatry, 190* (4): 319–325.

Forrester, D., Goodman, K., Cocker, C., Binnie, C. and Jensch, G. (2009) 'What is the impact of public care on children's welfare? A review of research findings from England and Wales and their policy implications', *Journal of Social Policy, 38* (3): 439–456.

Forrester, D., Westlake, D. and Glynn, G. (2012) 'Parental resistance and social worker skills: Towards a theory of motivational social work', *Child and Family Social Work, 17* (2): 118–129.

The Fostering Network (2017) 'Recruitment targets'. Available at: www.thefosteringnetwork.org.uk/advice-information/all-about-fostering/recruitment-targets.

Fox Harding, L.M. (1991) 'The Children Act 1989 in context: Four perspectives in child care law and policy (I)', *The Journal of Social Welfare and Family Law, 13* (3): 179–193.

Francis, J. (2007) 'Could Do Better!' Supporting the Education of Looked-after Children' in A. Kendrick (ed.), *Residential Child Care, Prospects and Challenges*, London: Jessica Kingsley.

Freeman, P. and Hunt, J (1998) *Parental Perspective on Care Proceedings*. London: The Stationery Office.

Fursland, E. (2010) *Facing Up to Facebook: A Survival Guide for Adoptive Families*. London: BAAF.

Fursland, E. (2011) *Foster Care and Social Networking: A Guide for Social Workers and Foster Carers*. London: BAAF.

Gallagher, B. (2000) 'The extent and nature of known cases of institutional child sexual abuse', *British Journal of Social Work, 30* (6): 795–817.

George, V. (1970) *Foster Care*. London: Routledge and Kegan Paul.

Gilbert, N., Parton, N. and Skivenes, M. (eds) (2011) *Child Protection Systems: International Trends and Orientations*. New York: Oxford University Press.

Gilligan, R. (1997) 'Beyond Permanence? The importance of resilience in child placement practice and planning', *Adoption and Fostering, 21*: 12–20.

Gilligan, R. (2000) 'Adversity, resilience and young people: The protective value of positive school and spare time experiences', *Children and Society, 14* (1): 37–47.

Gilligan, R. (2007) 'Spare time activities for young people in care: What can they contribute to educational progress?', *Adoption and Fostering, 31* (1): 92–99.

Glaser, D. (2000) 'Child abuse and neglect and the brain – a review', *The Journal of Child Psychology and Psychiatry and Allied Disciplines, 41* (1): 97–116.

Goodley, D. (2014) *Dis/Ability Studies, Theorising Disabilism and Ableism*. London: Routledge.

Goodman, R. and Scott, S. (2012) *Child and Adolescent Psychiatry*, 3rd Edition. Chichester: Wiley-Blackwell.

Goodyer, A. (2011) *Child-Centred Foster Care, A Rights-Based Model for Practice*. London: Jessica Kingsley.

Granqvist, P., Sroufe, L.A., Dozier, M., Hesse, E., Steele, M., van Ijzendoorn, M., Solomon, J., Schuengel, C., Fearon, P., Bakermans-Kranenburg, M., Steele, H., Cassidy, J., Carlson, E., Madigan, S., Jacobvitz, D., Foster, S., Behrens, K., Rifkin-Graboi, A., Gribneau, N., Spangler, G., Ward, M.J., True, M., Spieker, S., Reijman, S., Reisz, S., Tharner, A., Nkara, F., Goldwyn, R., Sroufe, J., Pederson, D., Pederson, D., Weigand, R., Siegel, D., Dazzi, N., Bernard, K., Fonagy, P., Waters, E., Toth, S., Cicchetti, D., Zeanah, C.H., Lyons-Ruth, K., Main, M. and Duschinsky, R. (2017) 'Disorganized attachment in infancy: A review of the phenomenon and its implications for clinicians and policy-makers', *Attachment and Human Development, 19* (6): 534–558.

Gray, M., Plath, D. and Webb, S.A. (2009) *Evidence Based Social Work, A Critical Stance*. London: Routledge.

Green, L. (2005) 'Theorizing sexuality, sexual abuse and residential children's homes: Adding gender to the equation', *British Journal of Social Work, 35* (4): 453–481.

Green, H., McGinnity, A., Meltzer, H., Ford, T. and Goodman, R. (2005) *Mental Health of Children and Young People in Great Britain, 2004*. London: Palgrave Macmillan.

Greenhow, S., Hackett, S., Jones, C. and Meins, E. (2017) 'Adoptive family experiences of post-adoption contact in an Internet era', *Child and Family Social Work, 22* (1): 44–52.

Griffiths, R. (2013) 'The Letterbox Club: Educational possibilities in a parcel', in S. Jackson (ed.), *Pathways through Education for Young People in Care: Ideas from Research and Practice*. London: BAAF.

Gupta, A. (2008) 'Ascertaining the wishes and feelings of the child in the children's guardian role', in B. Luckock and M. Lefevre (eds), *Direct Work, Social Work with Children and Young People in Care*. London: BAAF.

Hadfield, S.C. and Preece, P.M. (2008) 'Obesity in looked after children: Is foster care protective from the dangers of obesity?', *Child: Care, Health and Development*, 34 (6): 710–712.

Hadley Centre/Coram Voice (2015) *Children and Young People's Views on Being in Care, A Literature Review*. Bristol: University of Bristol.

Hale, B. and Fortin, J. (2015) 'Legal issues in the care and treatment of children with mental health problems' in A. Thapar, D. Pine, J.F. Leckman, S. Scott, M.J. Snowling and E. Taylor (eds), *Rutter's Child and Adolescent Psychiatry*, 6th Edition. Chichester: John Wiley & Sons.

Hammond, S.P. and Cooper, N.J. (2013) *Digital Life Story Work – Using Technology to Help Young People make Sense of their Experiences*. London: BAAF.

Hannon, C., Wood, C. and Bazalgette, L. (2010) *In Loco Parentis*. London: Demos.

Hansard (2016) 'Staying Put' 10 October 2016, Volume 615 Available at: https://hansard.parliament.uk/commons/2016-10-10/debates/E162D157-07AF-49DF-BD81-0F4C6744FBAE/StayingPut.

Harker, R., Dobel-Ober, D., Berridge, D. and Sinclair, R. (2004) *Taking Care of Education: An Evaluation of the Education of Looked After Children*. London: National Children's Bureau.

Harold, G., Hampden-Thompson, G., Rodic, M. and Sellers, R. (2017) *An Evaluation of the AdOpt Parenting, Research Report*. London: DfE.

Hart, R. (1992) *Ladder of Participation, Children's Participation: From Tokenism to Citizenship*. Innocenti Essays, 4.

Harwin, J., Alrouh, B., Ryan, M. and Tunnard, J. (2014) *Changing Lifestyles, Keeping Children Safe: An Evaluation of the First Family Drug and Alcohol Court (FDAC) in Care Proceedings*. London: Brunel University.

Helm, D. (2010) *Making Sense of Child and Family Assessment: How to Interpret Children's Needs*. London: Jessica Kingsley.

Henderson, P. and Thomas, D.N. (2013) *Skills in Neighbourhood Work*, 4th Edition. London: Routledge.

Herrick, M.A. and Piccus, W. (2005) 'Sibling connections: The importance of nurturing sibling bonds in the foster care system', *Children and Youth Services Review*, 27 (7): 845–861.

Higgins, M., Goodyer, A. and Whittaker, A. (2015) 'Can a Munro-inspired approach transform the lives of looked after children in England?' *Social Work Education*, 34 (3): 328–340.

Hill, C.M. (2009) 'The health of looked after children', in G. Schofield and J. Simmonds (eds), *The Child Placement Handbook, Research, Policy and Practice*. London: BAAF.

Hill, M. (1999) 'What's the problem? Who can help?', *Journal of Social Work Practice*, 13 (2): 135–145.

Hill, M. (2000) 'The residential child care context', in M. Chakrabarti and M. Hill (eds), *Residential Child Care: International Perspectives on Links with Families and Peers*. London: Jessica Kingsley.

Hill, M. (2002) 'Network assessments and diagrams: A flexible friend for social work practice and education', *Journal of Social Work*, 2 (2): 233–254.

Hill, M. (2009) 'The place of child placement research in policy and practice', in G. Schofield and J. Simmonds (eds), *The Child Placement Handbook, Research, Policy and Practice*. London: BAAF.

Hill, M. (2014) 'Introduction', in M. Hill (ed.), *John Triseliotis, Selected Writings on Adoption, Fostering and Child Care*. London: BAAF.

Hill, M., Lockyer, A. and Stone, F. (eds.) (2006) *Youth Justice and Child Protection*. London: Jessica Kingsley.

Hill, M., Nutter, R., Giltinan, D., Hudson, J. and Galaway, B. (1999) [1993] '*A Comparative Survey of Specialist Fostering in the UK and North America*', in M. Hill (ed.), *Signposts in Fostering, Policy, Practice and Research Issues*. London: BAAF.

HM Government (2015) *Working Together to Safeguard Children: A Guide to Inter-Agency Working to Safeguard and Promote the Welfare of Children*. London: The Stationery Office.

Holland, S., Burgess, S., Grogan-Kaylor, A. and Delva, J. (2011) 'Understanding neighbour-hoods, communities and environments: New approaches for social work research', *British Journal of Social Work, 41* (4): 689–707.

Holland, S., Faulkner, A. and Perez-del-Aguila, R. (2005a) 'Promoting stability and continuity of care for looked after children: A survey and critical review', *Child and Family Social Work, 10* (1): 29–41.

Holland, S., Scourfield, J., O'Neill, S. and Pithouse, A. (2005b) 'Democratising the family and the state? The case of family group conferences in child welfare', *Journal of Social Policy, 34* (1): 59–77.

Holman, B. (2002) *The Unknown Fostering: A Study of Private Fostering*. Lyme Regis: RHP.

House of Commons (2013) *Home Affairs Select Committee, Child sexual exploitation and the response to localized grooming, Second Report of Session 2013–14, Volume III*. London: The Stationery Office.

Howard League (2016) *Ending the Criminalisation of Children in Residential Care, Briefing One*. London: The Howard League for Penal Reform. Available at: http://howardleague.org/wp-content/uploads/2017/07/Ending-the-criminalisation-of-children-in-residential-care-Briefing-one.pdf.

Howe, D. (2011) *Attachment Across the Lifecourse, A Brief Introduction*. Basingstoke: Palgrave.

Howe, D., Brandon, M., Hinings, D. and Schofield, G. (1999) *Attachment Theory, Child Maltreatment and Family Support*. Basingstoke: Palgrave.

Howe, D. and Feast, J. (2000) *Adoption Search and Reunion*. London: The Children's Society.

Howe, D., Sawbridge, P. and Hinings, D. (1992) *Half a Million Women: Mothers who Lose their Children by Adoption*. London: Penguin.

Humphreys, C. and Kiraly, M. (2009) *Baby On Board: Executive Summary of Report of the Infants in Care and Family Contact Research Project*, Melbourne: University of Melbourne. Available at: http://research.cwav.asn.au/AFRP/OOHC/InfantsInCare/Baby%20On%20Board%20Report/Full%20Report.pdf.

Hunt, J., Waterhouse, S. and Lutman, E. (2008) *Keeping Them in the Family: Outcomes for Children Placed in Kinship Care through Care Proceedings*. London: BAAF.

Hunt, J. (2009) 'Family and friends care', in G. Schofield, G. and J. Simmonds (eds), *The Child Placement Handbook Research, Policy and Practice*. London: BAAF.

Hutchinson, B. (2005) 'The Professionalisation of Foster Care', in A. Wheal (ed.), *The RHP Companion to Foster Care*, 2nd Edition. Lyme Regis: Russell House.

Jack, G. (2015) '"I may not know who I am, but I know where I am from": The meaning of place in social work with children and families', *Child and Family Social Work, 20* (4): 415–423.

Jack, G. and Donnellan, H. (2013) *Social Work with Children*. London: Palgrave.

Jack, G. and Gill, O. (2009) 'The role of communities in safeguarding children and young people', *Child Abuse Review, 19* (1): 82–96.

Jackson, S. (1998) 'Looking after children: A new approach or just an exercise in form filling? A response to Knight and Caveney', *The British Journal of Social Work, 28* (1): 45–56.

Jackson, S. (2010) 'Reconnecting care and education: From the Children Act 1989 to Care Matters', *Journal of Children's Services,* 5 (3): 48–59.

Jackson, S. and Ajayi, S. (2007) 'Foster care and higher education', *Adoption and Fostering, 31* (1): 62–72.

Jackson, S. and Cameron, C. (2012) 'Leaving care: Looking ahead and aiming higher', *Children and Youth Services Review,* 34 (6): 1107–1114.

Jackson, S. and Martin, P.Y. (1998) 'Surviving the care system: Education and resilience', *Journal of Adolescence, 21* (5): 569–583.

James, A. (2013) *Socialising Children.* London: Palgrave.

James, A. and Prout, A. (eds) (1997) *Constructing and Reconstructing Childhood: Contemporary Issues in the Sociological Study of Childhood,* 2nd Edition. London: Falmer.

Jay, A. (2014) *Independent Inquiry into Child Sexual Exploitation in Rotherham: 1997–2013.* Rotherham: Rotherham Metropolitan Borough Council.

Jones, D. (2010) 'Child maltreament', in M. Rutter, D. Bishop, D. Pine, S. Scott, J. Stevenson, E. Taylor and A. Thapar (eds), *Rutter's Child and Adolescent Psychiatry,* 5th Edition. Oxford: Blackwell.

Jordan, B. (1981) "Achieving permanence: Prevention", *Adoption and Fostering, 5* (3): 20–22.

Juffer, F. and van IJzendoorn, M.H. (2005) 'Behavior problems and mental health referrals of international adoptees: A meta-analysis', *JAMA, The Journal of the American Medical Association,* 293 (20): 2501–2515.

Katz, E. (2015) 'Domestic violence, children's agency and mother–child relationships: Towards a more advanced model', *Children and Society,* 29 (1): 69–79.

Kay, H., Kendrick, A., Stevens, I. and Davidson, J. (2007) 'Safer recruitment? Protecting children, improving practice in residential child care', *Child Abuse Review 16* (4): 223–236.

Kelly, G. (2000) 'The survival of long-term foster care', in G. Kelly and R. Gilligan (eds), *Issues in Foster Care, Policy, Practice and Research.* London: Jessica Kingsley.

Kendall, P.C., Peterman, J.S. and Cummings, C.M. (2015) 'Cognitive-behavioral therapy, behavioral therapy, and related treatments in children', in A. Thapar, D. Pine, J.F. Leckman, S. Scott, M.J. Snowling and E. Taylor (eds), *Rutter's Child and Adolescent Psychiatry,* 6th Edition. Chichester: John Wiley & Sons.

Kendrick, A. (2008) 'Black and minority ethnic children and young people in residential care', in A. Kendrick (ed.), *Residential Child Care, Prospects and Challenges.* London: Jessica Kingsley.

Kendrick, A. (2013) 'Relations, relationships and relatedness: Residential child care and the family metaphor', *Child and Family Social Work,* 18 (1): 77–86.

Kenrick, J. (2009) 'Concurrent planning: A retrospective study of the continuities and discontinuities of care, and their impact on the development of infants and young children placed for adoption by the Coram Concurrent Planning Project', *Adoption and Fostering,* 33 (4): 5–18.

Kenrick, J. (2010) 'Concurrent planning (2): 'The rollercoaster of uncertainty', *Adoption and Fostering,* 34 (2): 38–48.

Kent, R. (1997) *Children's Safeguards Review.* Edinburgh: The Stationery Office.

Kerr, L. and Cossar, J. (2014) 'Attachment Interventions with Foster and Adoptive Parents: A Systematic Review', *Child Abuse Review,* 23 (6): 426–439.

Kirton, D. (2000) *'Race', Ethnicity and Adoption.* Buckingham: Open University Press.

Kirton, D., Beecham, J. and Ogilvie, K. (2007) 'Gaining satisfaction? an exploration of foster-carers' attitudes to payment', *British Journal of Social Work,* 37 (7): 1205–1224.

Kosonen, M. (1996) 'Maintaining sibling relationships – neglected dimension in child care practice', *British Journal of Social Work,* 26 (6): 809–822.

Laming, H. (2003) *The Victoria Climbié Inquiry, Report of an Inquiry*. London: Department of Health.

Larkins, C., Ridley, J., Farrelly, N., Austerberry, H., Bilson, A., Hussein, S., ... and Stanley, N. (2013) 'Children's, young people's and parents' perspectives on contact: Findings from the evaluation of social work practices', *British Journal of Social Work, 45* (1): 296–312.

Lee, A. and Hankin, B.L. (2009) 'Insecure attachment, dysfunctional attitudes, and low self-esteem predicting prospective symptoms of depression and anxiety during adolescence', *Journal of Clinical Child and Adolescent Psychology, 38*: 219–231.

Lefevre, M. (2008) 'Communicating and engaging with children and young people in care through play and the creative arts', in B. Luckock and M. Lefevre (eds), *Direct Work: Social Work with Children and Young People in Care*. London: BAAF.

Levy, A.J. (2011) 'Neurobiology and the therapeutic action of psychoanalytic play therapy with children', *Clinical Social Work Journal, 39* (1): 50–60.

Lin, Y.W. and Bratton, S.C. (2015) 'A meta-analytic review of child-centered play therapy approaches', *Journal of Counseling and Development, 93* (1): 45–58.

Livingstone, S. (2008) 'Taking risky opportunities in youthful content creation: Teenagers' use of social networking sites for intimacy, privacy and self-expression', *New Media and Society, 10* (3): 393–411.

Livingstone, S. (2009) *Children and the Internet*. Cambridge: Polity.

Lloyd, E.C. and Barth, R.P. (2011) 'Developmental outcomes after five years for foster children returned home, remaining in care, or adopted', *Children and Youth Services Review, 33* (8): 1383–1391.

Lowe, N., Murch, M., Borkowski, M., Weaver, A., Beckford, V. and Thomas, C. (1999) *Supporting Adoption: Reframing the Approach*. London: BAAF.

Luckock, B. and Lefevre, M. (2008) 'Introduction', in B. Luckock, B. and M. Lefevre (eds), *Direct Work, Social Work with Children and Young People in Care*. London: BAAF.

Lundström, T. and Sallnäs, M. (2012) 'Sibling contact among Swedish children in foster and residential care – Out of home care in a family service system', *Children and Youth Services Review, 34* (2): 396–402.

Lutman, E. and Farmer, E. (2012) 'What contributes to outcomes for neglected children who are reunified with their parents? Findings from a five-year follow-up study', *British Journal of Social Work, 43* (3): 559–578.

Macdonald, G. and Turner, W. (2005) 'An experiment in helping foster carers manage challenging behaviour', *British Journal of Social Work, 35* (8): 1265–1282.

Macdonald, G. and Turner, W. (2009) *Treatment Foster Care for Improving Outcomes in Children and Young People (Review)*. Chichester: The Cochrane Collaboration/Wiley.

Macdonald, G., Kelly, G.P., Higgins, K.M. and Robinson, C. (2016) 'Mobile phones and contact arrangements for children living in care', *British Journal of Social Work, 47* (3): 828–845.

Mackaskill, C. (2002) *Safe contact? Children in Permanent Placement and Contact with their Birth Relatives*. Lyme Regis: RHP.

Main, M. and Solomon, J. (1986) 'Discovery of an insecure-disorganized/disoriented attachment pattern', in T.B. Brazelton and M.W. Yogman (eds), *Affective Development in Infancy*. Westport, CT: Ablex Publishing.

Malet, M., Mcsherry, D., Larkin, E., Kelly, G., Robinson, C. and Schubotz, D. (2010) 'Young children returning home from care: The birth parents' perspective', *Child and Family Social Work, 15* (1): 77–86.

Marsh, P. (1998) 'Leaving care and extended families', *Adoption and Fostering, 22* (4): 6–14.

Marsh, P. and Crow, G. (1998) *Family Group Conferences in Child Welfare*. Oxford: Blackwell.

Marsh, P. and Triseliotis, J. (2014) [1993] 'The theory continuum: Prevention, restoration and permanence', in M. Hill (ed.), *John Triseliotis, Selected Writings on Adoption, Fostering and Child Care*. London: BAAF.

Mason, P., Ferguson, H., Morris, K., Munton, T. and Sen, R. (2017) *Leeds Family Valued Evaluation Report*. London: Department of Education.

Masson, J.M., Pearce, J., Bader, K., Joyner, O., Marsden, J. and Westlake, D. (2008) *Care Profiling Study*. London: Ministry of Justice.

Maughan, B. and Collishaw, S. (2015) 'Development and psychopathology: A life course perspective', in A. Thapar, D. Pine, J.F. Leckman, S. Scott, M.J. Snowling and E. Taylor (eds), *Rutter's child and adolescent psychiatry*, 6th Edition. Chichester: John Wiley & Sons.

Maxwell, A., Proctor, J. and Hammond, L. (2011) 'Me and my child': Parenting experiences of young mothers leaving care, *Adoption and Fostering*, 35(4): 29–40.

McBeath, B., Kothari, B.H., Blakeslee, J., Lamson-Siu, E., Bank, L., Linares, L.O., Waid, J., Sorenson, P., Jimenez, J., Pearson, E. and Shlonsky, A. (2014) 'Intervening to improve outcomes for siblings in foster care: Conceptual, substantive, and methodological dimensions of a prevention science framework', *Children and Youth Services Review*, 39: 1–10.

McClung, M. and Gayle, V. (2010) 'Exploring the care effects of multiple factors on the educational achievement of children looked after at home and away from home: An investigation of two Scottish local authorities', *Child and Family Social Work*, 15 (4): 409–431.

McConkey, R., Nixon, T., Donaghy, E. and Mulhern, D. (2004) 'The characteristics of children with a disability looked after away from home and their future service needs', *British Journal of Social Work*, 34 (4): 561–576.

McGhee, J., Bunting, L., McCartan, C., Elliott, M., Bywaters, P. and Featherstone, B. (2017) 'Looking after children in the UK – convergence or divergence?' *The British Journal of Social Work*, bcx103.

McKeigue, B. and Beckett, C. (2010) 'Squeezing the toothpaste tube: Will tackling court delay result in pre-court delay in its place?' *British Journal of Social Work*, 40 (1): 154–169.

McKeown, K. (2000) *A Guide to What Works in Family Support Services for Vulnerable Families*. Dublin: Department for Health and Children.

McNicoll, A. (2017) 'Children in poorest areas more likely to enter care', *Community Care Online*, Available at: www.communitycare.co.uk/2017/02/28/children-poorest-areas-likely-enter-care-finds-study/.

McPheat, G. (2007) 'Evalaution of City of Edinburgh Residential Child Care Recruitment and Development Centre', Unpublished MSc thesis. University of Strathclyde.

McPheat, G. and Vrouwenfelder, E. (2017) 'Social pedagogy: Developing and maintaining multi-disciplinary relationships in residential child care', *International Journal of Social Pedagogy*, 6 (1): 64–82.

McSherry, D., Malet, M.F. and Weatherall, K. (2013) *Comparing Long-Term Placements for Young Children in Care*. London: BAAF.

Medical Press (2017) 'Care system not to blame for increased risk of mental health issues in children'. Available at: https://medicalxpress.com/news/2017-06-blame-mental-health-issues-children.html.

Mellish, L., Jennings, S. Tasker, F., Lamb, M. and Golombok, S. (2013) *Gay, Lesbian and Heterosexual Adoptive Families*. London: BAAF.

Meltzer, H., Gatward, R., Goodman, R. and Ford, T. (2000) *Mental Health of Children and Adolescents in Great Britain*. London: The Stationery Office.

Meltzer, H., Gatward, R., Corbin, T., Goodman, R. and Ford, T. (2003) *The Mental Health of Young People Looked After by Local Authorities in England*. London: The Stationery Office.

Meltzer, H., Lader, D., Corbin, T., Goodman, R. and Ford, T. (2004) *The Mental Health of Children Looked After by Local Authorities in Scotland*. London: The Stationery Office.

Mercer, J. (2011) 'Reply to Sudbery, Shardlow and Huntington: Holding Therapy', *British Journal of Social Work, 42* (3): 556–559.

Midgley, N. and Kennedy, E. (2011) 'Psychodynamic psychotherapy for children and adolescents: A critical review of the evidence base', *Journal of Child Psychotherapy, 37* (3): 232–260.

Millham, S., Bullock, R., Hosie, K. and Haak, M. (1986) *Lost in Care*. Aldershot: Gower.

Millward, R., Kennedy, E., Towlson, K. and Minnis, H. (2006) 'Reactive attachment disorder in looked-after children', *Emotional and Behavioural Difficulties, 11* (4): 273–279.

Milner, J. and Bateman, J. (2011) *Working with Children and Teenagers Using Solution Focused Approaches*. London: Jessica Kingsley.

Milner, J., Myers, S. and O'Byrne, P. (2015) *Assessment in Social Work*, 4th Edition. London: Palgrave.

Miron, D., Bisaillon, C., Jordan, B., Bryce, G., Gauthier, Y., St-Andre, M. and Minnis, H. (2013) 'Whose rights count? Negotiating practice, policy, and legal dilemmas regarding infant–parent contact when infants are in out-of-home care', *Infant Mental Health Journal, 34* (2): 177–188.

Monck, E. and Rushton, A. (2009) 'Access to post-adoption services when the child has substantial problems', *Journal of Children's Services, 4* (3): 21–33.

Moorhead, J. (2014) 'Adoption parties: The best way for children and parents to meet?', *The Guardian*, 11 January.

Moran-Ellis, J. (2010) 'Reflections on the sociology of childhood in the UK current sociology', *Current Sociology, 58* (2): 186–205.

Morgan, R. (2005) *Being Fostered: A National Survey of the Views of Foster Children, Foster Carers, and Birth Parents about Foster Care*. Newcastle: Office of the Children's Rights Director.

Morgan, R. (2006a) *About Adoption: A Children's Views Report*. Newcastle: Office of the Children's Rights Director.

Morgan, R. (2006b) *Before Care: A Report of Children's Views on Entering Care by the Children's Rights Director for England*. Manchester: Ofsted.

Morgan, R. (2009a) *Keeping in Touch, A Report of Children's Experience by the Children's Rights Director for England*. Manchester: Ofsted.

Morgan, R. (2009b) *Life in Children's Homes*. Manchester: Ofsted.

Moyers, S., Farmer, E. and Lipscombe, J. (2005) 'Contact with family members and its impact on adolescents and their foster placements', *British Journal of Social Work, 36* (4): 541–559.

Munro, E. (1999) 'Common errors of reasoning in child protection work', *Child Abuse and Neglect, 23* (8): 745–758.

Munro, E. (2011) *The Munro Review of Child Protection, Final Report, A Child Centred System*. London: The Stationery Office.

Munro, E.R., Lushey, C., Maskell-Graham, D., Ward, H. and Holmes, L. (2012) *Evaluation of the Staying Put: 18 Plus Family Placement Programme*. London: DfE.

Munro, E.R. and Stein, M. (2008) 'Comparative exploration of care leavers transitions to adulthood: An introduction', in M. Stein and E.R. Munro (eds), *Young People's Transitions from Care to Adulthood: International. Research and Practice*. London: Jessica Kingsley Publishers.

Narey, M. (2011) 'The Narey Report on Adoption: Our blueprint for Britain's lost children', *The Times*, 5 July. Available at: www.thetimes.co.uk/article/the-narey-report-a-blueprint-for-the-nations-lost-children-7b2ktmcrf0w.

Narey, M. (2016) *Residential Care in England: Report of Sir Martin Narey's Independent Review of Children's Residential Care: July 2016.* London: DfE.

A National Voice (2011) *Children in Care Councils (CiCC) Mapping Project 2010 to 2011.* London: DfE.

The National Adoption Leadership Board (2014) *Impact of Court Judgements on Adoption, What the Judgements do and do not say,* Preston: NALB.

The National Implementation Service (NIS) (2017) Available at: www.evidencebasedinterventions.org.uk/about/national-implementation-service.

Neil, E., Beek, M. and Ward, E. (2014) *Contact after Adoption: A Longitudinal Study of Adopted Young People and Their Adoptive Parents and Birth Relatives.* London: BAAF.

Neil, E., Cossar, J., Lorgelly, P. and Young, J. (2010) *Helping Birth Families: Services, Costs and Outcomes.* London: BAAF.

Neil, E. and Howe, D. (2004) *Contact in Adoption and Permanent Foster Care: Research, Theory and Practice.* London: BAAF.

Nelson, S. (2015) *Tackling Child Sexual Abuse: Radical Approaches to Prevention, Protection and Support.* Bristol: Policy Press.

Norgrove, D. (2011) *Family Justice Review, Final Report.* London: The Stationery Office.

O'Connor, T.G. and Byrne, G.J. (2007) 'Attachment measures for research and practice', *Child and Adolescent Mental Health, 12* (4): 187–192.

Ofsted (2012) *Right on Time: Exploring Delays in Adoption.* Manchester: Ofsted.

OHCR (2016) 'Concluding observations on the fifth periodic report of the United Kingdom of Great Britain and Northern Ireland'. Available at: http://docstore.ohchr.org/SelfServices/FilesHandler.ashx?enc=6QkG1d%2fPPRiCAqhKb7yhskHOj6VpDS%2f%2fJqg2Jx b9gncnUyUgbnuttBweOlyIfyYPkBbwffitW2JurgBRuMMxZqnGgerUdpjxij3uZ0bj QBOLNTNvQ9fUIEOvA5LtW0GL.

Oliver, M., Sapey, B. and Thomas, P. (2012) *Social Work with Disabled Children,* 4th Edition. London: Palgrave.

O'Neill, T. (2008) 'Gender matters in residential child care', in A. Kendrick (ed.), *Residential Child Care, Prospects and Challenges.* London: Jessica Kingsley.

Osborne, C., Alfano, J. and Winn, T. (2013) 'Paired reading as a literary intervention for foster children', in S. Jackson (ed.), *Pathways through Education for Young People in Care: Ideas from Research and Practice.* London: BAAF.

O'Sullivan, A., Westerman, R. with McNamara, P. and Mains, A. (2013) 'Closing the gap: Investigating the barriers to educational achievement for looked after children', in S. Jackson (ed.), *Pathways through Education for Young People in Care: Ideas from Research and Practice.* London: BAAF.

Owen, M. (1999) *Novices, Old Hands and Professionals: Adoption by Single People.* London: BAAF.

Owen, C. and Statham, J. (2009) *Disproportionality in Child Welfare. The Prevalence of Black and Minority Ethnic Children within the 'Looked After' and 'Children in Need' Populations and on Child Protection Registers in England, DCSF Research Report DCSF-RR124.* Nottingham: DCSF.

Parker, R. (1966) *Decision in Foster Care.* London: Allen & Unwin.

Parker, R. (1999) *Adoption Research Messages.* London: DOH.

Parton, N. (2014) *The Politics of Child Protection, Contemporary Developments and Future Directions.* London: Palgrave.

Paskell, C. (2012) *Tackling Child Sexual Exploitation. Helping Local Authorities to Develop Effective Responses*. Barnardo's: Ilford.

Pawson, R. (2013) *The Science of Evaluation: A Realist Manifesto*. London: Sage.

Pearce, C. (2009) *A Short Introduction to Attachment and Attachment Disorder*. London: Jessica Kingsley.

PIU (Performance and Innovation Unit) (2000) *Prime Minister's Review: Adoption: Issued for Consultation*. London: Cabinet Office.

Piggot, J., Williams, C., McLeod, S. and Barton, J. (2004) 'A qualitative study of support for young people who self-harm in residential care in Glasgow', *Scottish Journal of Residential Child Care*: 45–54.

Pilgrim, D. (2017*) Key Concepts in Mental Health*, 4th Edition. London: Sage.

Pithouse, A. and Rees, A. (2015) *Creating Stable Foster Placements*. London: Jessica Kingsley.

Prior, V. and Glaser, D. (2006) *Understanding Attachment and Attachment Disorders. Theory, Evidence and Practice*. London: Jessica Kingsley.

Prison Reform Trust (2016) *In Care, Out of Trouble: How the Life Chances of Children in Care can be Transformed by Protecting them from Unnecessary Involvement in the Criminal Justice System. Report of an Independent Review Chaired by Lord Laming*. London: PRT.

Quinton, D. (2012) *Rethinking Matching in Adoptions from Care, A Conceptual and Research Review*. London: BAAF.

Quinton, D., Rushton, A., Dance, C. and Mayes, D. (1997) 'Contact between children placed away from home and their birth parents: Research issues and evidence', *Clinical Child Psychology and Psychiatry, 2* (3): 393–413.

Quinton, D., Rushton, A., Dance, C. and Mayes, D. (1998) *Joining New Families: A Study of Adoption and Fostering in Middle Childhood*. Chichester: John Wiley & Sons.

Quinton, D. and Rutter, M. (1988) *Parenting Breakdown: The Making and Breaking of Intergenerational Links*. Aldershot: Avebury.

Qvortup, J. (1994) '*Childhood Matters: An Introduction*', in J. Qvortup, G.M. Bardy, G. Sgritta and H. Wintersberger (eds), *Childhood Matters: Social Theory, Practice and Politics*. Aldershot: Avebury.

Randle, M. (2013) 'Through the eyes of ex-foster children: Placement success and the characteristics of good foster carers', *Practice, 25* (1): 3–19.

Rawlinson, K. (2017) 'British Sikh couple take legal action after being advised not to adopt', *The Guardian*, 27 June.

Rees, J. (2001) 'Making residential care educational care' in S. Jackson (ed.), *Nobody Ever Told Us School Mattered*. London: BAAF.

Ridley, J. and McCluskey, S. (2003) 'Exploring the perception of young people in care and care leavers of their health needs', *Scottish Journal of Residential Child Care, 2* (1): 55–65.

Roberts, L., Maxwell, N., Rees, P., Holland, S. and Forbes, N. (2016) 'Improving well-being and outcomes for looked after children in Wales: A context sensitive review of interventions', *Adoption and Fostering, 40* (4): 309–324.

Robinson, M., Lindaman, S., Clemmons, M., Doyle-Buckwalter, K., Ryan, M. (2009) 'I Deserve a Family': The evolution of an adolescent's behaviour and beliefs about himself and others when treated with Theraplay in residential care', *Child and Adolescent Social Work Journal, 26* (4): 291–306.

Rogers, C. (1951) *Client-Centered Counselling*. Boston: Houghton-Mifflin.

Rogers, A. and Pilgrim, D. (2015) *A Sociology of Mental Health and Illness*, 5th Edition. Maidenhead: Open University Press.

Rogoff, B. (1990) *Apprenticeship in Thinking: Cognitive Development in Social Context*. Oxford: Oxford University Press.

Rogoff, B. (2003) *The Cultural Nature of Human Development*. Oxford: Oxford University Press.

Rojek, C., Peacock, G. and Collins, S. (1988) *Social Work and Received Ideas*. London: Routledge.

Rowe, J. and Lambert, L. (1973) *Children who Wait*. London: BAAF.

Ruch, G., Turney, D. and Ward, A. (2010) *Relationship-Based Practice: Getting to the Heart of Practice*. London: Jessica Kingsley.

Rushton, A. (2003) *A Scoping and Scanning Review of Research on the Adoption of Children Placed from Public Care*. London: SCIE.

Rushton, A., Dance, C., Quinton, D. and Mayes, D. (2001) *Siblings in Late Permanent Placements*. London: BAAF.

Rushton, A. and Dance, C. (2006) 'The adoption of children from public care: A prospective study of outcome in adolescence', *Journal of the American Academy of Child & Adolescent Psychiatry*, 45 (7): 877–883.

Rushton, A., Monck, E., Leese, M., McCrone, P. and Sharac, J. (2010) 'Enhancing adoptive parenting: A randomized controlled trial', *Clinical Child Psychology and Psychiatry*, 15 (4): 529–542.

Rutter, M. (1981) *Maternal Deprivation Reassessed*, 2nd Edition. Harmondsworth: Penguin.

Rutter, M. (2000) 'Psychosocial influences: Critiques, findings, and research needs', *Development and Psychopathology*, 12 (3): 375–405.

Rutter, M., Kreppner, J. and Sonuga-Barke, E. (2009) 'Emanuel miller lecture: Attachment insecurity, disinhibited attachment, and attachment disorders: Where do research findings leave the concepts?', *Journal of Child Psychology and Psychiatry and Allied Disciplines*, 50 (5): 529–543.

Rutter, M. and Rutter, M. (1993) *Developing Minds, Challenge and Continuity Across the Life Span*. London: Penguin.

Rutter, M. and Stevenson, J. (2010) 'Using epidemiology to plan services, a conceptual approach', in M. Rutter, D. Bishop, D. Pine, S. Scott, J. Stevenson, E. Taylor and A. Thapar (eds), *Rutter's Child and Adolescent Psychiatry*, 5th Edition. Oxford: Blackwell.

Ryan, V. (2007) 'Filial therapy: Helping children and new carers to form secure attachment relationships', *British Journal of Social Work*, 37 (4): 643–657.

Ryan, T. and Walker, R. (2007) *Life Story Work: A Practical Guide to Helping Children Understand Their Past*. London: BAAF.

Ryburn, M. (1999) 'Contact between children placed away from home and their birth parents: A reanalysis of the evidence in relation to permanent placements', *Clinical Child Psychology and Psychiatry*, 4 (4): 505–518.

Rycroft-Malone, J., Seers, K., Titchen, A., Harvey, G., Kitson, A. and McCormack, B. (2004) 'What counts as evidence in evidence-based practice?', *Journal of Advanced Nursing*, 47 (1): 81–90.

Saleebey, D. (2006) *The Strengths Perspective in Social work*, 4th Edition. London: Pearson.

Schaffer, H. and Rudolph, R. (1990) *Making Decisions About Children. Psychological Questions and Answers*. Oxford: Blackwell.

Schofield, G. (2009) 'Long-term foster care' in G. Schofield and J. Simmonds (eds), *The Child Placement Handbook Research, Policy and Practice*. London: BAAF.

Schofield, G. and Beek, M. (2009) 'Growing up in foster care: Providing a secure base through adolescence', *Child and Family Social Work*, 14 (3): 255–266.

Schofield, G. and Beek, M. (2014) *Promoting Attachment and Resilience*. London: BAAF.

Schofield, G., Beek, M., Sargent, K. and Thoburn, J. (2000) *Growing up in Foster Care*. London: BAAF.

Schofield, G., Biggart, L., Ward, E., Scaife, V., Dodsworth, J., Haynes, A. and Larsson, B. (2014) *Looked after Children and Offending: Reducing Risk and Promoting Resilience.* London: BAAF.

Schofield, G. and Stevenson, O. (2009) 'Contact and relationships between fostered children and their birth families', in G. Schofield and J. Simmonds (eds), *The Child Placement Handbook: Research, Policy and Practice.* London: BAAF.

Schofield, G., Ward, E., Warman, A., Simmonds, J. and Butler, J. (2008) *Permanence in Foster Care – A Study of Care Planning in England and Wales.* London: BAAF.

Schwehr, B. (2016) 'Guide to the law on deprivation of liberty of children', Community Care Online. Available at: www.communitycare.co.uk/2016/07/14/guide-law-deprivation-liberty-children/.

SCIE (2004) *Research Briefing 9: Preventing Teenage Pregnancy in Looked after Children, Research Briefing 9.* London: SCIE.

Scott, J., Ward, H. and Hill, M. (2007) 'The health of looked after children in residential child care', in A. Kendrick (ed.), *Residential Child Care: Prospects and Challenges.* London: Jessica Kingsley.

Scottish Executive (2005) *Getting It Right for Every Child, Proposals for Action Edinburgh.* Edinburgh: Scottish Executive.

Scottish Executive (2007) *Looked after Children and Young People: We Can and Must do Better.* Edinburgh: Scottish Executive. Available at: www.gov.scot/Resource/Doc/162790/0044282.pdf.

Scottish Government (2007) *Getting It Right for Every Child in Foster Care and Kinship Care - A National Strategy.* Edinburgh: Scottish Government. Available at: http://hub.careinspectorate.com/media/107723/sg-girfec-in-foster-care-and-kinship-care_national-strategy.pdf.

Scottish Government (2013) *Staying Put Scotland Providing Care Leavers with Connectness and Belonging.* Edinburgh: Scottish Government.

Scottish Government (2017a) *Children's Social Work Statistics Scotland 2015/16.* Edinburgh: Scottish Government. Available at: www.gov.scot/Publications/2017/03/6791/downloads.

Scottish Government (2017b) *Children's Social Work Statistics Scotland 2015/16, Additional Tables.* Edinburgh: Scottish Government: Available at: www.gov.scot/Topics/Statistics/Browse/Children/PubChildrenSocialWork/CSWSAT1516.

Sebba, J., Berridge, D., Luke, N., Fletcher, J., ... O'Higgins, A. (2015) *The Educational Progress of Looked After Children in England: Linking Care and Educational Data.* Oxford: Rees Centre/University of Bristol.

Sellick, C. and Connolly, J. (2002) 'Independent Fostering Agencies uncovered: The findings of a national study', *Child and Family Social Work, 7* (2): 107–120.

Selman, P.F. (2004) 'Adoption: A cure for (too) many ills?', in F. Bowie (ed.), *Cross-Cultural Approaches to Adoption.* London: Routledge.

Selwyn, J. and Nandy, S. (2014) 'Kinship care in the UK: Using census data to estimate the extent of formal and informal care by relatives', *Child and Family Social Work, 19* (1): 44–54.

Selwyn, J., Quinton, D., Harris, P., Wijedasa, D., Nawaz, S. and Wood, M. (2010) *Pathways to Permanence for Black, Asian and Mixed Ethnicity Children.* London: BAAF.

Selwyn, J., Sturgess, W., Quinton, D. and Baxter, C. (2006) *Cost and Outcomes of Non-Infant Adoptions.* London: BAAF.

Selwyn, J., Wijedasa, D. and Meakings, S. (2014) *Beyond the Adoption Order: Challenges, Interventions and Adoption Disruption.* London: DfE.

Sempik, J. (2010) *Looked after Children: EP22 – The Mental Health of Looked after Children under 5 years.* NICE guidance.

Sen, R. (2010) 'Managing contact in Scotland for children in non-permanent placement', *Child Abuse Review, 19* (6): 423–437.

Sen, R. (2015) 'Not all that is solid melts into air? Care-experienced young people, friendship and relationships in the "digital age"', *The British Journal of Social Work, 46* (4): 1059–1075.

Sen, R. (2016) 'Building relationships in a cold climate: A case study of family engagement within an "edge of care" family support service', *Social Policy and Society, 15* (2): 289–302.

Sen, R. (2017) *Child Sexual Exploitation, Awareness, Identification, Support and Prevention.* University of Sheffield/South Yorkshire Teaching Partnership: Sheffield. Available at: www.sheffield.ac.uk/polopoly_fs/1.760056!/file/CSEPracticeResourceSen_June2017-1.pdf.

Sen, R. and Broadhurst, K. (2011) 'Contact between children in out-of-home placements and their family and friends networks: A research review', *Child and Family Social Work, 16* (3): 298–309.

Sen, R., Lister, P.G., Rigby, P. and Kendrick, A. (2014) 'Grading the graded care profile', *Child Abuse Review, 23* (5): 361–373.

Sen, R., Kendrick, A., Milligan, I. and Hawthorn, M. (2008) 'Lessons learnt? abuse in residential child care in Scotland', *Child and Family Social Work, 13* (4): 411–422.

Sen, R. and McCormack, J. (2011) 'Foster carers' involvement in contact: Other professionals' views', *Practice, 23* (5): 279–292.

SEU (Social Exclusion Unit) (1998) *SEU Truancy and School Exclusion, Cm3957.* London: The Stationery Office.

SEU (Social Exclusion Unit) (2003) *A Better Education for Children in Care.* London: SEU.

Shah, S. (2016) *Key Changes to Family Justice (England).* London: Coram/BAAF.

Shaw, C., Brodie, I., Ellis, A., Graham, B., Mainey, A., de Sousa, S. and Willmott, N. (2010) *Research into Private Fostering.* London: DCSF.

Shaw, J. (2014) *Residential Children's Homes and the Youth Justice System.* London: Palgrave.

Shaw, M., Broadhurst, K., Harwin, J., Alrouh, B., Kershaw, S. and Mason, C. (2014) 'The emergence of child protection as a public health issue: How would a more prevention-oriented approach alter the provision of services and the family–professional relationship?', *Family Law, 44* (12): 1705–1708.

Shemmings, D. (2016) 'A quick guide to attachment theory', *The Guardian*, 15 February.

Shemmings, D. and Shemmings, Y. (2011) *Understanding Disorganized Attachment.* London: Jessica Kingsley.

Shlonsky, A. and Benbenishty, R. (2014) 'From evidence to outcomes in child welfare', in A. Shlonksy and R. Benenishty (eds), *From Evidence to Outcomes in Child Welfare: An International Reader.* Oxford: Oxford University Press.

Simmonds, J. (2017) 'Why are people so suspicious about adoption?' *Community Care Online.* Available at: www.communitycare.co.uk/2017/03/07/people-suspicious-adoption/

Simpson, J. (2016) 'A divergence of opinion: How those involved in child and family social work are responding to the challenges of the Internet and social media', *Child and Family Social Work, 21* (1): 94–102.

Sinclair, I. (2005) *Fostering Now: Messages from Research.* London: Jessica Kingsley.

Sinclair, I. (2006) 'Residential care in the UK', in C. McCauley, P. Pecora and W. Rose (eds), *Enhancing the Well-Being of Children and Families through Effective Interventions: International Evidence for Practice.* London: Jessica Kingsley.

Sinclair, I., Baker, C., Lee, J. and Gibbs, I. (2007) *The Pursuit of Permanence: A Study of the English Child Care System.* London: Jessica Kingsley.

Sinclair, I. and Gibbs, I. (1998) *Children's Homes: A Study in Diversity.* Chichester: John Wiley & Sons.

Sinclair, I., Gibbs, I. and Wilson, K. (2004) *Foster Carers: Why They Stay and Why They Leave.* London: Jessica Kingsley.

Sinclair, I., Baker, C., Wilson, K. and Gibbs, I. (2005a) *Foster Children: Where They Go and How They Get On.* London: Jessica Kingsley.

Sinclair, I., Wilson, K. and Gibbs, I. (2005b) *Foster Placements: Why They Succeed and Why They Fail.* London: Jessica Kingsley.

Skinner, A. (1992) *Another Kind of Home: A Review of Residential Child Care.* Edinburgh: The Scottish Office.

Smart, C., Neale, B. and Wade, A. (2001) *The Changing Experience of Childhood.* Cambridge: Polity.

Smeeton, J. and Boxall, K. (2011) 'Birth parents' perceptions of professional practice in child care and adoption proceedings: Implications for practice', *Child and Family Social Work, 16* (4): 444–453.

Smith, M. (2009) *Rethinking Residential Child Care: Positive Perspectives.* Bristol: Policy.

Smith, M., Fulcher, L. and Doran, P. (2013) *Residential Child Care in Practice, Making a Difference.* Bristol: Policy.

Spring Consortium (2017) 'Delivering the children's social care innovation programme'. Available at: http://springconsortium.com/about-the-programme/.

Sroufe, L.A., Carlson, E.A., Levy, A.K. and Egeland, B. (1999) 'Implications of attachment theory for developmental psychopathology', *Development and Psychopathology, 11* (1): 1–13.

Stalker, K. (2008) 'Disabled Children in Residential Settings', in A. Kendrick (ed.), *Residential Child Care, Prospects and Challenges.* London: Jessica Kingsley.

Stalker, K. and McArthur, K. (2012) 'Child abuse, child protection and disabled children: A review of recent research', *Child Abuse Review, 21* (1): 24–40.

Stanley, N., Riordan, D. and Alaszewsk, H. (2005) 'The mental health of looked after children: Matching response to need', *Health and Social Care in the Community, 13* (3): 239–248.

Stanley, N. (2007) 'Young people's and carers' perspectives on the mental health needs of looked-after adolescents', *Child and Family Social Work, 12* (3): 258–267.

Stein, M. (2008) 'Transitions from care to adulthood: Messages from research for policy and practice', in M. Stein and E.R. Munro (eds), *Young People's Transitions from Care to Adulthood: International. Research and Practice.* London: Jessica Kingsley Publishers.

Stein, M. (2012) *Young People Leaving Care. Supporting Pathways to Adulthood.* London: Jessica Kingsley.

Stein, D.J., Phillips, K.A., Bolton, D., Fulford, K.W.M., Sadler, J.Z. and Kendler, K.S. (2010) 'What is a mental/psychiatric disorder? From DSM-IV to DSM-V', *Psychological Medicine, 40* (11): 1759–1765.

Stevenson, L. (2015) 'One in four care leavers taking advantage of 'Staying Put' reforms', *Community Care Online.* Available at: www.communitycare.co.uk/2015/08/24/one-four-care-leavers-taking-advantage-staying-put-reforms/.

Stevenson, L. (2017) 'Foster carers facing "poverty" over inadequate Staying Put funding', *Community Care Online.* Available at: www.communitycare.co.uk/2017/06/01/foster-carers-facing-poverty-inadequate-staying-put-funding/.

Storø, J. (2013) *Practical Social Pedagogy, Theories Values and Tools for Working with Children and Young People.* Bristol: Policy.

Stuart, M. and Baines, C. (2004) *Progress on Safeguards for Children Living Away from Home.* York: Joseph Rowntree Foundation.

Taylor, E. (2015) 'Pharmacological, medically-led and related treatements', in A. Thapar, D. Pine, J.F. Leckman, S. Scott, M.J. Snowling and E. Taylor (eds), *Rutter's Child and Adolescent Psychiatry,* 6th Edition. Chichester: John Wiley & Sons.

Thoburn, J. (2009a) 'International contexts and comparisons', in G. Schofield and J. Simmonds (eds), *The Child Placement Handbook, Research, Policy and Practice.* London: BAAF.

Thoburn, J. (2009b) *Reunification of Children in Out-of- Home Care to Birth Parents or Relatives: A Synthesis of the Evidence on Processes, Practice and Outcomes.* Munchen, Deutsches Jugendinstitut.

Thoburn, J. and Courtney, M.E. (2011) 'A guide through the knowledge base on children in out-of-home care', *Journal of Children's Services, 6* (4): 210–227.

Thoburn, J., Norford, E. and Rashid, S. (2000) *Permanent Family Placement for Children of Minority Ethnic Origin.* London: Jessica Kingsley.

Thomas, N. (2007) 'Towards a theory of children's participation', *International Journal of Children's Rights, 15* (2): 199–218.

Thomas, C. and Beckford, V. with Lowe, N. and Murch, M. (1999) *Adopted Children Speaking.* London: BAAF.

Thorpe, D. and Bilson, A. (1987) 'The leaving care curve', *Community Care,* 22: 24–26.

The Transparency Project (2015) 'It's wrong to measure the success of local authorities in terms of adoption numbers', Available at: www.transparencyproject.org.uk/its-wrong-to-measure-the-success-of-local-authorities-in-terms-of-adoption-numbers/.

The Transparency Project (2016) 'English Councils confirm they set targets' Available at: www.transparencyproject.org.uk/english-councils-confirm-they-set-targets-for-the-number-of-children-to-be-adopted/.

Treseder, P. (1997) *Empowering Children and Young People – Training Manual.* London: Save The Children.

Triseliotis, J. (1973) *In Search of Origins.* London: Routledge and Kegan Paul.

Triseliotis, J. (2002a) [1998–99] 'Is permanency through adoption in decline?', in M. Hill (ed.), *Shaping Childcare Practice in Scotland: Key Papers in Adoption and Fostering.* London: BAAF.

Triseliotis, J. (2002b) 'Long-term foster care or adoption? The evidence examined', *Child and Family Social Work, 7* (1): 23–33.

Triseliotis, J. (2010) 'Contact between looked after children and their parents: A level playing field?', *Adoption and Fostering, 34* (3): 59–66.

Triseliotis, J. (1991) 'Perceptions of permanence', *Adoption and Fostering, 15* (4): 6–15.

Triseliotis, J. (2013) 'Children's Views', in M. Hill (ed.), *John Triseliotis: Selected Writings on Adoption, Fostering and Child Care.* London: BAAF.

Triseliotis, J., Borland, M. and Hill, M. (2002) [1998] 'Foster carers who cease to foster', in M. Hill (ed.), *Shaping Childcare Practice in Scotland.* London: BAAF.

Triseliotis, J., Shireman, J. and Hundleby, M. (1997) *Adoption: Theory, Policy and Practice.* London: Cassell.

Triseliotis, J., Borland, M., Hill, M. and Lambert, L. (1995a) *Teenagers and the Social Work Services.* London: The Stationery Office.

Triseliotis, J., Sellick, C. and Short, R. (1995b) *Foster Care Theory and Practice.* London: B.T. Batsford.

Triseliotis, J., Feast, J. and Howe, D. (2005) *The Adoption Triangle Revisited: A Study of Adoption, Search and Reunion Experience.* London: BAAF.

UNCRC (United Nations Convention on the Rights of the Child) (1989) *Convention on the Rights of the Child*.

Ungar, M. (2015) 'Resilence and culture: The diversity of protective processes and positive adaptation', in L. Theron, L. Liebenberg and M. Ungar (eds), *Youth Resilience and Culture, Commonalities and Complexities*. New York and London: Springer Heidelberg.

Utting, W. (1991) *Children in the Public Care: A Review of Residential Child Care*. London: The Stationery Office.

Utting, W. (1997) *People Like Us: The Report of the Review of the Safeguards for Children Living Away from Home*. London: The Stationery Office.

Van IJzendoorn, M.H. and Juffer, F. (2006) 'The Emanuel Miller memorial lecture 2006: Adoption as intervention. Meta-analytic evidence for massive catch-up and plasticity in physical, socio-emotional, and cognitive development', *Journal of Child Psychology and Psychiatry, 47* (12): 1228–1245.

Venkatapuram, S. (2011) *Health Justice: An Argument from the Capabilities Approach*. Cambridge: Polity.

Wade, J., Biehal, N., Clayden, J. and Stein, M. (1998) *Going Missing: Young People Absent from Care*. Chichester: John Wiley & Sons.

Wade, J., Biehal, N., Farrelly, N. and Sinclair, I. (2011) *Caring for Abused and Neglected Children: Making the Right Decisions for Reunification or Long-term Care*. London: Jessica Kingsley.

Wade, J. and Dixon, J. (2006) 'Making a home, finding a job: Investigating early housing and employment outcomes for young people leaving care', *Child and Family Social Work, 11* (3): 199–208.

Wade, J., Dixon, J. and Richards, A. (2010) *Special Guardianship in Practice*. London: BAAF.

Wade, J. and Munro, E.R. (2008) 'UK', in M. Stein and E.R. Munro (eds), *Young People's Transitions from Care to Adulthood: International Research and Practice*. London: Jessica Kingsley Publishers.

Wade, J., Sinclair, I., Stuttard, L. and Simmonds, J. (2014) *Investigating Special Guardianship: Experiences, Outcomes and Challenges, Research Report*. London: DfE.

Wade, J., Sirriyeh, A., Kohli, R. and Simmonds, J. (2012) *Fostering Unaccompanied Asylum-Seeking Young People: Creating a Family Life across a 'World of Difference'*. London: BAAF.

Wagner, G. (1990) *A Positive Choice: Report of the Independent Review of Residential Care*. London: The Stationery Office.

Wainwright, J. and Ridley, J. (2012) 'Matching, ethnicity and identity: Reflections on the practice and realities of ethnic matching in adoption', *Adoption and Fostering, 36* (3–4): 50–61.

Walker, M. (2005) 'A social and policy understanding of the changing perceptions of children and childhood', in A. Wheal (ed.), *The RHP Companion to Foster Care*. London: RHP.

Walker, M., Hill, M. and Triseliotis, J. (2002) *Testing the Limits of Foster Care: Fostering as an Alternative to Secure Accommodation*. London: BAAF.

Walker, S. (2003) *Social Work and Child and Adolescent Mental Health*. Lyme Regis: RHP.

Wang, E.W., Lambert, M.C., Johnson, L.E., Boudreau, B., Breidenbach, R. and Baumann, D. (2012) 'Expediting permanent placement from foster care systems: The role of family group decision-making', *Children and Youth Services Review, 34* (4): 845–850.

Ward, A. (2007) *Working in Group Care: Social Work and Social Care in Residential and Day Care Settings*. Bristol: Policy Press.

Ward, H. (ed.) (1995) *Looking After Children: Research into Practice*. London: The Stationery Office.

Ward, H. and Brown, R. (2013) 'Decision-making within a child's timeframe: A response', *Family Law Journal*, 43: 1181–1186.

Ward, J. and Smeeton, J. (2017) 'The end of non-consensual adoption? Promoting the wellbeing of children in care', *Practice*, *29* (1): 55–73.

Wardhaugh, J. and Wilding, P. (1993) 'Towards an explanation of the corruption of care', *Critical Social Policy*, 37: 4–31.

Warner, N. (1992) *Choosing with Care: The Report of The Committee of Inquiry into The Selection, Development and Management of Staff in Children's Homes*. London: The Stationery Office.

Wastell, D. and White, S. (2012) 'Blinded by neuroscience: Social policy, the family and the infant brain', *Families, Relationships and Societies*, *1* (3): 397–414.

Watson, D.L., Latter, S. and Bellew, R. (2015a) 'Adopted children and young people's views on their life storybooks: The role of narrative in the formation of identities', *Children and Youth Services Review*, 58: 90–98.

Watson, D., Latter, S. and Bellew, R. (2015b) 'Adopters' views on their children's life story books', *Adoption and Fostering*, *39* (2): 119–134.

Welbourne, P. and Leeson, C. (2012) 'The education of children in care: A research review', *Journal of Children's Services*, *7* (2): 128–143.

Weyts, A. (2004) 'The educational achievements of looked after children: Do welfare systems make a difference to outcomes?', *Adoption and Fostering*, 28 (3): 7–19.

Wheal, A. (2005) 'Personal support', in A. Wheal (ed.), *The Leaving Care Handbook, Helping and Supporting Care Leavers*. Lyme Regis: RHP.

WHO (World Health Organization) (1992) *International Statistical Classification of Diseases, Injuries and Causes of Death*, 10th Edition. Geneva: WHO.

WHO (World Health Organization) (2017) 'Classifications'. Available at: www.who.int/classifications/icd/en/.

Wilkins, M. and Farmer, E. (2015) *Reunification: An Evidence Informed Framework for Return Home Practice*. London: NSPCC.

Willis, R. and Holland, S. (2009) 'Life story work: Reflections on the experience by looked after young people', *Adoption and Fostering*, *33* (4): 44–52.

Willow, C. (2015) *Children Behind Bars: Why the Abuse of Child Imprisonment Must End*. Bristol: Policy Press.

Wilson, K. and Ryan, V. (2005) *Play Therapy, A Non-Directive Approach for Children and Adolescents*. Oxford: Baillière Tindall.

Wilson, K., Sinclair, I., Taylor, C., Pithouse, A. and Sellick, C. (2004) *Fostering Success: An Exploration of the Research Literature in Foster Care*. London: Social Care Institute for Excellence.

Winter, K. (2006) 'Widening our knowledge concerning young looked after children: The case for research using sociological models of childhood', *Child and Family Social Work*, *11* (1): 55–64.

Woodhead, M. (1997) 'Psychology and the cultural construction of childrens' needs', in A. Prout and A. James (eds), *Construction and Reconstruction of Childhood*, 2nd Edition. London: Falmer.

Wootton, B.F. (1959) *Social Science and Social Pathology*. London: George Allen and Unwin.

Wright, M.O. and Masten, A.S. (2015) 'Pathways to resilience in context', in L. Theron, M. Liebenberg and M. Ungar (eds), *Youth Resilience and Culture, Commonalities and Complexities*. New York and London: Springer Heidelberg.

Zeanah, C.H. and Gleason, M.M. (2011) 'Reactive attachment disorder: A review for DSM-V', *American Psychiatric Association*. Washington, DC.

Zeanah, C.H. and Smyke, A.T. (2015) 'Disorders of attachment and social engagement related to deprivation' in A. Thapar, D. Pine, J.F. Leckman, S. Scott, M.J. Snowling and E. Taylor (eds), *Rutter's Child and Adolescent Psychiatry*, 6th Edition. Chichester: John Wiley & Sons.

INDEX

CPSIA information can be obtained
at www.ICGtesting.com
Printed in the USA
LVOW13s2331130418
573480LV00015B/359/P